MISSION CRITICAL
MEETINGS

MISSION CRITICAL
MEETINGS

81 Practical Facilitation Techniques

AVA S. BUTLER

Mission Critical Meetings: 81 Practical Facilitation Techniques

Copyright © 2014 Ava S. Butler. All rights reserved. No part of this book may be reproduced or retransmitted in any form or by any means without the written permission of the publisher.

Published by Wheatmark®
1760 East River Road, Suite 145
Tucson, Arizona 85718 USA
www.wheatmark.com

ISBN: 978-1-60494-037-5 (paperback)
ISBN: 978-1-32787-038-2 (ebook)
LCCN: 2014934746

rev201401

This book is dedicated to my dear husband, Richard. You inspire me on so many levels and I treasure every day we have together.

Contents

Preface

Over my decades as an organizational development consultant, I have learned to appreciate the importance of meeting effectiveness. Meetings are mission critical to almost every aspect of organizational life. Without effective meetings, an organization's chances of success are greatly diminished. But despite the importance of meetings, most of them are irrelevant. This is unfortunate and completely avoidable.

I've learned so much from all my mentors, clients, and colleagues over the years. I'm so grateful for all they've taught me. This book is my opportunity to share what I've learned and is my small contribution to growing the next generation of meeting facilitators.

MISSION CRITICAL
MEETINGS

1

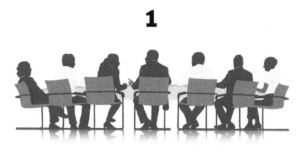

The Foundations

The Importance of Meetings in Organizational Success

Meetings are commonplace in every organization, but most of them are underutilized at best. In most organizations, employees perceive meetings as the primary time waster. However, when used correctly, meetings are a powerful mechanism for expressing ideas, gathering information, making decisions, and communicating changes.

Meetings are a place where people experience and observe an organization's culture, and organizations use meetings to define and perpetuate their cultures. Is time valued or wasted? Are people's ideas encouraged and used or dismissed? Are problems addressed proactively or ignored? Are participants expected to guard their turf or work together toward the good of all? Is open, timely communication expected or discouraged?

Furthermore, new innovations, as well as global and increasingly sophisticated competition, drive organizations to reevaluate and challenge the basic concepts that have delivered past success. Organizations thus utilize participative methods, involving all levels, in a more dynamic, higher-impact process of planning, decision making, and implementation. And organizations primarily use meetings to employ and integrate these improvements.

Despite the ever-continuing use of technology and social media, meetings remain essential when working with people. Staff meetings, strategy sessions, project team meetings, and so on remain an integral part of organizational life.

Even if coworkers widely describe the meetings you facilitate as disasters, there is hope.

You can transform even the most boring, inefficient, and unproductive meetings. Changing your meetings not only produces happier participants, but also fosters an increased likelihood that the teams, groups, and organization you serve will survive and even prosper in the future.

Is This Book for Me?

Mission Critical Meetings is designed to benefit all people who facilitate meetings, regardless of their level within their organization. If you recognize any of the conditions on the following checklist, this book will help you to profoundly increase the efficiency, productivity, and effectiveness of the meetings that you lead or facilitate.

____Things take longer than we want, and we often run out of time, especially on the most important items.

____There is not enough input from some people and too much input from a few.

____Participants don't speak up in the meetings but talk among themselves afterward.

____People say "I told you so" a lot in our department.

____Our team is under scrutiny to be more effective.

____New competition is forcing us to rethink our business.

____We want to be world-class competitors.

____Our group seems stuck.

____Our meetings do not produce the results we need.

____Participants find excuses not to attend our meetings.

____We have a new group forming, and we want to get off on the right track.

____I wish we could accomplish more in less meeting time.

____Meeting participants yawn and sleep in our meetings.

____I'm asked to facilitate a lot of meetings, and I want to do a better job.

____I have an idea of what I need to do in order to improve our meetings, but I don't know how to do it.

How This Book Will Help You

People hold meetings to accomplish something—to obtain some result. The meeting is a means to an end. The effectiveness of meetings directly impacts the quality of its intended results.

Mission Critical Meetings provides the tools required to build the relevant and necessary structure for any type of meeting and is designed to:

- Serve as a quick reference for selecting the most appropriate techniques to use in the meetings you lead or facilitate
- Provide step-by-step instructions for how to apply and use these techniques

This book is like a carpenter's toolbox. It holds the specific tools you need to effectively deal with diverse meeting situations. It not only provides the basic hammer, nails, and hand-saw, but also the more sophisticated specialty tools required to complete nearly any potential meeting objective. At the same time, this book could be considered a cookbook. The techniques serve as the ingredients necessary to accomplish complex tasks. Just as the recipe for perfect lasagna calls for particular layers of ingredients in a certain order, meeting facilitation techniques build on each other to create the perfect agenda.

The techniques described in *Mission Critical Meetings* are designed for all types of meetings and provide the capability to efficiently:

- Improve meeting productivity
- Boost creativity and teamwork
- Brainstorm ideas
- Gather information
- Make decisions
- Implement decisions
- Evaluate meeting effectiveness

You use some techniques in every meeting, some in conjunction with other techniques, and some only in special situations. Some techniques are very basic, and some are more advanced. All of the techniques in this book have a specific purpose and move meetings toward their ultimate goals.

Knowledge of the specific meeting facilitation techniques described in this book will give you a greater depth and understanding of processes. It will also increase your personal confidence and better equip you to improvise with clarity. This ability to improvise is an important skill for meeting facilitation. Even though meeting agendas and their techniques are designed and structured, in practice they become far more fluid and require flexibility, skill, and creativity.

How to Use This Book

Skim through the Book

Look for what you know already and what you need or want to know. There may be techniques that are familiar to you or that you have used in a slightly different way. Concentrate on the parts of the book that are most pertinent to you and the meetings you are currently planning. The novice facilitator may read the book cover to cover and refer to techniques again and again when planning specific meetings. The more experienced reader will likely focus on new ideas and more complex techniques.

Think of This Book as Your Toolbox

Every experienced facilitator has a well-developed toolbox of specific meeting techniques to use in given situations. The variations, combinations, and adaptations of these processes are almost endless. As you prepare for each meeting, refer to this book to help you accomplish your goals.

Develop and Customize Your Own Techniques

Just as a chef continues to learn new recipes and customize standard recipes for his or her own tastes, you should continuously develop and customize techniques to meet your own style and the evolving needs of your organization or clients. You may find that you can modify or copy a technique described in one section to meet another objective. Be creative. Challenge yourself to learn how to combine techniques into a perfect meeting.

Pick up ideas wherever you can. The more options you can create, the better a facilitator you will become.

Accommodating Individual Styles

People don't think, learn, or interact in the same ways. The ways in which people think impact the information they communicate. Therefore, for meetings to be efficient and successful, the effective meeting facilitator must utilize techniques that reinforce and tap into these different personal styles.

Some people need significant time to think before they are ready to share their ideas publicly. Others want to think out loud, using speech to form their thoughts. Still others prefer to share their ideas through writing. A large number of people require visual aids to understand ideas; that is, they have to see ideas. Others are tactile or hands-on learners. Some people feel comfortable making quick decisions, and others don't.

Every person has seven possible personal learning styles. They include visual-spatial, musical, interpersonal, intrapersonal, mathematical-logical, bodily-physical (kinesthetic), and linguistic. Naturally, each of us excels in a few of these areas. Unsurprisingly, meetings almost exclusively tap the linguistic style. The key to a successful meeting, however, is to use techniques that appeal to a wider range of personal learning styles and aptitudes. Not only will your meetings be more interesting, but they will also be far more effective. Moreover, capitalizing on these different learning styles is easier than you think. Each technique in this book incorporates one or more of these individual styles. Here are some examples.

Visual-Spatial

- Use visual aids, diagrams, charts, and illustrations. (Charting, technique 12; Mind Mapping, technique 29; Process Flowcharting, technique 44; Dots, technique 56; Force Field Analysis, technique 67; Team Effectiveness Chart, technique 80)
- Ask participants to draw their perspectives. (Art, technique 13)

Musical

- Use appropriate music before the meeting, during breaks, after the meeting, and as a review technique. (Music, technique 18)

Interpersonal (Relationships between People)

- Allow people to talk among themselves in small groups. (Small Groups, technique 20)
- Use quick exercises to allow people to get to know each other better. (Introductions, technique 1)

Intrapersonal (Relationship of Person with Him- or Herself)

- Allow quiet time for thinking. Write down ideas independently and silently. (Writing, technique 19)
- Ask reflective questions. (Shredded Questions, technique 9; Open-Ended Questions, technique 34)
- Set personal goals. (Individual Action Planning, technique 66)

Mathematical-Logical

- List key points in sequence. (Storyboarding, technique 30)
- Prioritize choices and concerns. (Expectations Survey, technique 39; Multivoting, technique 54; One Hundred Votes, technique 57; Nominal Prioritization, technique 58)
- Analyze issues or choices, step-by-step. (Criteria Matrix, technique 60; Force Field Analysis, technique 67)
- Compare and contrast issues. (Impact and Changeability Analysis, technique 61)
- Use flowcharts. (Process Flowcharting, technique 44)

Bodily-Physical (Kinesthetic)

- Write ideas on cards and move them into appropriate categories. (Card Clusters, technique 31)
- Create movement during your meeting. (Movement, technique 16)

Linguistic

- Lead focused group discussions. (Content Experts, technique 45; SWOTs, technique 51)
- Use analogies and metaphors. (Analogies and Metaphors, technique 14)

Attributes of an Effective Meeting Facilitator

An effective meeting requires an effective facilitator. Meeting facilitation is a skill, and skills can be learned. The techniques described in the following chapters are designed to enhance your skills as a facilitator. But exceptional facilitators go beyond technical skill in creating an atmosphere of success. The relationship these people create with a group is far less tangible but is easy to see, hear, and feel.

I work with a lot of groups and observe a lot of meetings. With some groups, I instantly sense that I'm in a place where people work together to get results and have a good time doing so. Other groups have the feel of a detention center. I have found that the personal attributes of the meeting facilitator can greatly enhance any group's success, as exemplified by two facilitators I recently observed leading meetings.

Gary gave the impression that there was always a right answer. It was by the book from the start. His meeting was very serious and rigidly militaristic. Participants quickly stifled any laughter. When the group wanted to alter the agenda, Gary became very defensive. The group was unable to stimulate any creative new ideas, and the meeting was dull, dull, dull. People seemed tired, looked at their watches, and in some cases even nodded off. As I watched his meeting progress, I kept thinking, "Lighten up, Gary!"

Rachel, on the other hand, seemed to enjoy life and her job. She was relaxed and exuded confidence. Her participants seemed positively impacted by her energy. Her meeting was serious and focused but was also embraced with trust and lightheartedness. Once, when the group got stuck, she asked for ideas on how to move forward. Together, the group modified the technique to accomplish the goal. When she asked for feedback at the end of the meeting, she listened to the group's comments without rebuttal.

Even though Gary and Rachel have basically the same skill and experience levels, the differences in their meetings were profound, as were the results. The most significant variables between them were their individual styles and personal attributes. With few exceptions, personal attributes cannot be taught. A strong skill base can help create a foundation for these attributes to flower, but the rest is up to the individual. Following is a list of the attributes that I have found to support effective meeting facilitators. As you read them, you'll notice that they are interrelated, building on and supporting each other.

Good Sense of Humor

Humor can get a meeting going, cut the tension, and revive your group in even the most demanding situations. There will be times in your meetings when something less than ideal will happen, and you as the facilitator need to handle the resulting stress with confidence, style, and grace. If you can't laugh at yourself and laugh in difficult situations, you will find meeting facilitation to be very trying indeed.

Assertiveness

As the facilitator, you need to have the ability and the guts to state difficult truths when necessary. If you are afraid to say what needs to be said, when it needs to be said, you won't be as effective or credible.

The challenge of assertiveness is knowing when to push forward and when to pull back. You need to know when to step in to keep the group on track and when to let things work themselves out on their own.

As you know, there is a big difference between assertiveness and aggressiveness. Please don't confuse the two when facilitating meetings.

Intuition

Meeting facilitation is not a skill that involves applying a simple formula and arriving at the right answer. You must identify what is best for each situation. One could argue that intuition comes from experience, and I agree. But it also includes the ability to act on a hunch.

Creativity

You will need to assemble techniques in new and creative ways every time you facilitate a meeting. This is true for a group meeting for the first time or for the two hundredth time. Agendas are created by pulling theories, experiences, and ideas from every direction you know and some that you don't. Outside the box thinking is the best way to develop the agendas and processes for each of your meetings.

Flexibility

The meeting facilitator who is wedded to his or her first idea, or to his or her ideas in general, is going to encounter trouble. You must think on your feet, accept new and better ideas from others, and change or modify course as required. This sometimes means working outside the boundaries of what you already know and feel comfortable with.

Confidence and Enthusiasm

Without facilitator confidence and enthusiasm, a group quickly prepares for a boring, unproductive experience. The ability to appear articulate and knowledgeable in front of a group of people is essential in creating a positive atmosphere from the start. When a meeting begins to slump, which inevitably occurs, the facilitator must help everyone keep going. This does not mean ill-advised enthusiasm for enthusiasm's sake but heartfelt enthusiasm to keep the group involved and moving forward.

Team Player

If you want to be in the limelight, meeting facilitation is not the job for you. You are the moderator, the interpreter, and the timekeeper but not the star. Your recognition comes from the work you allow others to accomplish and the success you help build in the organizations you serve.

Many groups alternate facilitators. This is an excellent method for building a broad base of skill and commitment across the team. Some individuals will inevitably be better than others. Being a team player means sharing your insights to support the development of facilitation skills throughout your group instead of hoping to be seen as the hero or heroine.

High Self-Esteem

If a meeting is not going well, people usually blame the facilitator. Sometimes this is justified, sometimes not. Regardless, when a group or individual takes their frustration out on you, you can't take it personally. You must be able to separate your skill, your experiences, and your job from your worth as a human being.

Sincerity

Sincerity, according to the thesaurus, is the opposite of hypocrisy. You, as the facilitator, need to truly care about your group and its success.

Dedicated to Learning

Good meeting facilitators are dedicated to continuously building their skills. The more tools you have available to you, the less likely you will be to panic when a certain technique doesn't work the way you planned. Knowledge of communication, group dynamics, problem solving, systems thinking, leadership, quality improvement, and decision-making models are all areas to target for development. The more you understand, the more assured and skilled you will be when confronted with the infinite range of situations that will surely come your way.

What about the Participants?

At this point, you might be saying to yourself, "It's great if I possess all of these wonderful attributes, but don't meeting participants have a responsibility, too? Shouldn't successful meeting participants have certain attributes as well?"

You're right. Meeting success is a team responsibility. The same attributes that apply to meeting facilitators apply to meeting participants. It would be fantastic if every meeting participant you came in contact with had the same attributes that make you a great facilitator. But it's not a perfect world, and you are going to have to deal with all types of people in all types of situations. The full spectrum of people will populate your meetings just as they populate the earth.

It's your responsibility as a meeting facilitator to apply your experience and skill to maximize the outcome of every meeting you lead. You will have difficult participants and problems making meetings work. However, if you apply the techniques described in this book, 99 percent of the behavior problems so common to meetings will never happen because the techniques take care of the problems before they occur. These tested techniques provide the processes to maximize the positive and minimize the negative. They not only work but are specifically designed to bring out the best in all people. They inspire participants to trust the process, and, in turn, trust you. Since you will have the skills described in this book, it will even look easy.

Summary

The unparalleled speed of organizational change necessitates using the full potential of the organization. Meetings provide occasions where decisions are made, priorities set, and changes agreed upon. Meetings define and perpetuate organizational culture. If your meetings aren't changing, it's likely that your company is slow to change as well. Because meetings are so critical, effective meeting facilitators have become an essential link in the chain of people who deliver organizational success.

Meeting facilitators create the agendas and techniques that constitute meeting structure. This allows meeting participants to focus on the content of their discussions and leave the management of those conversations to the facilitator. It is not the facilitator's job to define the content or outcomes of any meeting; instead, the facilitator defines the structure, processes, and techniques required so that the participants can effectively accomplish the goals of their agendas.

Successful meeting facilitators possess certain attributes. They are self-confident, flexible, and humorous. They are enthusiastic and sincere. They are assertive, creative, and intuitive.

They work well with a team and are dedicated to learning. These attributes are at best difficult to teach.

Meeting facilitators also possess the expertise to successfully facilitate a participative meeting. These skills are accessible to almost anybody with the will to learn. The quest for new and more effective techniques never ends. Even the most experienced meeting facilitator will want to acquire new levels of skill and knowledge.

The specific techniques described in this book exemplify the skills of meeting facilitation. When assimilated, practiced, perfected, and expanded upon, they will become part of an indispensable set of tools to make meetings work as well as position you on the cutting edge of change and organizational success.

2

Before the Meeting

Chapter 1 describes the importance of meetings in organizational success, the fundamentals of personal learning styles, and the distinctive attributes of an accomplished meeting facilitator. These fundamentals and attributes, when coupled with effective premeeting planning and use of the specific facilitation techniques discussed in this book, will lead you to become a more competent meeting leader. This chapter extends the concepts from chapter 1 into practical advice that will help you prepare for the meetings you will facilitate. I will outline specific meeting components and provide an efficient and flexible template that you can use for planning all your meetings. Chapter 2 includes sections that will describe how to:

- Skillfully plan your meetings
- Build concise and flexible meeting agendas
- Best prepare the physical meeting environment
- Efficiently report meeting content and results

This step-by-step, component-based approach simplifies the process of designing effective meetings and will increase your level of success.

Planning Your Meeting

What you do before your meetings is every bit as important as what you do in them. In fact, without effective premeeting planning and organization, the quality of your meetings will certainly suffer, and some will very likely fail. Most facilitators plan to some degree.

Many consider their meetings planned if they create an agenda, send it out, book a room, and order the coffee. But proficient premeeting planning needs to go beyond these basics. The level of planning a facilitator attains before the meeting separates the true professional from the rank amateur. And meeting results speak for themselves. Detailed planning is essential for consistent success because, as the old saying goes, the devil is in the details.

Let's use Sam's meeting as an example. Sam has facilitated a number of meetings, and he thought his meeting was well prepared. He had clarified its purpose and prepared an agenda, and he had set the time and place. Figure 2-1 illustrates Sam's meeting agenda.

MEETING AGENDA

GOAL: Prepare the management presentation asking for approval of new equipment.

TO: Nancy Bartlett, Jacob French, Kim Preston, Anna Saiano, Andre Washington, Clinton Williams

FROM: Sam Ballard

DATE: June 5, 2014

TIME: 2:00–5:00 p.m.

PLACE: Conference Room B

AGENDA:	TIME:
1. Prioritize statistical data	60 minutes
2. Prepare a presentation to management	120 minutes

Figure 2-1. Sam's original meeting agenda.

The goal of Sam's group was to prepare a management presentation asking for approval to purchase new equipment. He had sent out an agenda, assembled the right people, and estimated a three-hour time frame. He purposely started his meeting at 2:00 p.m., giving the group an additional half hour if the meeting happened to take more time. (Quitting time was at 5:30 p.m.)

Premeeting Planning Questions

This section will help you avoid the premeeting planning mistakes that Sam and many other meeting facilitators typically make. Use the following premeeting planning questions to prepare for every meeting you facilitate. Five categories of questions will help you focus on the major elements of every meeting: foundation, specific agenda items, logistics, reporting, and evaluation.

This checklist demonstrates the questions you need to ask to build your meeting agendas and will tune you in to your meetings like never before.

1. Foundation Questions

☑ What is the purpose and/or goal(s) of this meeting?

This sounds like a basic question, but you'd be surprised how often the meeting's purpose, goals, and expected outcomes are not clear and not agreed upon. This lack of clarity means your meeting will be doomed before it starts.

☑ Is a meeting the best way to accomplish these goals?

Even the best-run meeting can be a waste of time if it is not necessary in the first place. You might decide, based on the given situation, to invite some people for only part of the meeting, meet with participants one-on-one, or just send an e-mail asking for written input. Always keep in mind that your ultimate goal is to work for the success and best interests of the organization you serve. Meetings are not always the best answer.

☑ Who owns the meeting?

The meeting facilitator is not always the owner of the meeting. The owner is often a line manager or executive who delegates the facilitation of the meeting to a team member or outside facilitator. Regardless of who facilitates, the meeting owner needs to approve the agenda, its processes, and the participants. Failure to align with the owner in advance means you might be criticized publicly in the midst of your meeting, a situation you obviously want to avoid.

☑ Who should be involved in planning this meeting?

Including key participants in planning your meetings provides better and more complete information and pays profound dividends in the meeting itself. This activity allows you to discover danger spots, problems, or any potential conflicts, as well as gain insights into better ways to accomplish tasks. It creates shared ownership of meeting goals and ultimately improves the likelihood of meeting success. This collaboration is especially critical in long meetings with large groups of people and meetings of special importance.

Often, for critical meetings such as strategy sessions, a formal planning team is assembled that includes the owner and other handpicked participants. The planning team meets in advance of the meeting to agree on the goals and processes and also gets together during breaks or lunch at the meeting itself to address issues or correct the meeting's course as required.

☑ What specific issues or agenda items need to be addressed?

☑ What information needs to be gathered and disseminated before the meeting?

☑ How should this information be gathered? And by whom?

☑ Who needs to attend this meeting?

☑ Of these people, does everyone need to attend the entire meeting?

☑ How should the agenda be ordered to ensure that everyone's time is used wisely?

☑ What is the best date and location for the meeting?

With ongoing groups, plan the time and place of your next meetings at the end of the previous meeting whenever possible.

☑ What correspondence/prework needs to be sent to the participants before the meeting?

☑ What plans are required to ensure no interruptions happen to the meeting?

Some groups are notorious for having interruptions that diminish productivity. Plan ahead so you have a method to assure that there are no interruptions, except for emergencies. This means having a method to take messages at off-site locations and a no-interruptions policy inside the meetings. See Ground Rules, technique 3, for details on how to implement a no-interruptions policy.

2. Specific Agenda Item Questions

☑ What is the overall purpose of each issue or agenda item?

Because this information will be transferred directly to your agenda, structure each issue or agenda item as a statement that clearly expresses both its subject and purpose. For example, "Tax report" only states the subject of the agenda item and is therefore potentially confusing. "Agree how to improve the tax report" much more clearly describes both the subject and purpose. Defining this purpose also provides the context for answering the following agenda item questions. Eliminate any issues/agenda items not worthy of meeting time.

☑ How, specifically, will each issue or agenda item be accomplished?

Envision exactly how the meeting conversations will flow, what questions will need to be answered, and what problems might occur. Identify the substeps required to achieve each agenda item to an appropriate level of detail.

☑ What are the most appropriate facilitation techniques for each substep?

Refer to the corresponding how-to chapters in this book to identify the specific techniques that will best support your agenda item goals.

Note that not every substep will require a specific technique. Sometimes, for example, simple group discussion will be adequate. Make sure that you are choosing techniques because they are the best techniques, not because they are the ones you feel most comfortable with or like the best.

☑ What meeting productivity techniques are required for this meeting?

See chapter 3 for ideas on controlling meeting behavior, keeping your meeting on track, improving the clarity of communication, stimulating and maintaining energy, and increasing participation.

☑ What are the time requirements for each issue or agenda item?

Time requirements are based on the estimated time to complete each substep within an issue or agenda item. To accurately estimate meeting time, it is extremely important to break each agenda item down into its substeps for analysis. Visualize how the discussions, exercises, and techniques you have selected will transpire. Design the agenda in such a way that you can control the momentum yet be flexible enough to accommodate the inevitable timing errors in your agenda.

☑ What handouts, overheads, and other visual aids need to be prepared?

☑ Who should facilitate or present each issue or agenda item?

The meeting facilitator or meeting owner is not always the appropriate person to be responsible for each specific agenda item. Delegate and share responsibility as much as possible.

☑ How should each issue or agenda item be introduced?

Determine what background information participants will need. Consider using Three P Statements, technique 8, to introduce new agenda items.

3. Logistical Questions
☑ What room arrangements and other preparations are necessary?
    ___ Room
    ___ Charts and easels? How many?
    ___ Tables, chairs (numbers and configurations)?
    ___ Audio-visual equipment?
    ___ Computer use?
    ___ Microphones? Fixed or roving?
    ___ Video/audio links?
    ___ Translations?
    ___ Car parking?
    ___ Plants/flowers?
    ___ Music?
    ___ Travel arrangements?
    ___ Accessibility for participants with special needs?
    ___ Internet access?
    ___ Name tags/placecards
    ___ Arrangements for messages?
    ___ Other

Physical Environment

Communication experts state that nonverbal communication comprises 55 percent of the total message. If your physical environment is not conducive to productivity and creativity, the chances of your meeting accomplishing its goals are slim. Think about the difference in atmosphere between a greasy diner and a gourmet French restaurant. The moment you walk through the door you instantly get a feel for the type of meal you will have. The same is true when you walk into a meeting room.

Ensure that the physical environment for all your meetings is properly prepared. This doesn't mean that your preparation has to be expensive. It simply means that you should make a conscientious effort to provide a meeting environment that feels good to both you and your participants.

Windows

Some people believe that windows distract participants from discussions and the agenda at hand. But, in fact, the opposite is true. Natural light can have a wonderful effect on energy and productivity. Whenever possible, open the shades. This creates a feeling of openness—for fresh air and fresh ideas.

Atmosphere

A dull room can result in dull minds. Create as bright and energetic an atmosphere as possible. As appropriate, add life and color to your meeting rooms by hanging pictures and posters, or even attaching kites to the ceiling or walls. Display flip charts or project plans from previous meetings. You might bring in plants or flowers. Consider playing prerecorded music in the background before your meetings begin and during breaks. Balance your imagination with common sense for what is appropriate for your audience and your organizational culture.

Room Arrangement

Strive for a room arrangement that promotes discussion. Everyone should be able to have eye contact with everyone else. A meeting with auditorium-style seating nonverbally communicates to your participants that they are there for a lecture. Refer to figure 2-3 for seating options.

U - Shaped	Herringbone	Round Tables

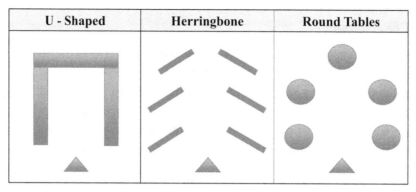

Figure 2-3. Seating options for participative meetings.

Whenever possible, use chairs that will be comfortable for many hours and will provide adequate ergonomic support.

Temperature

Do your best to reserve a room where the participants can control the thermostat themselves. Participants who are too hot or too cold will not be able to focus on the meeting agenda.

Refreshments

☑ What refreshments should be served?
____ Breakfast, lunch, snacks, dinner?
____ Special food requirements?
____ Catering?

It is often a good idea to include food and beverages in your meetings. Because sugar causes a quick energy high followed by a long crash, try to avoid it. If your group can't resist doughnuts and brioches, be sure to include lighter foods such as fruit or gluten-free items. Those participants on special diets will appreciate the options. If you plan to provide coffee, be sure to provide tea, water, and possibly soft drinks as well. Place the food and beverages near the door, on the table(s), or somewhere people will feel comfortable serving themselves during the meeting.

4. Reporting Questions

☑ What level of documentation is necessary?

Determine ahead of time what level of detail the meeting notes will require. Some meeting groups will need a detailed record of all discussions while most will only want a record of decisions and next steps. Note that documenting decisions makes it easy to refer to them later if the group forgets what has already been decided or slips into the mistake of wanting to remake decisions that have already been taken.

☑ What is the best way to arrange for meeting notes to be documented and distributed?

For key meetings, consider having an administrative assistant in the room to record the meeting highlights in real time. A laptop computer is the best method for minimizing effort and maximizing time effectiveness. If you don't have someone in the room to help you in real time, take photos of flip charts or take the actual flip charts with you to type up. Note that you may want to save some of the flip charts for use in future meetings. Whichever method you choose, establish who will be responsible for the minutes at the beginning of the meeting or before the meeting begins. Gain agreement on the level of detail required.

Distribute the meeting notes as quickly as possible. Meeting follow-up loses momentum when there are no notes to quickly reinforce decisions and next steps. The meeting notes will make more sense and be far more valuable if delivered in or near real time. It should never take more than a few days to process and deliver them. Take the time to ensure that they are clear enough to make sense to you and the participants a few weeks after the meeting.

5. Evaluation Questions

☑ What is the best way to evaluate the effectiveness of your meetings?

Creating Your Agenda

Many experts would argue that the meeting agenda, if properly prepared, is the most important and powerful component of any meeting. It is, at the very least, your road map to success. The agenda is a fundamental and essential element of every meeting, serving as your preparation tool and script notes.

Once you have answered the premeeting planning questions, you can effectively build your agenda. This process includes:
- Finalizing the order and flow of the agenda
- Reviewing the selected techniques, processes, and time frames for each agenda item
- Identifying alternative techniques in the event they are needed
- Obtaining final input/approval from key participants
- Sending out the agenda to all participants

Using the chart in figure 2-4 as a model, prepare your agenda. It is a good idea to create a master template on your computer that you can customize every time you plan a meeting.

MEETING AGENDA	
MEETING GOAL OR PURPOSE:	
TO: (List of attendees)	
FROM: (Person who is sending the agenda)	
DATE:	
TIME: (Including starting and ending times)	
PLACE: (Include instructions if necessary)	
AGENDA ITEMS:	**TIME:**

Figure 2-4. Meeting agenda template.

You should have already collected all of the information required to complete your agenda, except perhaps the final order of agenda items, in your premeeting planning questions. When considering the most suitable order for your agenda, rely on logic and input from those you have involved in the planning process. Keep in mind the primary goal(s) of the meeting and diversify the tasks and pace to keep things fresh.

To be consistently successful, you will want to prepare two different agendas for all your meetings. That's right, two! You will prepare one for your meeting participants, which is the same one that you send out in advance and display during the meeting, and you will also want to prepare a more detailed agenda for yourself as a facilitator's guide. Writing a facilitator's guide is a useful process and articulates the specific details of the facilitation techniques you will utilize in your meeting. It acts as your recipe for success.

Figure 2-2 showed Sam's improved agenda. Below is his correlating facilitator's guide for that meeting.

FACILITATOR'S GUIDE

GOAL: Prepare a management presentation asking for approval of new equipment.

TO: Jacob French, Nancy Bartlett, Anna Saiano, Andre Washington, Philip Nugent, Kim Preston, Clinton Williams, Allan Cluquot

FROM: Sam Ballard

DATE: June 3, 2014

TIME: 2:00–5:00 p.m.

PLACE: Conference Room B

AGENDA ITEMS	WHO:	TIME:
Review the agenda, agree on time frames and processes Post agenda with time frames (flip chart made in advance)	Sam	5 minutes 2:00–2:05
Review compiled statistical data (A) Individuals with next steps to gather specific information (from the last meeting) share their analysis with the group	Sam to set up	5 minutes 2:05–2:10
(B) Individuals share their reports. Gain feedback from the team as we go. 10 min. each	Nancy, Jacob, Kim	30 minutes 2:10–2:40
Determine what data is most pertinent to management team (A) Discuss and agree what types of data will be most important to the management team. "What will it take to convince them that our case is a sound one?"	Sam to lead	15 minutes 2:40–2:55

AGENDA ITEMS *continued*	WHO:	TIME:
(B) Discuss any issues or concerns the management team will have, i.e.: "What else is happening in the business that we need to consider?" "What difficult questions will we likely encounter?"		15 minutes 2:55–3:10
(C) Determine how to address/incorporate those concerns.		15 minutes 3:10–3:25
Break		10 minutes 3:25–3:35
Plan the presentation (A) Determine the flow and story of the presentation. Write draft heading of each slide on large post-it notes. Move post-its around on wall according to the brainstormed flow of the presentation's story.	Sam to lead	15 minutes 3:35–3:50
(B) Small groups work to create details of presentation slides Group 1: Jacob, Kim, Andre Group 2: Nancy, Anna, Clinton (Names written on flip chart in advance) Sam to float between the two groups	Sam to set up exercise, followed by small group work	20 min. 3:50–4:10
(C) Small group report outs and feedback	Small group reps	15 minutes 4:10–4:25
Check flow and messaging of the presentation Place all draft slides in sequence to create the story line. "How well do these slides work together to create a consistent and compelling story?" "What is the best flow of our presentation?"	Sam to lead	15 minutes 4:25–4:40

AGENDA ITEMS *continued*	WHO:	TIME:
Determine who will give the presentation to management These people will finalize the document and present the group's proposal to management.	Sam to lead	5 minutes 4:40–4:45
Schedule time for presenters do a run-through of their presentation with this group [At least a half day before the actual presentation.]	Sam to lead	5 minutes 4:45–4:50
Evaluate the meeting What went well, opportunities for improvement—both with the meeting and the presentation preparation in general.	Sam to lead	10 minutes 4:50–5:00

Figure 2-5. Sam's facilitator's guide.

Figures 2-6 and 2-7 demonstrate another example of a meeting agenda and facilitator's guide for a different type of meeting.

MEETING AGENDA

MEETING GOAL:	To create a shared understanding of the why, what, and how of the New Product Development team.
TO:	Martha D'Alessandro, Blair Dee, James Hollows, Omar Ismat, Joseph Nguyen, Ian Pate, Brett Phillipson
FROM:	Jessica Landry
DATE:	March 14, 2014
TIME:	9:00–11:30 a.m.
PLACE:	Emerald conference room

AGENDA ITEMS *continued*	TIME:
Welcoming remarks	20 minutes
Review the history of how this idea came to be	10 minutes
Understand the role of this team	15 minutes
Describe the major components in the process	20 minutes
Break	10 minutes
Discuss information in small groups	20 minutes
Report back and respond to small group discussions	30 minutes
Schedule the next meeting	5 minutes
Evaluate the meeting	15 minutes
Close	5 minutes

Figure 2-6. Participant's meeting agenda for a new product development launch.

MEETING AGENDA

MEETING GOAL:	To create a shared understanding of the why, what and how of the New Product Development team.
TO:	Martha D'Alessandro, Blair Dee, James Hollows, Omar Ismat, Joseph Nguyen, Ian Pate, Brett Phillipson, Sarah Vigil
FROM:	Jessica Landry
DATE:	March 14, 2014
TIME:	9:00–11:30 a.m.
PLACE:	Emerald conference room

AGENDA ITEMS	WHO:	TIME:
Welcoming remarks:		

AGENDA ITEMS *continued*	WHO:	TIME:
Opening remarks from the divisional director	Martha	5 minutes 9:00–9:05
Review the agenda and ground rules (flip charts prepared in advance)	Jessica	5 minutes 9:05–9:10
Introductions: (prepared flip chart) • Name, job, experience with the project to date	Jessica to set up/all to introduce themselves	10 minutes 9:10–9:20
Review the history of how this idea came to be Review history (use overhead with prepared slides) Outline the 5 major steps and time frames (another overhead)	Martha	10 minutes 9:20–9:30
Understand the role of this team Answer these questions using visual aids/handouts • Why have a team? • Why were you in particulate asked to participate? • What will you be responsible to do? • How much time will it take? • What are the expected results?	Martha	15 minutes 9:30–9:45
Describe the major components in the process Review the 5 major components and time frames Explain all components in some detail, especially the immediate next steps (use 2 overheads as visuals) Remember to ask for questions and concerns	Omar	20 minutes 9:45–10:05
Break	All	10 minutes 10:05–10:15

AGENDA ITEMS *continued*	WHO:	TIME:
Discuss information in small groups: Ask participants to break into 2 small groups of 4. (Cluster participants into two teams based on seating proximity.) Explain the purpose of the exercise: to have a few minutes to discuss what we covered amongst yourselves Share the instructions: (written on a flip chart) • Pick a recorder (2 min.) • Discuss: What are your reactions? and What are your questions? (15 min.) • Recorder writes responses on flip chart—one flip chart per question	James to set up then small groups	20 minutes 10:15–10:35
Report back and respond to the small group discussions Two recorders report back the summary of their group's reactions and questions	Recorders	10 minutes 10:35–10:45
React to group's responses and answer their questions	Martha, Omar	20 minutes 10:45–11:05
Schedule the next meeting Determine where to meet and when	Jessica to lead	5 minutes 11:05–11:10
Evaluate the meeting Summarize what was covered in the meeting. Refer to the posted agenda Chart the group's comments to these questions • What went well with our first meeting? • What are our opportunities for improvement for our next meeting	Jessica to lead	15 minutes 11:10–11:25
Closing remarks from the director	Martha	5 minutes 11:25–11:30

Figure 2-7. Facilitator's guide for the new product development launch meeting.

Now you're galloping toward meeting success. If you feel that this level of detail is over-kill, question your paradigms. Ironically, the more detailed your facilitation planning becomes, the less bogged down in detail your meeting will actually be.

It may seem like a long and involved process, but if you follow the above procedures, all of your hard work will result in a professional meeting. Remember to gain approval for your completed agenda from the meeting owner (if it's not you) and also from the key participants as appropriate.

More Inside Information

Setting the Stage

Plan to arrive at the meeting location early to make sure that everything is set up the way you expected. Prepare your flip charts and other visual aids in advance so you have time to take care of any last-minute details. Be ready to greet people as they arrive. You will find that this added preparation time will help you feel more relaxed, set a positive and productive tone for the meeting, and increase your overall effectiveness.

Expect Changes

Even though you have planned your meeting down to the minute, rest assured that things will never go exactly as planned. Agenda items and their issues will sometimes take more time and sometimes less, a person who is crucial to your meeting's success will not show up or will have to leave early, or something critical will happen in the organization that overrides your original agenda. You will see signs of boredom, frustration, and interpersonal conflict that you will not have planned for and will need to address.

Does this mean that planning is a waste of time? Quite the opposite. Your planning will give you an educated basis for making decisions about how best to move forward and will help you negotiate changes with the participants as necessary. The more techniques you know and the more experience you have, the better you will be able to remain flexible and effective in the real world of your meetings.

Be open to change, and don't be afraid to make the uncomfortable statement or ask the difficult question. You will almost always find that coworkers will appreciate and respect your flexibility and courage. For example, you might observe, "It seems that Joan and Enrique have some strong disagreements about this topic. Is it best for us all to continue this debate, or would it be more appropriate for the two of you to continue your discussion after the meeting?" … "Some of you are looking confused. What can we do to make things clearer?" … "This conversation is taking longer than I anticipated. Should we continue and postpone another part of the agenda to another date, wrap this conversation up, or continue our meeting past its deadline?"

Continuous Improvement

Take a few minutes after each meeting to review what went well and what you would do differently if you had it to do again. Jot down a few specific notes. This quick and simple process, combined with the formal feedback you receive from your meeting participants, will help you to continually improve your effectiveness as a meeting facilitator.

Changing Your Style

If you have a history of dull, autocratic meetings and now suddenly decide to change your style, discuss the changes you propose with your meeting groups first. Ask for their input and ideas. If you change without proactively saying something, people are likely to be resistant and highly suspicious.

Summary

The quality of your meetings is relative to the quality of your planning. If you don't clearly define the purpose and goals of your meeting, time will be wasted. If you don't labor over the details of each proposed agenda item, the techniques you select might not work effectively, and your timelines may be unpredictable.

As a meeting facilitator, you are responsible for making your meetings as successful as possible. Sometimes these efforts are relatively simple, and other times they can be difficult and stressful. But you can succeed!

3

Twenty Techniques to Improve Meeting Productivity

Everyone on Anne's manufacturing team is complaining about having to attend another one of her meetings. "Why should we go? Nothing ever gets accomplished. Most of us just sit there and waste away while she tries to control totally meaningless and unfocused conversations, bickering, and finger-pointing. It's a waste of time!"

Anne couldn't agree more. "It's obvious that everybody, including me, is frustrated. I just don't know where to start!"

Joe's group is light years ahead of Anne's. "We have a great organization! Everybody works well together and is committed to continuous improvement. And our improved performance shows the value of participation! This year we're targeting our meetings as an area for improvement and are eager to learn new techniques to help us reach our goals. But we're not sure how to begin."

This chapter outlines twenty fundamental techniques for facilitating successful meetings. These essential productivity techniques provide specific, uncomplicated processes to define meeting behavior, keep meetings on track, improve the clarity of communication, and maintain maximum energy. Employing these procedures not only saves time and increases effectiveness and efficiency, but also adds immediate power to every meeting agenda by eliminating time wasters, focusing discussions, expanding the quality of input, and significantly increasing participation and results.

Specific techniques for defining and controlling meeting behavior include:
1. Introductions
2. Clearing
3. Ground Rules
4. Pulse Check

For keeping your meeting on track, use:
5. Parking Lot
6. Verbal Warnings
7. The Bell
8. Three P Statements
9. Shredded Questions
10. Self-Management
11. Go/No Go

For improving the clarity of communication, apply:
12. Charting
13. Art
14. Analogies and Metaphors

When you want to stimulate and maintain high energy, utilize:
15. Breaks
16. Movement
17. Toys
18. Music

When you want to increase participation, employ:
19. Writing
20. Small Groups

"I want to be sure that everyone in our group is acquainted and feels comfortable with each other. How can I structure personal introductions to include the entire group as well as add value to the participative process?"

1. Introductions

What Are Introductions?

Introductions assure that all participants know each other. People want to know who else is there and what they have to contribute. People will not work as openly if they do not know who is in the room.

Introductions include everyone at the beginning of your meeting. They create equal ground and highlight the expectations for participation.

When to Use Introductions

- When your meeting participants aren't acquainted with each other
- When you want to increase participants' knowledge of each other

How to Use Introductions

1. Include Introductions on your agenda. Allow about one minute of time for each participant.

2. Decide which type of Introductions is most appropriate for your group.

   OPTION A: "Tell us your name and something personal about yourself that most of the group doesn't know, for example, a hobby, something about your family, somewhere you have lived, and so on."

   OPTION B: "Tell us your name and what you do in two sentences."

   OPTION C: "Pair up with someone you don't know and haven't met yet. Introduce yourselves and talk for a few minutes to get to know each other better. Then you will introduce each other to the group." Suggest some guidelines, such as questions to ask from option A and B.

   NOTE: Allow an extra ten minutes for this option.

OPTION D: "Please share your name, background, and the skills you have that will contribute to the meeting, such as expertise in operations or budgeting."

> NOTE: This option is especially pertinent when new groups form to accomplish a specific objective.

NOTE: Options A through D can be combined with Movement, technique 16, where a ball is thrown from person to person during their introductions.

OPTION E: When a new person joins a group of people who already know each other, you can say, "I would like to introduce [the person's name]. [The person's name] comes to us from [the place, company, or division], where she was responsible for [whatever the person was responsible for]. I'm sure [the person's name] will be a positive addition to our group with her expertise in [specific skills, expertise]."

You can then ask the person to add to what you've said. Ask all other participants to introduce themselves.

3. Use Introductions as planned.

Summary

Introductions ensure that everyone in your group is acquainted with each other while supporting participation.

1. Place Introductions on your agenda, allowing one minute for each participant.

2. Determine which type of Introduction is best suited for the specific situation.

3. Use Introductions as planned.

"It seems like when our meetings begin, everybody is still focused on what they just left behind—their work, their weekend, their vacation, or whatever. It really takes a long time for us all to get settled. What can we do to get focused sooner?"

2. Clearing

What Is Clearing?

Clearing is a productivity technique that allows the members of your group to clear their minds and focus on the meeting. It provides a transition from what participants just left behind to the meeting itself. Clearing significantly decreases the time it takes participants to settle themselves at the beginning of the meeting, providing earlier focus and greater effectiveness.

This technique involves participants sharing what they are thinking about/distracted by with the meeting group. Once a person has voiced what is on his or her mind, these thoughts are more easily put aside. You may have noticed this in your own life. For example, after sharing your frustration about a current project with a colleague, you find that your frustration diminishes and you are better able to focus on your work. Left unacknowledged, your frustration mounts, further impeding your effectiveness. One-on-one meetings usually include a few minutes of informal conversation before focusing on the formal topic. However, group meetings usually do not have this Clearing time built in. As a result, meeting participants take longer to settle into the formal business at hand.

Clearing also allows participants to let the other meeting members know in a constructive way if anything is getting in the way of full participation.

The goal of Clearing is not to solve problems or address the concerns that arise but rather to allow people to simply state their issues. The few moments of venting time provided by this technique effectively help people focus and concentrate on the meeting sooner.

Clearing alone will not be enough to transform the effectiveness of your meetings. You will want to use a variety of other techniques as well, which will vary depending on the group and the specific agenda of the meeting. However, the Clearing technique, coupled with Ground Rules, technique 3, usually provides a solid foundation for focused meetings.

When to Use Clearing

- When participants' other obligations keep their minds on topics other than the meeting
- When participants come to the meeting without taking a few minutes to relax or talk together informally

How to Use Clearing

1. Explain to participants the purpose of Clearing. For example: "Clearing is a technique for transitioning from your previous thoughts and activities to our meeting. If you agree, we'll use Clearing at the beginning of each meeting to help us get focused more quickly. The goal of Clearing is not to solve problems but instead to simply state what you have on your mind. By doing so, you are better able to put those issues aside and give your full attention to the meeting."

2. Explain the instructions for Clearing. Post the instructions on a chart or overhead, like figure 3-1 below.

CLEARING INSTRUCTIONS

- Everyone gets a turn.

- One minute maximum per person.

- Briefly share issues, positive or negative, currently on your mind.

- Use statements instead of questions.

- Listen without problem solving.

- It's OK to pass or say "I'm clear."

- Keep it quick.

Figure 3-1. Instructions chart for Clearing.

3. Begin the Clearing exercise. Be sure everyone gets a turn. The first time your group does this activity, you may want to start, thus giving the other participants an example to follow.

   OPTION: If your group is large, ask participants to clear informally with others next to them. If people are sitting at tables, each table can clear independently.

   NOTE: If someone brings up an issue worthy of group discussion, put it on your Parking Lot chart, technique 5, or otherwise note it for later discussion. Unless there is some emergency, like an impending lawsuit or supplier disaster, do not change your agenda to accommodate these issues. It would be rare for serious problems to come up in the Clearing session. Simple venting and sharing of personal news will be more common. For example, "Our department's financial report is due in two weeks, and we have two months of data to analyze. Needless to say, I'm feeling a little stressed."

"We just won the Edmondson account. We've been working on them for over a year, and their business will put us in line for their parent company's business next year."

"I'm having problems with my back again. Please excuse me if I stand up during parts of the meeting. Sitting exacerbates the problem."

4. After everyone has had a turn, thank the group and move on to the next agenda item.

    NOTE: The first time you use Clearing with a specific group, note that you will ask for feedback about the technique at the end of the meeting. By then the group will be able to see if Clearing helped the session run more smoothly. At the end of the meeting, take a few minutes to ask the group:

    *   "What were your observations about our meeting effectiveness?"
    *   "What value did Clearing add?"
    *   "Do you think we should keep Clearing as a regular exercise?"

    NOTE: If your group agrees, start each meeting with a brief Clearing session.

    OPTION: Use Clearing sporadically, when participants seem to be restless at the beginning of the meeting.

Summary

Clearing helps participants focus on the meeting by allowing them to put their other concerns and responsibilities aside until the meeting is over.

1. Explain the purpose of Clearing.

2. Explain the instructions for Clearing.

3. Begin the Clearing exercise. Be sure everyone gets a turn.

4. After everyone has had a turn, move on to the next agenda item.

"Sometimes people act inappropriately at our meetings. They come in late, interrupt others, ramble from topic to topic, dominate discussions, are hostile to the ideas and opinions of others, and have side conversations. Is there an easy way to handle these situations?"

3. Ground Rules

What Are Ground Rules?

Ground Rules, as a productivity technique, help establish and maintain acceptable standards of meeting behavior. Using this technique virtually eliminates behavior problems before they begin. When behavior problems do occur, preestablished Ground Rules support your request for change.

This technique involves discussing and posting meeting Ground Rules in a way that continually reminds meeting participants of the rules and regulations of their meeting.

If standards of behavior are not discussed and agreed upon ahead of time, it is very difficult to censure a person's behavior because the group has never defined acceptable and unacceptable behaviors. Ground Rules provide this definition and become the group's standards of behavior. They support meeting productivity, creativity, and participation and help keep the meeting on track.

When to Use Ground Rules

- When you want to use your meeting time wisely
- When you expect conflict because of specific personalities or volatile issues
- When the group has a lot to accomplish in a short period of time
- When there is a history of unproductive behavior at previous meetings
- When a group is working together for the first time

How to Use Ground Rules

1. At your meeting, introduce the idea and state the purpose of having Ground Rules. For example: "Ground Rules are designed to act as an agreement outlining how we will conduct ourselves during the meeting. Once we have agreed on them, we will post our ground rules near the front of the room and refer to them as needed. Anyone can remind us of our Ground Rules when he or she sees that we are getting off track."

NOTE: If you want to establish Ground Rules with a preexisting group, talk with the group, or at least a sampling of participants, about the idea before you put the issue on the agenda. For example: "It seems to me that we have established some unproductive norms, such as jumping from subject to subject, starting late, and so on. [Use your own meetings' examples without pointing fingers.] I would like to take a few minutes at our next meeting to determine what standards we would like to establish for ourselves in the future. What do you think of this idea?"

2. Using chart paper, show the group draft Ground Rules, as in figure 3-2.

EXAMPLES OF GROUND RULES:

- Listen to and honor all opinions and concerns
- One conversation at a time
- Focus on the task at hand
- Help us stay on track and on schedule
- Avoid detail overload—keep remarks brief and to the point
- Work toward honest consensus
- Think out of the box
- Avoid personal agendas
- Stay future-oriented—don't dwell on the past
- Offer solutions, not complaints
- All items written on charts as a record
- No lectures
- Cellular phones off
- Fun is allowed

Figure 3-2. Ground Rules examples.

3. Ask the group members what Ground Rules they would like to use as their own. Chart (write down on chart paper) their ideas.

   OPTION A: Use a fresh piece of paper to chart their ideas.

   OPTION B: Leave plenty of room on the page of example Ground Rules you presented. Write modifications and additions directly on that page.

4. When you and your group feel that the list of Ground Rules is complete, ask if there are any Ground Rules that anyone cannot live with or support. Change them as necessary. Be sure that everyone agrees to all the Ground Rules.

NOTE: In potentially volatile situations or with a very dysfunctional group, ask each person individually, in round-robin fashion, if he or she is willing to personally support the Ground Rules.

5. If appropriate, ask participants what measures they, as a group, think should be taken if the Ground Rules are not followed. This helps secure agreement on how to handle potential problems when they occur and makes everyone responsible for meeting success. Agree on something that fits the personality of the group, can be done by any participant, and serves as clear and immediate feedback. For example, one group agreed to point in the direction of the posted ground rules as a nonverbal reminder. Another group decided to use a more direct approach and created this formula:

   "We agreed to [indicate the pertinent Ground Rule]. It seems like we're/you're [state the disruptive behavior]. What do you think?"

   Here are two specific examples:

   "We agreed to avoid detail overload. It seems like you are giving us more information than we need at this point. Would it be okay if we move on?"

   "We agreed to listen to and honor all opinions and concerns. It seems like you are not taking Julie's perspective seriously. What do you think?"

6. Post the Ground Rules in a prominent place at every meeting held with that same group. (The chart may need to be rewritten if your original is too messy or crumpled.)

7. Refer to the Ground Rules as needed and review them when new members join the group. Modify them as necessary.

Summary

Ground Rules act as preferred standards of behavior. Establish Ground Rules at the beginning of your meeting, and refer to them when needed throughout your meeting.

1. Introduce the idea and state the purpose of having Ground Rules.

2. Show examples of Ground Rules.

3. Lead the group in creating its own Ground Rules. Chart the ideas.

4. When the list of Ground Rules is complete, ask if there are any Ground Rules that anyone cannot live with or support.

5. Agree on what measures the group will take if someone doesn't follow the Ground Rules.

6. Post the Ground Rules.

7. Refer to the Ground Rules as needed.

"I know that from time to time there is some skepticism within our group. But I don't know how to identify which specific issues are causing the most concern and how much our success is impacted. I wish I had a way of measuring the attitudes of our group. Do you have any ideas?"

4. Pulse Check

What Is Pulse Check?

Pulse Check is a technique to determine the mood, attitude, temperature, or pulse of your group. It involves asking individuals to articulate their feelings toward a particular issue. Their ratings are used to determine the overall pulse of the group and act as a springboard for discussion about how people are feeling and why.

Negativity, left unchecked, can feed on itself. What may start with one or two people can quickly spread to the rest of the group. For this reason, it is wise to identify and address any concerns proactively. Pulse Check information will help identify any possible negative energy surrounding an issue and support its transformation into a positive force from the start. Because Pulse Check will also expose positive attitudes, it can help you sustain positive energy.

This technique should be used to help you feel the pulse of your group on an issue, positive or negative, so that you can use it to the group's greatest advantage and benefit.

When to Use Pulse Check

- When you want to check how your group feels about a specific issue
- When you suspect that there will be low energy and enthusiasm for your meeting
- When the group has had negative experiences in the past and you want to stimulate more positive experiences in the future

How to Use Pulse Check

1. Introduce the Pulse Check.

   For example: "Let's take our group's pulse by identifying our present attitudes about [name the specific issue, concern, or even the meeting itself]. We will do this by secret ballot and tally. Then we will have a brief discussion of our findings and look for ways to turn any negative energy or concerns toward a positive outcome."

2. Gather pulse ratings from each individual at the meeting.

    a. Pass out small pieces of paper to all participants and ask them to select a number from one (low) to ten (high) that reflects their expectations for a successful outcome about the issue at hand. Have them write this number on the paper.

    NOTE: You may participate unless you are a neutral facilitator.

    OPTION: If the group has a high level of trust, ask for verbal reports or ask each person to come forward to tick his or her number on the chart.

    OPTION: You may also do this through electronic voting.

    b. Ask participants to fold their papers and pass them to one or two designated people near the front of the room.

    NOTE: Designate people who are in a logical location for this. You could also ask participants to pass their paper to persons at corner points of the room or to a designated person at each table. Do what seems logical given the layout of your room and the size of your group.

    c. Ask the designated people to read the numbers aloud. Record numbers by adding tick marks on a prepared chart similar to figure 3-3.

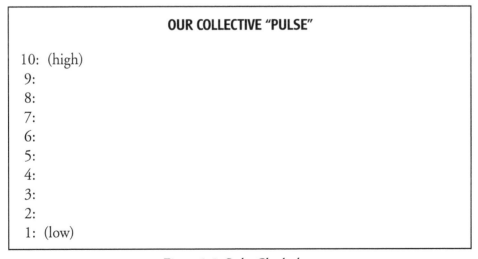

Figure 3-3. Pulse Check chart.

    d. Identify the group's average score. Add all the numbers together and divide by the total number of voters to arrive at the mean or average score.

    NOTE: Unless you are quick at math, bring a calculator. If you don't have a calculator, ask another participant to do the math for you.

    e. Ask volunteers to give some specific reasons why they awarded the ratings that they did.

3. Discuss your group results.

    a. Ask the group, for example:

- "What in particular stands out to you?"
- "What are your reactions to this information?"
- "How might these results impact our work together?"
- "What can we do to exceed the expectations of the group?"
- "How can we use this information to help us make xxxx more successful?"

    NOTE: Modify these questions to best meet the specific needs of your group.

    b. Summarize the key points from the group discussion. Chart key points as appropriate.

4. Take action according to the suggestions of the group.

Summary

1. Introduce Pulse Check.

2. Gather pulse ratings from each individual at the meeting.

3. Discuss the group results. Summarize the key points from the group discussion.

4. Take action according to the suggestions of the group.

"Our meetings are continually spinning off onto tangents unrelated to our original agenda. We never accomplish what we originally set out to do, and everyone is frustrated, including me. What can I do?"

5. Parking Lot

What Is a Parking Lot?

Parking Lot is a productivity technique for effectively dealing with distracting but important nonagenda items that arise during the course of your meeting.

Nonagenda items always seem to find their way into meetings. It is important to honor and recognize the existence of these important nonagenda items, but without interrupting the focus and goals of your meeting agenda. Parking Lot involves recording these tangential issues on paper, ensuring that they will be remembered and addressed, but without interrupting the ongoing conversation.

Parking Lot is another basic productivity technique that can be used to support your group's Ground Rules, technique 3, for keeping on track.

When to Use a Parking Lot

- When the meeting gets off track with issues worthy of discussion or action but unrelated, or tangential, to the current agenda item

How to Use a Parking Lot

1. At or before the beginning of each meeting, place a chart labeled Parking Lot on the wall. Refer to figure 3-4.

PARKING LOT		
What	**Who**	**By When**

Figure 3-4. Parking Lot chart.

The first time you use Parking Lot, explain its purpose to the participants at the beginning of your meeting. Gain their approval to use this technique as needed throughout your meeting.

For example: "As you know, our meetings often get off the subject, and we end up spending our time on issues outside our agenda. I suggest that from now on, when this starts to happen, we record the tangential issue on a Parking Lot chart for later discussion. That way, we will remember to come back to the issue later but still be able to accomplish our meeting's goals. What do you think? I encourage you all to help me note when our conversations are getting off track."

2. When the conversation wanders off track with an issue worthy of consideration but off the topic under discussion, briefly stop the meeting and write a quick synopsis of the issue, with permission from the group, on the Parking Lot chart.

   NOTE: With issues that are trivial, politely remind the group that the meeting is getting off track. If you are not sure if an issue is worthy of the unfinished business list, ask the group members what they think.

3. As one of the last agenda items for your meeting, go back to your Parking Lot list and decide, as a group, how to address each item. Some issues may be appropriate for discussion at your next meeting. Others may be more appropriately handled by a subset of the group or even by an individual. Some issues will no longer seem important and will be dropped.

   NOTE: During this discussion, document who will do what by when. This ensures that issues will be addressed. For example: "Sam and Rebecca, make recommendations for a new building site at the next meeting." "Carl, send information on product exposure through e-mail by Friday, September the eighth." Write the information directly on your Parking Lot chart and include it in the minutes of your meeting.

   NOTE: Be sure to save enough time at the end of your meeting to do this step. If you fail to go back to your Parking Lot before the end of the meeting, you lose credibility. People will be reluctant to have their issues permanently left and forgotten on the Parking Lot chart.

Summary

Parking Lot is a technique for dealing with the tangential issues that threaten to take your meeting off track.

1. Post a chart labeled Parking Lot on the wall.

2. When the conversation wanders off track, briefly stop the meeting and write a quick synopsis of the issue on the Parking Lot chart.

3. As one of the last agenda items for your meeting, go back to your Parking Lot list. Decide, as a group, how to address each item.

"I agree that each agenda item should have a time limit, but as we get into our conversation, some-times we forget how much time has gone by. More often than not, our allotted time is gone before we've come to any conclusions. How can we avoid this problem?"

6. Verbal Warnings

What Are Verbal Warnings?

Verbal Warnings help groups pace their discussions. This technique involves verbalizing how much discussion or work time remains within a predetermined and agreed-upon dead-line.

Assigning time frames to each agenda item greatly enhances meeting effectiveness. The Verbal Warnings technique further increases meeting success by managing discussion time. It focuses discussions because it regulates the discussion time frames, although this control feature needs to remain flexible enough to expand and contract as the specific discussion dictates.

By regulating the time frames, this technique gives the meeting facilitator a powerful tool to help accurately estimate future meeting agenda time parameters.

When to Use Verbal Warnings
- When you want to keep your meetings on track
- When you are nearing the completion of each item on your agenda

How to Use Verbal Warnings
1. Introduce the Verbal Warnings technique and determine who will track the time at the beginning of each meeting.

   The first time you use this technique, you might say, for example, "In order to help us meet our agreed-upon schedule, we need to keep better track of our time. I suggest that from now on, we ask one person to be our official timekeeper at every meeting. That person will be responsible for giving us Verbal Warnings about how much time we have left. For instance, during a discussion scheduled for forty-five minutes, the timekeeper would give us warnings at thirty minutes, fifteen minutes, seven minutes, and two minutes. If he or she felt we were using our time wisely, he or she might only give us a seven- and a two-minute warning instead. What do you think about the idea? Who would like to be our timekeeper today?"

NOTE: Even if you are an external facilitator, it is generally better to share responsibility for the meeting's success by using a timekeeper. However, if you think that a separate timekeeper will be overkill, then be the timekeeper yourself.

NOTE: When small group discussions are used, each group elects its own timekeeper.

2. Give Verbal Warnings for each agenda item as is needed.

3. Negotiate times as necessary.

When the predetermined time is insufficient, ask the group or small groups how much more time they need. Negotiate with the group(s) for more time as is appropriate.

NOTE: This might mean negotiating not just how much time is needed for that agenda item but also what will be dropped from that meeting's agenda if time runs out.

Conversely, be sure to watch for opportunities when less time is needed for an agenda item than is originally planned. If you are observant and proactive in this way, your group will be able to use this extra time for other agenda items or meeting business.

Summary

The Verbal Warnings technique helps your meeting groups pace their discussions by verbalizing how much time remains within the predetermined time frames for each agenda item.

1. Introduce Verbal Warnings and determine who will be the meeting's timekeeper.

2. Give Verbal Warnings for each agenda item as is needed.

3. Negotiate times as necessary.

"I have trouble calling our meetings to order. No one can hear me when other people are talking, even with a microphone. This is a problem before we begin, when we come back from breaks, and when we are using small group discussions. I nearly end up with laryngitis. There has to be an easier way."

7. The Bell

What Is the Bell?

The Bell is an effective and simple productivity technique to communicate to meeting participants that it is time to reconvene. Using the Bell can save your voice and make you heard above the crowd.

When to Use the Bell

- When you want to indicate that the meeting is starting
- When you want to bring small groups back together into a large group again
- When the situation has gotten out of control or off the subject

How to Use the Bell

1. It is a good idea to mention the purpose and use of the Bell the first time you use it with a meeting group. Be sure you ask your participants for their support in helping you keep the meeting on schedule.

   NOTE: Purchase a small dinner bell or customer service bell for your meetings. Both are inexpensive and easy to locate. Customer services bells can typically be found at your local office supply store, but you can use any bell that is not too shrill and obnoxious. Be sure that your bell can be heard above the sound of participants' voices.

2. Simply ring the bell at all appropriate times to reconvene your meeting group.

Summary

The Bell is a technique to communicate that it is time to begin. It acts as a friendly and easily heard reminder that it is time to focus energy on the meeting.

1. Introduce the Bell technique.

2. Ring the Bell at appropriate times to reconvene your meeting group.

"Even though I think I've been clear, my meeting participants often question me about the specific function and value of meeting activities. They certainly have every right to know what is going on and why. Is there a technique I can use to better explain what will happen, how it will happen, and why it will happen?"

8. Three P Statements

What Are Three P Statements?

The Three P Statements productivity technique explains the focus, methodology, and value of a given upcoming agenda item. It informs your meeting group of what to expect and what will be accomplished from the start.

Three P Statements are used to help a meeting group adequately prepare for the meeting itself, a presentation, a new agenda item, or a discussion topic. Three P is an acronym of sorts that translates into *purpose*, *process*, and *payoff*, and the technique involves answering three basic and critical questions in statement form: What will we do? How will we do it? Why is it important?

Purpose states what you plan to accomplish. Stating this intention or purpose answers some fundamental questions. Why are we here? What is the goal? How will the information be used?

Process describes how the meeting will address the topic under consideration and answers additional important questions. How will we proceed? What techniques will we use? What steps will we take? How long will this last? What is expected of me? What is expected of the group?

Payoff informs your participants of the benefit, or what they will get from the discussion, and resolves the following questions. Why bother? What is in it for me to participate? What are the real benefits? How will this affect our group's goals?

Not only does the Three P Statements technique provide essential information to your meeting group, it also provides you as the facilitator with critical planning information. If you can't identify the purpose, process, and payoff for any given topic of discussion, do not proceed. If you do, the likelihood of failure will be high.

When to Use Three P Statements
- When you are planning the agenda for your meeting
- When you are starting your meeting
- When you are beginning a new agenda item in your meeting
- When you are making a formal presentation

How to Use Three P Statements

1. When you are planning for your meeting, apply the three P statements template to the proposed topics of your agenda:

   a. What is the *purpose* of this topic?

   b. What *process* will we use to discuss it?

   c. What is the anticipated *payoff* (benefit or result) from the discussion?

   Consider using this template to organize your Three P Statements:
   In order to (*purpose*), we will (*process*), so that (*payoff*).

   NOTE: Modify this template to meet your specific situation.

   An example using this format is: "In order to decide how to best meet our customers' needs, we will conduct a focus group with our key customers. This will give us information on what they see as the top priorities for improvement in the next fiscal year."

2. Use the Three P Statements as planned.

   NOTE: Remember that Three P Statements can be used to help you plan your meeting agendas, open your meetings, introduce new agenda items during your meetings, or make formal presentations or suggestions. They are also helpful if the group becomes unfocused or confused about what you are doing and why.

Summary

Three P Statements is a technique to articulate the purpose, process, and payoff of the proposed topics on your meeting agenda.

1. When planning for your meetings, apply the Three P Statements template to each issue of your agenda: In order to (*purpose*), we will (*process*), so that (*payoff*).

2. Use the Three P Statements to help plan your agenda, open your meetings, introduce new agenda items, or make formal presentations or suggestions.

"It seems as if conversations at our meetings always go around in circles. We talk about different aspects of the same question all at the same time. Is there a specific technique we can use that will give us some structure and control over this?"

9. Shredded Questions

What Are Shredded Questions?

The Shredded Questions technique outlines an orderly process for addressing a specific meeting issue or agenda item. This technique ensures that every appropriate facet or element of the specific issue under discussion will be examined thoroughly and efficiently.

Generally, the facets of meeting issues include:
- Facts and background
- Feelings and reactions
- Brainstorming or creative alternatives
- The pros of each alternative
- The cons of each alternative
- Agreement on the decision
- Implementation and next steps

Unstructured discussions can result in all facets being discussed simultaneously, and the consequences of this lack of structure are measured in wasted time and disappointing results. Shredded Questions break each issue or agenda item down into a series of specific questions drawn from each of the facets; as a result, discussions become ordered, focused, and more successful.

Shredded Questions save valuable meeting time and dramatically improve the quality and the results of the meeting discussions where the technique is applied. This shredding technique also allows you as a facilitator to more effectively estimate agenda timelines.

When to Use Shredded Questions
- When you want to efficiently examine all aspects of a specific issue or agenda item
- When your group will be discussing complex issues
- When discussions seem to go around in circles

How to Use Shredded Questions

Before the Meeting

1. Determine the purpose and desired end result of your specific agenda item.

2. Determine the best questions to guide your proposed discussion.

   a. Be sure to include questions that will consider all appropriate facets of the agenda topic.

   NOTE: Eliminate inappropriate categories based on the goal(s) of that particular agenda item.

   Facts and background include purely factual information. Some example questions to elicit facts might be: What is the history of this issue? What are the key points? What specific details are important for us all to understand? What data and analysis are available? What do the experts say? What do our customers think? What are the facts?

   NOTE: Facts and background are typically collected first and need to be comprehensive. Be sure to obtain them from all available perspectives, including individuals who may not be in your meeting. This step creates a foundation for all further discussion on the issue under consideration.

   Feelings and reactions include intuitions, feelings, and emotional reactions. Sample questions might be: What was the high point/low point for you? What was the collective mood at the time? How do you feel about it? What are you excited about? What are you worried about? What is your gut feeling?

   NOTE: Emotions and feelings are important information. When taken into consideration, they strengthen and support decisions. If ignored, they can jeopardize those decisions. It is imperative to include emotional information and energy along with the facts.

   Creative alternatives are the result of brainstorming and offer possible solutions to a given problem. Example questions include: What alternatives or options do we have? What ideas come to mind? How can we best address this issue?

NOTE: Refer to the Old-Fashioned Way, technique 28, or other specific brainstorming techniques described in chapter 5.

The **pros** of each alternative reveal the positive side of the brainstormed ideas. Ask, for example: How will this make a difference in the way we do business? What are the positive aspects of this option? What are the benefits of this alternative?

The **cons** of each alternative reveal the negative side of the brainstormed ideas. Questions you might ask include: What are the negatives we should consider? What are the budgetary requirements? What are the personnel requirements?

NOTE: The last two questions could be perceived as either a pro or con depending on the situation.

NOTE: Both facts and feelings can be used to assess the viability of any creative alternative.

Agreement on the decision, or decisions, should be reached by consensus, agreed upon, and mutually owned by all participants. To lead a group to a decision, you might ask: "Now that we have analyzed all the information, what should we do?" "What is our decision?"

NOTE: See chapter 7 for ten specific techniques to help your group make decisions.

Next steps provide the follow-through to ensure that the decision (or decisions) made is effectively implemented and monitored. You might say, for example: "What are the next steps?" "Who do we need to communicate with?" "How will we measure our success?" "What are the steps we need to take to implement these changes?" "What can we do to make sure that the program is implemented properly?"

NOTE: Consider Chart Actions, technique 63, to support the next steps.

b. Develop your key questions and sequence them in a logical manner.

c. Be sure to use Open-Ended Questions. See Open-Ended Questions, technique 34, for details.

3. Prepare any visual aids you will use in the meeting.

During the Meeting

1. Introduce the issue or agenda item for discussion. Describe the intended result and purpose. Explain why this issue is important.

2. Explain the Shredded Questions technique, and ask the group for help in answering only one question at a time.

   You might say, for example: "Let's try to keep our discussion focused on one aspect of this issue at a time. Here are the questions I've prepared to help us accomplish this. [Display your questions on an overhead or chart.] I'd appreciate your help in answering the questions one by one. This will save us both time and frustration."

   NOTE: Letting the group see all the questions from the beginning will help them focus and remain patient.

3. Lead the discussion, either as a large group or in small groups. Record the points of the discussion on charts. Post each chart so that it can be viewed throughout the meeting.

   NOTE: Alter your preplanned questions if they are not working as expected. Ask your group for help in modifying or resequencing the questions if necessary.

Summary

Shredded Questions dissect the facets or elements of an issue and address them one by one. These facets include facts and background, feelings and reactions, brainstorming for creative alternatives, the pros and cons of each alternative, agreement on the decision, and implementation and next steps.

Before the Meeting

1. Focus on a specific agenda item. Determine its purpose and intended result.

2. Determine the best questions to guide the conversation.

3. Prepare any visual aids you will use in the meeting.

During the Meeting

1. Introduce the issue or agenda item for discussion, describing the purpose and intended result.

2. Explain the Shredded Questions technique, and ask the group for help in answering only one question at a time.

3. Lead the discussion, modifying questions if necessary. Chart all comments.

"How can I stimulate the participants in our group to become more involved and take more responsibility for our meeting's success?"

10. Self-Management

What Is Self-Management?

Self-Management is a productivity technique for stimulating participant involvement and sharing responsibility for and ownership of meeting success.

Participants in the meeting accomplish this by breaking apart the different roles of the meeting facilitator and sharing them among themselves. These roles include a facilitator, recorder, minute taker, and timekeeper, as well as a facilitator in small group discussions.

When group members share the facilitation duties, their involvement and ownership increases automatically. Self-Management increases meeting success by sharing responsibility and also stimulates better focus, commitment, and participation.

Every meeting needs to focus on both process and content. The process and facilitation of a meeting support the content. It is very difficult to focus on both of them simultaneously. Group leaders will find that separating the two enables them to focus on content most effectively.

Regardless of whether you delegate these roles or do them all yourself, please know that they must be performed, and it's helpful to think of them all consciously throughout your meeting.

When to Use Self-Management

- When you want to separate the content of the meeting from the process of facilitation
- When you want fuller group participation in your meetings
- When you use small group discussions within your meetings

How to Use Self-Management

1. Describe the Self-Management technique and its purpose to the group.

   For example: "We want our meetings to be more successful. As each person's involvement in the process increases, contribution and ownership increase as well. By breaking down and sharing the meeting facilitation roles, we can accomplish this result. What do you think?" ... "A successful meeting facilitator has several roles and responsibilities. These include ..." (Use a chart or overhead similar to figure 3-5.)

MEETING ROLES

Facilitator: Facilitates the meeting. Takes a leadership role in planning the meeting.

Recorder: Records all comments, ideas, and decisions on chart paper.

Minute Taker: Prepares the minutes.

Timekeeper: Keeps track of time limitations.

Figure 3-5. Meeting roles chart for Self-Management.

2. Select participants to fill the meeting roles.

You might say, for example: "In order to share responsibility for the success of our meeting, I'd like to suggest that at each meeting we rotate these roles. What do you think?" "I've planned to lead this meeting, but who would like to be our recorder?" "our minute taker?" "our timekeeper?" "Thanks, everyone. Let's see how our meeting runs with this new shared responsibility."

OPTION: You may assign these responsibilities before the meeting and announce them in the meeting.

a. **The facilitator** facilitates the meeting, using different participative processes to accomplish each agenda item.

As stated above, the manager or group leader does not have to facilitate the meeting. In fact, it is a good idea to rotate this responsibility. Be sure to assign facilitator responsibilities for the next meeting before your current meeting ends so the new facilitator can adequately prepare.

NOTE: If you are the manager or group leader and you delegate the facilitation role, please meet with the facilitator before the meeting to ensure that you agree on the agenda, processes, and time frames.

b. **The recorder** records the group's comments, ideas, and decisions on chart paper.

Often the facilitator acts as the recorder. But when the group is large or the conversation is difficult to facilitate, it is better to have a separate recorder. Give recorders spelling amnesty. Correct spelling is not critical; however, it is critical that recorders accurately capture the thoughts of all members of the group.

c. **The minute taker** prepares and sends the minutes of the meeting shortly after it is finished.

The minutes of the meeting should include highlights of the discussions, the decisions made, and next steps. See chapter 2 for more details.

d. **The timekeeper** keeps track of the time limitations. (See Verbal Warnings, technique 6, for timekeeper instructions.)

3. When your meetings utilize small group discussions, each group should have its own facilitator, timekeeper, and recorder.

NOTE: It is a good idea to move around and listen to what is happening within the groups to assure that everyone's thoughts are documented, everyone is getting a chance to be heard, and the groups are on track.

Summary

Self-Management is a technique for increasing participation and ownership by sharing meeting responsibility. This is accomplished by sharing the roles of facilitator, recorder, minute taker, and timekeeper among members of the group.

1. Describe the Self-Management technique and its purpose.

2. Select participants to fill the four meeting facilitator roles.

3. In small group discussions, each group should nominate its own facilitator, recorder, and timekeeper.

"What is the easiest way to ascertain if our meeting group is ready to move to the next agenda item or next part of our current discussion? Sometimes I'm not sure."

11. Go/No Go

What Is Go/No Go?

Go/No Go is a productivity technique that helps your meeting group decide whether or not to move forward. This can mean moving to the next agenda item, the next section of a complex question, the next step, or the next question, or making any decision that requires a yes or no vote.

If an ongoing discussion is incomplete, and this often occurs with complex issues, moving forward prematurely slows down or even undermines success. The Go/No Go technique involves a simple voting procedure to make this determination.

When to Use Go/No Go

- When you want agreement from the group that it is time to move on
- When you need agreement from the group to do something

How to Use Go/No Go

1. When you feel that it is time for the group to move on, take a vote.

   You might say to the group, "All in favor of moving forward to the next section/ agenda item say go." … "All in favor of not moving forward say no go."

2. If there are No Go votes, address the concerns of the negative voters before moving forward. Ask, "What needs to happen before you will feel comfortable moving forward?" Examples of No Go reasons include a need to further explore a fact or gather additional information. Address No Go issues in the appropriate manner.

3. Revote as necessary.

   OPTION: Instead of voting, simply confirm your recommendation to move forward with the group. For example, "I think we are ready to move on, do you agree?" Look for verbal and nonverbal confirmation and react accordingly.

OPTION: Ask the manager or group leader in the meeting to make the Go/No Go decision.

Summary

Go/No Go is a technique to help your team decide as a group when it is time to move forward. This can relate to the next agenda item, the next section of a complex question, or any decision requiring a yes or no vote.

1. Take a Go/No Go vote to gain consensus.

2. When there are No Go votes, address the concerns of the negative voters before moving forward.

3. Revote as necessary.

"Even though I think my instructions are clear, participants frequently ask me to repeat what I say. Also, points that are made in the meeting are often repeated later on. This is frustrating and always seems to slow us down. Can you suggest a technique that will eliminate these problems?"

12. Charting

What Is Charting?

Charting is a productivity technique for increasing the effectiveness of communication in your meetings by using visual aids to support your efforts.

Because many studies demonstrate the low accuracy of communication, it is important to use meeting facilitation techniques that sustain and reinforce the accuracy of memory. Many people are visual learners, and they will concentrate better and remember much more when you use visual aids.

Charting significantly improves the accuracy of your communication, whether it is instructions, agendas, questions, data collection, discussions, or presentations. Charting responses to conversations also shows participants that their comments are being captured accurately.

When to Use Charting

- When you want to improve the accuracy of communication in your meetings
- When giving instructions/directions
- When you want to accurately document the points made during a discussion, either to use in the future or to confirm that you have heard each individual's comments and opinions correctly

How to Use Charting

Five types of information benefit from Charting in meetings. These include: agendas and ground rules, discussion questions, small group and individual exercise instructions, discussion points, and decisions and actions.

Agendas and Ground Rules

Chart and post your agenda and ground rules where they can be seen throughout the meeting.

NOTE: As you proceed through your agenda, check off where you are on the chart. This helps people know where they are and where they're going. It gives them a sense of accomplishment. Refer back to your charted agenda from time to time, summarizing what has happened and what will happen.

Discussion Questions

Post discussion questions on either an overhead or chart to help keep your group on track. See Shredded Questions, technique 9, for specific ideas.

Small Group and Individual Exercise Instructions

During small group and individual exercises, chart and post all instructions and time frames.

NOTE: You should prepare these instructions before the meeting on either charts or overheads. Overheads usually work better with larger groups because people can read them more easily at a distance and from different positions in the room. Charts are better for smaller groups and/or when the information needs to be seen throughout the meeting. If small groups will meet in different rooms, prepare instruction charts for each room.

- Break instructions down into logical steps
- Write legibly and as large as possible to ensure that everyone can read what you write
- Use dark colors (so the chart can be read from longer distances)
- State time frames (i.e., ten minutes) and finishing times (i.e., 9:25) for each step

Discussion Points

Use chart paper to record discussions from all agenda items. This keeps conversations from going around in circles, avoids repetition of the same points, and provides excellent data from which to prepare the minutes of your meeting. It also ensures that participants know they are being heard correctly.

NOTE: Have small groups record their discussions on chart paper for their report back to the rest of the groups.

NOTE: If you plan to use your charts for a different purpose later in the meeting, such as voting on priorities, set your chart up for this purpose from the start. Leave room on the chart so your next exercise, that is, the voting, can be done without messiness or confusion.

Decisions and Actions

Record all group decisions and actions or next steps on charts for inclusion in the minutes of the meeting.

Summary

Charting is a productivity technique for improving retention and understanding through the use of visual aids.

Clearly chart and post your agenda, ground rules, discussion questions, small group and individual instructions, discussion points, and decisions and actions.

"My participants sometimes seem to get bogged down in their own logic. This inhibits their creativity and negatively impacts the energy of the group. I am looking for a way to get people to think more creatively so we can develop a deeper understanding of an issue. Is there a technique that will help us see things through different eyes?"

13. Art

What Is Art?

Art is a technique for helping your meeting participants think and express themselves differently.

When people articulate their thoughts in atypical ways, they tend to produce a broader spectrum of information. And sometimes the most unlikely methods of expression produce the most revealing information because such methods encourage people to use the part of their brain that taps and stimulates their perception differently.

Art involves having participants express their thoughts and ideas visually on paper. If used correctly, this type of artistic expression will increase the effectiveness of your meetings by providing new insights and boosting creativity, energy, and fun.

When to Use Art

- When people need to visualize their future, a change, or a decision
- When you want to clarify a point that is difficult to articulate
- When you want to summarize what has been completed
- When you want more creative input

How to Use Art

1. As a part of one or more relevant agenda items, ask your participants to draw or otherwise visually depict their ideas on paper. This can be done individually or in small groups, and the Art can be literal or figurative. Provide the necessary paper and a wide variety of colored markers.

   OPTION: You may also bring other art materials, such as scissors, magazines to cut up, colored paper, and whatever else comes to mind.

   NOTE: Be sure that your instructions highlight that ideas are the goal of the exercise. Artistic skill is irrelevant.

NOTE: You may perceive Art as a high-risk idea and thus be hesitant to use it. But try it. The technique works well at all levels of an organization and can provide very creative and revealing information. You will be impressed with its effectiveness and high fun factor.

The following are some specific examples of how to initiate Art:

- To share information about staff responsibilities, you might say, "Create a visual aid to explain how you spend your time in a typical week."

  OPTION: Use collages. Ask people to prepare a visual of the things they accomplished in the last year—for example, pie charts of percentages of time use or projects accomplished.

- To gain an understanding of the group's current situation, say, for example, "Draw a picture of what it feels like to work here."

- To create a vision of the group's preferred future, you could say, "Imagine we have been able to accomplish all we discussed and agreed to today. Think of our group in five years. [Choose a number based on your circumstances.] What will it look like?" Or you might say, "Draw an animal that describes our group as it is today. Draw another animal that describes the perfect group of the future."

  NOTE: Use this information to create a list of words that describe your group's preferred future.

- To gain information on the attitudes in your department, you might say, "Show us, either literally or figuratively, our department's attitude toward the new management philosophy."

2. After the Art work is completed (usually fifteen to twenty minutes is enough), have the artists present and explain their work.

   NOTE: Take photos of the drawings and include them in the minutes of the meeting.

3. Ask the group members to summarize what they learned from the Art process.

For example, you might say, "What in particular stood out to you during this last exercise?" "What conclusions can we draw?"

Summary

Art is a technique that helps your meeting participants think and express themselves differently—that is, visually on paper. This type of artistic expression can lead to a deeper understanding of an issue and also increases a group's creativity, energy, and enjoyment.

1. Ask all participants to draw their ideas on paper. The pictures they draw can be literal or figurative.

2. Ask the individual or small-group artists to explain their work.

3. Have the group members summarize what they learned from the exercise and what conclusions can be drawn.

"Sometimes critical information isn't understood in our meetings as clearly as I would like. Important points seem to get lost because they are either complicated, dull, or both. What alternatives do we have to get key points across?"

14. Analogies and Metaphors

What Are Analogies and Metaphors?

The Analogies and Metaphors technique helps your meeting participants focus and crystalize their thinking and understanding of an issue. It can also be used to emphasize key points of a topic under discussion. This technique is especially applicable for information that is difficult to understand or explain in simple terms. Analogies and Metaphors involve using figurative language to explain and clarify the meaning of a specific issue. In addition to this primary goal, it can also help people to learn and think in new ways.

An analogy is a comparison that points out the similarity between the like features of two different things. For example, one could make an analogy between a heart and a pump or between a brain and a computer.

An example of an analogy was used in chapter 1. This book is like a carpenter's toolbox. It gives you the specific tools you need to effectively deal with diverse meeting situations. It not only provides the basic hammer, nails, and handsaw but also the more sophisticated specialty tools required to complete nearly any potential meeting objective.

A metaphor is a figure of speech that applies a term or phrase to something in order to suggest a resemblance. "Drowning in paperwork" and "walking on thin ice" are examples of metaphors.

The facilitator can use the Analogies and Metaphors technique as a communication strategy or as an exercise for participants.

When to Use Analogies and Metaphors

- When a key point is difficult to understand on its own
- When you want to make a point or explain something in a different way
- When you want to emphasize a point
- When you want to express personal perspectives in an impersonal but powerful way

How to Use Analogies and Metaphors As a Communication Strategy

Before the Meeting

1. Identify the point you want to emphasize or explain.

2. Think of your audience. What is important to your audience? What can they relate to? Football, skiing, computers, food?

3. Brainstorm possible analogies and metaphors for use in the meeting.

4. Choose one or two of the best to use in your meeting.

In the Meeting

1. Use the Analogies and Metaphors as planned.

   NOTE: It is a good idea to continually look for and think about effective ways to communicate ideas during your meetings. Tune in to your participants, improvise, and react with creative ideas as the situation presents itself.

How to Use Analogies and Metaphors as an Exercise for Meeting Participants

1. Introduce the topic and the Analogies and Metaphors technique. Explain why you are asking the group to create these Analogies and Metaphors and how they will be used.

   For example: "Our primary supplier has asked us for feedback on working with them, and I'm meeting with their president on Thursday. As you know, he sometimes has a difficult time relating to our specific needs, so I thought it would be helpful if I could use a few analogies or metaphors in our meeting. I'd like your help in coming up with some ideas."

   NOTE: Other situations where you might use this technique include: sharing information between participants about a project, their jobs, or the experience of working in that group or with a specific customer.

2. Ask the group to think silently for five minutes about Analogies and Metaphors on a specific subject. Present an overview of the meaning of the two terms with a few examples on a chart or overhead, as in figure 3-6.

CREATE AN ANALOGY OR METAPHOR TO DESCRIBE XX

Spend five minutes thinking silently and individually about xx. What analogies and/or metaphors come to mind?

Analogy = A comparison that points out the similarity between the like features of two different things. One can make an analogy between a heart and a pump, or a computer and a brain.

Metaphor = A representation or figurative expression. The application of a word or phrase to an object or concept it does not literally mean, in order to suggest comparison with another object or concept. A rose is often a metaphor for love, the rising sun for birth.

Figure 3-6. Instructions chart for Analogies and Metaphors.

3. Ask your participants to share their best analogies and metaphors with the group. This can be in either small groups or as a large group.

4. Ask the group what they can be conclude from the information. For example, "What points stuck out in your minds?" "What conclusions can we draw?"

OPTION: If appropriate for the goals of the agenda item, have the group pick one or two of their analogies and/or metaphors that best summarize how they feel.

Summary

The Analogies and Metaphors technique helps your meeting participants focus and increase their understanding of an issue because analogies and metaphors can explain and clarify the meaning of a complex issue. They also help people learn and think in new ways. The facilitator can use this technique as a communication strategy or as an exercise for the participants.

As a Communication Technique

Before the Meeting

1. Identify the point you want to emphasize.

2. Focus on topics that your audience will be able to relate to.

3. Brainstorm possible analogies and metaphors for use in the meeting.

4. Choose one or two of the best to use in your meeting.

During the Meeting

Use the Analogies and Metaphors as planned.

As an Exercise for Meeting Participants

1. Introduce Analogies and Metaphors and the topic under consideration.

2. Give the group members time to create their own Analogies and Metaphors.

3. Have the participants share the information.

4. Have the group summarize or draw conclusions.

"We seem to run out of steam long before our work has been completed. Do you have any ideas?"

15. Breaks

What Are Breaks?

Breaks are designed to support high energy and focus throughout your meeting.

Meetings are notorious for pushing on too long. The energy level of the group decreases as the meeting progresses, and concentration and creativity suffer as a result. This problem is especially common when participative meeting techniques are not utilized. Research shows that people work better for longer periods of time when they are able to take short and frequent Breaks. These Breaks, five or ten minutes an hour, are far more beneficial than less frequent, longer Breaks.

Breaks give the group time to stretch and discuss the agenda informally. The facilitator can use Breaks to ask for informal feedback on the meeting's processes and results and prepare for the next items on the agenda.

When to Use Breaks

- When your meetings run more than one hour
- When the group is stalled
- When the group is in conflict and needs a few minutes to cool down
- When you need time to regroup your thoughts—for example, if things are going badly
- When you see or feel the group's energy waning

How to Use Breaks

- Schedule Breaks for longer meetings, and take unplanned Breaks, with approval from the group, when appropriate.

- Use Breaks to ask for feedback informally from your participants. Ask open-ended questions like, "What are your reactions to the work we've done so far?" This information will help you modify the agenda and processes if necessary.

- Breaks are a good time to talk with people who tend to be antagonistic or disruptive in the meeting. Often meeting facilitators will try to avoid these people, perceiving them as problems. Instead, use Breaks to individually ask the person for his or her input. For example, to a person who seems to be resistant to the agenda you could say, "Tell me more about your concerns about the meeting today." You might learn valuable information and, at the very least, you will align yourself with the person by showing sensitivity for his or her concerns.

- Breaks are an excellent opportunity to talk to anyone who has been dominating the meeting discussions; you might say, "I would like your help. I know that you feel very comfortable sharing your ideas and opinions, but not everyone in the group feels as comfortable as you. It's very important for us to hear everybody's ideas. I was wondering if you would help me do this by holding your ideas a few minutes until we have heard from the others. If your points of view haven't been stated by the others, then give us your ideas. What do you think? How would that work for you?"

- This is a great time to deal with a conflict between a small number of group participants. You can say in this situation, "I know this issue is important to both of you, but I wonder if this meeting is the best place to resolve it. It seems like it doesn't include everyone, so I don't think it's a good use of everyone's time. What do you think?"

- Use this time to prepare for the next agenda items. Move charts, rearrange tables, and so on.

NOTE: Remember to post the time (to the minute) when the meeting will reconvene. It is critical to start on time after your breaks. If you don't, you and your meetings lose credibility and momentum.

NOTE: If your meeting is exceedingly dull, Breaks are not going to be enough to perk it up. You will need to look for other techniques to support your goals. Review the other techniques in this section for ideas. Don't hesitate to ask the group members for their help if you are unsure about how to address the problem of a boring, unproductive meeting.

OPTION: Consider adding a short break to the end of small group exercises. This gives the slower groups time to catch up, while allowing the others time to officially rest.

Summary

Breaks help keep your participants energized and focused. Schedule breaks at regular intervals, and take unscheduled breaks when needed. Use your own time wisely during breaks to talk with individual participants and prepare for the next items on the agenda.

"What other techniques can I use to keep people alert and involved in our meetings?"

16. Movement

What Is Movement?

Movement is another technique designed to keep energy high and attention focused. Any purposeful Movement can reenergize your group while at the same time supporting your meeting objectives.

When to Use Movement

- When your meetings last more than a few hours
- When you want to encourage participants to talk with new people
- When you anticipate that the group's energy level will deteriorate, such as after lunch
- When the group appears to be physically uncomfortable

How to Use Movement

1. Periodically encourage participants to sit in different places, next to different people. These changes can take place after Breaks and are especially important if your meeting lasts through both the morning and afternoon.

   OPTION: For small group discussions, have people consistently move to different parts of the room so that they interact with different people. This tends to be mentally stimulating and discourages the formation of cliques and alliances. This Movement also informally builds teamwork. This is most commonly done in one of two ways:

   a. Create predetermined discussion groups. Cluster participants with the maximum diversity of position, level within the organization, longevity on the job, and general perspective. Plan these groups, perhaps with the help of other participants, before the meeting.

   b. Create subgroups by asking participants to count off. See Small Groups, technique 20, for details.

2. Use a light ball during round-robin exercises to keep the group active.

   a. Explain the procedure. For example: "The person who has the ball is the one who speaks. When that person is done speaking, he or she will throw the ball to some-one else, anyone he or she chooses who has not yet spoken. Make sure that the ball gets around to everyone, thus giving everyone a chance to speak."

b. Arbitrarily toss the ball to someone, asking that person to start. If your ball happens to be physically nearer someone else, ask that person to choose who should start by throwing the ball to him or her. Unless you are an outside facilitator, you should also speak on the subject.

c. When everyone has spoken, summarize and move on with your agenda.

3. Ask participants to physically move to cluster around wall charts used during specific components of your agenda.

Summary

Movement is a technique for keeping energy high as well as assuring that participants talk with as many other participants as possible during the meeting.

1. Encourage participants to sit in different parts of the room and to work with different people in small groups.

2. Use a light ball as a group discussion tool.

3. Ask participants to physically move to cluster around wall charts used during specific components of your agenda.

"After an hour or so I start to see the signs. People start to fidget, they seem uncomfortable, and they lose concentration. We take frequent Breaks and use Movement in our meetings as well, but I'd like to learn another alternative for getting active people to sit still enough to listen and participate for extended periods of time."

17. Toys

What Are Toys?

The use of Toys is another technique designed to keep people focused and attentive for long periods of time.

"Sit still and pay attention!" Many of us learned this strict rule of behavior as children, but it isn't helpful advice for everybody. Not all people listen better when they are sitting still and at attention. In fact, some listen much better and for longer periods of time when they can do something with their hands. Toys is an uncomplicated and effective technique that involves allowing meeting participants to play with quiet toys during the meeting.

The Toys technique is not designed to replace Breaks, technique 15, or Movement, technique 16, but to work with them in concert to help keep your participants relaxed, comfortable, attentive, involved, and productive.

When to Use Toys

- When people must sit and concentrate for a long time
- When your meeting participants rarely sit as part of their job
- When you want to introduce an element of fun into your otherwise serious meetings

How to Use Toys

Before the Meeting

1. Go to your local toy store and purchase some simple toys. The cost will be minimal. Buy only toys that won't require any mental concentration, won't make noise, and won't distract others in the group.

   Examples of excellent toys are:
   - Koosh balls
   - Silly Putty
   - Colored pens and paper for doodling
   - Magnet toys

- Finger puppets
- Play-Doh

NOTE: Don't be afraid to try this technique with serious or upper-level groups. They may need Toys the most. However, if using Toys will be counter to the culture of your organization, test the idea with a few participants first.

2. Randomly place your Toys on the table(s) as you prepare the room for your meeting. If the tables are large, be sure that some Toys will be within easy reach of everybody who will attend the meeting.

In the Meeting

1. As your meeting begins, explain that the Toys are there purposely for participants to play with during the meeting. Emphasize that this activity can occur at any time and without permission but is an individual exercise. People who choose to use Toys shouldn't distract others from thinking or participation. This technique can be linked to the ground rule "fun is allowed." See Ground Rules, technique 3, for details.

2. At the end of the meeting, ask participants to leave the Toys for the next meeting. (Unless you want to give them away as mementos.)

NOTE: The first time you use Toys in your meeting, ask for reactions from your meeting participants at the end of the meeting.

Summary

The use of Toys is a productivity technique for keeping people relaxed, focused, and attentive for long periods of time.

Before the Meeting

1. Purchase some simple Toys at your local toy store. Be sure to buy only Toys that don't require any mental concentration.

2. Randomly place the Toys on the table(s) as you prepare the meeting room.

In the Meeting

1. As the meeting begins, explain that the Toys are there to be played with during the meeting.

2. Ask the participants to leave the Toys as the meeting ends.

"Sometimes I think that the energy swings in my meetings are due to the lack of diversity in my facilitation. And this sameness becomes a source of tedium for my participants. What can I do to change the atmosphere and the pace or create a different mood in my meetings?"

18. Music

What Is Music?

Music is another technique designed to keep your meeting group's energy high. Music can set the stage for increased creativity and productivity by a simple change of mood. Well planned, Music alters the ambience and tone of a meeting, thereby changing its pace and sparking the interest and attention of your participants. This reenergizes your group and provides an atmosphere that helps participants remain productive and mentally refreshed over longer periods of time.

When to Use Music

- When you want to change the atmosphere to help you reinforce a point
- When you want people to relax and focus on your meeting
- When you want to emphasize a theme or point
- When you want to review material in a different way

How to Use Music

Use Music Before the Meeting and During Breaks

Before the Meeting

Select music that will suit your audience and support the mood you want to create. Think about the diversity of participants in your meeting and choose music that will appeal to the majority. Prepare to bring appropriate music to the meeting, either on your laptop or otherwise. Instrumental music tends to be better because lyrics may distract conversations and thoughts.

In the Meeting

1. Turn the music on as you are setting up for the meeting and as each break begins.

2. When you stop the music, it signifies that the meeting is ready to begin.

Use Music During the Meeting to Introduce, Emphasize, or Reinforce a Point or Issue

Before the Meeting

1. Select a piece of lyrical or instrumental music that literally or emotionally underscores a planned agenda item or piece of information.

2. If possible, bring a broad selection of Music with you to your meetings. This will enable you to improvise with this technique as the situation presents itself. Music can help to cool tempers, negate conflict, introduce humor, stimulate optimism, and awaken creativity.

In the Meeting

Play the Music during the appropriate part of your agenda.

OPTION: Let the participants select or create a theme song for a specific project or for their group. They may want to alter the words to an existing song to suit their purposes.

Use Music Along with Visual Aids as a Review or Summary

This can be done at the completion of the day, the beginning of a subsequent day, or at the end of a project.

Before the Meeting

1. Select a piece of Music that will be generally pleasing to your audience and appropriate for your review.

2. Sequentially prepare the visual aids, such as charts, graphs, slides, and overheads that you will use in the review.

3. Decide how to best display your visual aids. These could be displayed throughout the room, but using the overhead projector in the front of the room will give you more control.

4. Practice your timing and sequencing with the actual music you will use during your meeting.

In the Meeting

1. Prepare the group for the summary. You might say, for example: "We are going to review the highlights of yesterday's planning meeting using Music as a backdrop. This

review will remind us of where we left off and prepare us for our next agenda item, which is prioritizing the decisions we made."

2. Start the music and begin your review, using your overheads, charts, and other graphics. Present the material in a way that leads your participants through the information you are reviewing.

    NOTE: Remember to keep it quick and simple. Let the Music and visuals speak for themselves. You will not need a voice-over.

3. Turn off the Music when you finish the summary.

Summary

Music is a technique designed to keep meeting energy high. It changes the mood, allows your participants to better prepare and concentrate, and creates diversity in your presentation of information.

Use Music before Meetings and During Breaks

Before the Meeting

Select the appropriate Music for your audience.

During the Meeting

1. Turn on the Music as you set up for the meeting or begin a break.

2. Turn off the Music when you want the meeting to begin or reconvene.

Use Music to Introduce, Emphasize, or Reinforce a Point or Issue

Before the Meeting

1. Select Music that underscores a planned agenda item or piece of information.

2. Plan to bring a broad selection of Music so you will be able to improvise based on the situation.

During the Meeting

Play the Music during the appropriate part of your agenda

Use Music with Visual Aids as a Review or Summary Technique

Before the Meeting

1. Select the appropriate piece of Music.

2. Sequentially prepare the visual aids that you will use in the review.

3. Decide how to best display this material to the group.

4. Practice your timing and sequencing with the actual Music you will use during your meeting.

During the Meeting

1. Prepare your meeting group for the summary.

2. Start the Music and begin your review as planned.

3. Turn the Music off when you finish the summary.

"I know that meetings are designed for two-way communication, but sometimes a verbal discussion doesn't seem like the best way to utilize the time of my meeting participants. This usually happens when the agenda is long, the group is large, only a few people participate, or the information requested is delicate or volatile. Is there an alternative to group discussions?"

19. Writing

What Is Writing?

As a productivity technique, Writing increases individual participation. This process involves obtaining specific and thoughtful written information from all participants before or instead of a verbal discussion.

Many people prefer to think before they speak. Others need time to formulate their ideas, especially concerning complex issues. Allowing a short time for quiet contemplation combined with asking participants to write their comments down on paper increases individual input and the number and variety of ideas. This technique not only meets the needs of these participants but is also the fastest, most efficient method of gathering information.

Writing can also be used before the meeting to gather specified information from the group. This can further improve time spent in the meeting itself.

When to Use Writing

- When you need to brainstorm or gather information quickly
- When you have participants who are uncomfortable speaking in front of a group
- When you have participants in the group who tend to dominate conversations
- When you want to collect information before the meeting
- When information needs to be exchanged, but face-to-face dialogue is not necessary

How to Use Writing

Before the Meeting

1. Consider how and when Writing will be used as you plan the details of your agenda. Many options exist, including:

   As a brainstorming technique:
   - Card Clusters, technique 31

As a technique for gathering premeeting information:

- Questionnaires, technique 37

As a technique for gathering information on individual perspectives of a problem:

- Nominal Group Process, technique 43

As a technique for gathering personal perspectives about how a group has worked together:

- Prouds and Sorries, technique 46
- Keep/Throw, technique 47

As a technique for evaluating the meeting:

- Written Questions, technique 81

2. Purchase and prepare the necessary supplies. This includes an adequate number of sticky notes (or cards and tape) and felt-tip pens.

During the Meeting

Use the information as planned.

Summary

Writing is a productivity technique designed to gather information quickly, thereby using meeting time wisely. This technique also ensures full participation.

Before the Meeting

1. Consider Writing as a technique as you plan the details for each item on your agenda.

2. Bring the necessary supplies.

During the Meeting

Use the information as planned.

"Sometimes it seems impossible to hear from everyone in our meetings. The group is too large, the agenda is too long, or the time is too short. How can I be sure that everyone gets a chance to speak his or her mind?"

20. Small Groups

What Are Small Groups?

Small Groups make it possible to gain input from everyone in the meeting. This productivity technique involves breaking a large group into smaller, more manageable groups of participants.

Small Groups stimulate fuller participation, require less time, and tend to create higher energy and better results. They can be combined with Writing, technique 19, to create a thoughtful, participative discussion.

When to Use Small Groups

- When your meeting involves more than five people
- When some participants are uncomfortable speaking in front of groups of people
- When an issue requires in-depth discussion
- When you want to increase participation without increasing time commitments

How to Use Small Groups

Before the Meeting

1. When creating the agenda, determine if and when Small Groups are best for specific parts of your meeting.

2. Determine the question(s) you want each Small Group to address.

   NOTE: See Shredded Questions, technique 9, or Open-Ended Questions, technique 34, for ideas.

3. Determine how best to create the Small Groups. Groups of three to six people are ideal.

OPTION A: Ask participants to count off in your meeting. For example, if your group includes thirty-five people, create seven groups of five persons each. Participants should count off one through seven to create these groups.

OPTION B: Ask the participants to cluster with two or three people sitting near them. You may want to help form these Small Groups to avoid having any people left without a group or unevenly distributed groups.

> NOTE: This option is particularly effective if participants do not know each other yet, or if your meeting has just started and there is no present need for Movement, technique 16, at this time.

OPTION C: Create lists of Small Groups before the meeting, usually working for maximum diversity within each group. There may be times when you want groups based by region, level in the organization, or intact work groups. But generally, maximum diversity gives groups a broader outlook and creates a sense of team across traditional boundaries. If the meeting calls for several small-group discussions, you can create several lists. For example, groups for agenda item 1, groups for agenda item 2, and so on. Post these lists and consider giving copies to all participants. This will avoid confusion whenever new Small Groups form.

> NOTE: If you are not the leader of the group, gain approval from the leader on the Small Groups and their participants in advance.

OPTION D: When your group has a long history together and seems tired of these other options, ask them to break into groups in nontraditional ways, like by birthday. For example: "All those born in the first quarter of the year, January, February, and March, form a group in this corner of the room," and so on.

> NOTE: This can also help informally create rapport among the group. Give people a few minutes to share birthdays before starting their official tasks. Before the report back ask if anyone has the same birthday, or if anyone has a birthday that day.

This technique can be modified as you wish. Create Small Groups based on anything that would work for the group.

4. Plan and prepare to communicate specific instructions for each Small Group exercise.

   Include Self-Management instructions, technique 10. Create visual aids to help the groups stay on track. See Charting, technique 12, for details.

   OPTION A: All groups answer the same question(s).

   OPTION B: All groups answer different question(s).

   OPTION C: A few groups answer one question while other groups answer a different question.

   NOTE: Determine when to ask the same or different questions based on the number of questions that need to be answered and the relative importance of each question to the goals of the agenda item.

5. Plan how best to have the Small Groups report back their ideas to the larger group.

   Report back options include:

   OPTION A: Each Small Group reports back a concise summary of its discussion using chart papers or overhead as a visual aid.

   OPTION B: Each Small Group reports back its best one or two ideas using a chart or overhead as a visual aid.

   OPTION C: Each Small Group reports one idea, without duplicating ideas from other groups. Keep going around to each group until all ideas have been covered.

6. Decide how to use all the information created by the Small Groups.

During the Meeting

1. Explain the purpose and process of the Small Groups technique.

2. Break the large group into Small Groups and give them their specific instructions.

3. Each Small Group discusses and reports back on the specific topic under consideration.

4. Use the resulting information as planned.

Summary

Small Groups is a technique for gaining information from all participants in your meeting. This technique saves time and increases participation. Use Small Groups as part of specific agenda items in your meeting.

Before the Meeting

1. Determine if and when Small Groups are best for your meeting.

2. Determine the question(s) you want each group to address.

3. Determine how best to create the Small Groups.

4. Plan and prepare all instructions, including visual aids.

5. Plan how best to have the Small Groups report back their ideas to the others.

6. Decide how to use the information after the report back.

During the Meeting

1. Present the topic and the purpose of using Small Groups.

2. Break participants into Small Groups.

3. Complete Small Group discussions and report backs.

4. Use the resulting information as planned.

Chapter 4

Seven Techniques to Boost Creativity and Teamwork

Miguel is part of a new, experimental project team, and some managers within the organization are skeptical about the idea. Miguel believes that "helping get this department out of the mess it's in is going to be a lot of work. And it's going to take a lot more than a single jump-start to keep things moving in the right direction. We know that we need to change our old mind-set, but we're not exactly sure how to go about doing it." New and creative ideas are essential to any organization's future competitiveness. The rules and ideas that defined organizational success in the past often no longer apply.

Moreover, teamwork is just as critical as creativity. The nature of work is too interdependent for any one person or function to effectively address complex organizational issues. The better a group or cross-functional team works together, the more efficient and successful it becomes.

This chapter describes seven techniques that stimulate the creativity and teamwork that are essential to every successful participative meeting. Whole books exist on team-building exercises. You may want to consult them, too.

The techniques outlined in this chapter include:

21. Thinking Outside the Box
22. New Glasses
23. Incrediballs
24. Team Learning
25. Two Truths and a Lie
26. Milestones
27. The Funeral

"One of my meeting groups is very analytical and established in the way its members deal with each other and the problems they face. The group members definitely need a push to help them start thinking in new ways. Do you have any ideas?"

21. Thinking Outside the Box

What Is Thinking Outside the Box?

Thinking Outside the Box is a technique designed to help your participants see the value of thinking in new and different ways.

People think and problem solve within their personal paradigms—the sets of beliefs each of us hold. These structure our thinking and the ways in which we view the world. Without challenging our paradigms, we restrict our ability to perceive a fuller picture of the world and thereby limit our ability to excel.

When to Use Thinking Outside the Box

- When your group seems to be stuck
- When you know the group's thinking will need to be challenged in order to effectively solve a problem or be more competitive
- When your group needs to look at things in different ways

How to Use Thinking Outside the Box

Before the Meeting

1. Determine how you want to use and introduce Thinking Outside the Box.

2. Create an overhead or chart as follows:

**Connect all the dots using no more than four straight lines
and without retracing your steps**

Figure 4-1. Instructions for the nine-dot exercise.

During the Meeting

1. Introduce the exercise. You might say, for example, "This next agenda item is going to take some creative thinking. To get us warmed up, let's do a quick exercise."

   NOTE: When you introduce and explain the exercise, don't use the words *thinking outside the box*, as that would provide too obvious a hint for the solution to the puzzle. Use the words *nine-dot exercise* instead.

2. Explain the exercise with the help of your chart or overhead. Ask participants to individually solve the puzzle.

3. Demonstrate how to solve the puzzle (see diagram on the following page). After a few minutes, ask if anyone has solved the problem. Invite one person who has solved the puzzle (be sure to verify that he or she has done so successfully first) to come forward and demonstrate the solution.

   NOTE: If no one has solved the puzzle, complete it yourself on the chart or overhead.

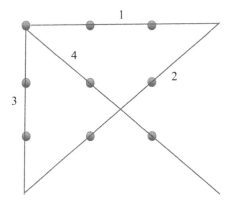

Figure 4-2. The successfully completed nine-dot exercise.

4. Debrief the exercise by asking the following questions: "What made it difficult to think outside the box?" "What is the value of thinking outside the box for us here today?" "What are the dangers of thinking outside the box?" "How can we remind ourselves to think outside the box?"

NOTE: This exercise is well-known. If your participant group is familiar with it, use the thinking outside the box terminology as a quick reminder. It may still be worthwhile to use the nine-dot model as a visual reminder from time to time.

Summary

Thinking Outside the Box is an excellent exercise to help people understand the limitations of their own boundaries and help them think in new and creative ways.

Before the Meeting

1. Determine how you will use and introduce Thinking Outside the Box.

2. Create the chart or overhead with instructions for the exercise.

During the Meeting

1. Introduce Thinking Outside the Box.

2. Explain the exercise and ask your participants to individually solve the puzzle.

3. Demonstrate how to solve the puzzle.

4. Debrief the exercise.

"Some of my group's participants seem resistant to change and insist on looking at problems in the same old ways. Is there a simple technique that can help them snap out of their old habits and perceptions?"

22. New Glasses

What Are New Glasses?

The New Glasses technique helps your meeting participants look at the meeting agenda's topics through new eyes and supports them in leaving their biases and old perspectives behind. It is an instantaneous energizer and also serves as a good technique for the tactile learner.

This simple technique involves literally asking each participant to put on a pair of silly glasses to help him or her look at a problem or issue through new eyes.

When to Use New Glasses

- When you know participants have preconceived ideas about topics on the agenda
- When you lead a strategic planning, reengineering, or any other type of meeting where changes will be made

How to Use New Glasses

Before the Meeting

1. Buy each participant in your meeting group a pair of silly glasses. These can be purchased at a costume shop or children's toy store. Buy several varieties and wrap them up as presents.

   OPTION: Don't wrap the glasses up; instead, place them at each seat as they are.

During the Meeting

1. Hand out the presents to all participants.

   OPTION A: Distribute the presents after your group agrees on the meeting ground rules (see Ground Rules, technique 3), especially if you have a ground rule for thinking with an open mind.

   OPTION B: Distribute the presents at any point during the meeting when the group will be challenged to look at the world through new eyes.

2. At the appropriate time, ask the participants to open their presents and give them a try. Explain their purpose. Tell them that the glasses will allow them to look at the world through new eyes. Explain that if, at any time during the meeting, the participants feel they are falling into old ways of looking at the world, they should put their glasses on. Or if they think that any other person is falling into old habits and perspectives, they may ask that person to put on his or her glasses.

    NOTE: The glasses also serve as another toy (see Toys, technique 17) to fiddle with during the meeting and will usually be the source of needed humor periodically throughout the meeting.

Summary

The New Glasses technique reminds your meeting group that they need to look at the topics at hand through new eyes.

Before the Meeting

Buy every participant a pair of silly glasses and wrap them up as presents.

During the Meeting

1. Hand out the presents.

2. Ask all participants to open their presents and give their New Glasses a try. Explain that the glasses are designed to help them look at the world with new eyes. The New Glasses are worn when anyone feels that he or she or any other person in the group is falling into old ways of thinking.

"More than ever before, our group needs to start making some radical improvements in the way we do our business. We haven't worked particularly well together in the past, and I need to get these people together and jolted fast. Do you have any suggestions?"

23: Incrediballs

What Are Incrediballs?

The Incrediballs technique motivates people to work together as a team and challenges them to think about ways to work together differently and more efficiently. The exercise presents participants with increasingly difficult and seemingly impossible deadlines, which stimulates creative thinking and solutions. The Incrediballs technique will graphically display the power and importance of both teamwork and creative thinking.

When to Use Incrediballs

- When your group is about to begin a process improvement or reengineering project
- When your group members are stuck in the way they think and work together

How to Use Incrediballs

Before the Meeting

1. Put Incrediballs (or team exercise) on your agenda. Allow thirty to forty minutes.

   NOTE: Your group must have more than five and fewer than thirty participants. If your group is very large, ask for a smaller group of volunteers. The rest of the group can observe.

2. Purchase three tennis balls and number the balls 1, 2, and 3 with a marker.

During the Meeting

1. Set up the exercise.

   a. Explain the purpose of Incrediballs. For example: "This exercise is designed to help us look at how we work together and how we might want or need to work together in the future; plus, we will have some fun."

   b. Ask the Incrediballs participants to move from their seats to stand in a circle.

NOTE: This may mean moving tables and chairs aside or moving to a different space large enough for the group to form a circle.

Then you might say, "For the next ten minutes you are no longer members of [the name of your organization here] but of a newly formed organization. What should be the name of your new organization?" (Use the group's chosen new name for the rest of the exercise.) "Usually an organization would define its vision, mission, goals, and objectives before its organizational processes are created. But for the purposes of this exercise, we'll presume that the essential, preliminary work is completed, and you're ready to design your organizational processes."

NOTE: Ask participants who are already familiar with Incrediballs to be the time-keeper and observer for you.

OPTION: If your group is larger than thirty people, ask for fifteen to twenty volunteers to participate in Incrediballs and for the others to be observers. Thirty is the preferred maximum number for Incrediballs.

2. Give the ball to someone (Mr. or Ms. X) in your group who doesn't usually take a leadership role. Ask Mr. or Ms. X to throw the ball to someone else, who then throws it to someone else, who in turn throws it to someone else, and so on. Ask the participants to remember who throws the ball to them and who they throw it to. The last person to receive the ball returns it to Mr. or Ms. X. Give the group a practice run with one ball.

NOTE: Groups usually make mistakes the first time, so let them get the sequence down with another practice session before going on.

3. Once they have completed the practice run without error, explain to the group that increased production requires that they triple their output, and their efforts will now be timed. Explain the three requirements of the exercise. Tell the group, for example, "Your organization is doing so well that demand for your product has tripled, but you have decided that your staffing levels will remain the same. So from now on you must work with all three balls." Hold up the balls which you have pre-numbered 1, 2, and 3. "Not only that, but from now on, your customers will time your work. And finally, your customers have given you three simple requirements:

- You must maintain the same person-to-person sequence
- People must contact the balls in the order the balls are put into play
- The process begins and ends with Mr. or Ms. X"

NOTE: These requirements can also be posted.

NOTE: These requirements are designed to create perceived walls around what can and cannot be done. In reality, they are to be taken as three separate requirements and to be observed very creatively. In fact, they must be observed very creatively for the group to achieve its goal.

If your group asks you for clarification or approval, tell them, "Your customers are not available at this time. They left only these three instructions and felt sure that your group would understand the requirements correctly." As they complete the exercise with three balls, time them.

NOTE: Ask Mr. or Ms. X to say "start" and "stop" to assist you in timing the group correctly.

NOTE: Use either your phone's stopwatch feature or a watch with a second hand.

4. Begin the exercise and record the time. Write the time on a nearby chart or board and share the time verbally with the group. Then explain that because competitors have cut their production time in half, it is necessary for the group to do the same. For example, "Your customers have just found a competitor who can produce the same product in half the time. They'd like to continue to work with you, but you must produce your product in at least the same time as your competitors. The customer requirements remain the same. You are allowed as much time as you need to discuss how you plan to accomplish this goal. Let me know when you are ready, and I will time your process again." After the group completes its task, communicate and record the time.

5. Repeat step 4 a few times, each time requiring that the time be cut in half until the time is down to under one second (one second is not a misprint).

NOTE: If the group needs prodding during this part of the exercise, tell them that another group you worked with recently did the exercise in less than one second.

6. When the group achieves the goal of one second, ask them to give themselves a round of applause and go back to their seats.

7. Debrief the experience as a group. Customize questions based on your situation. Here are sample debriefing questions: "How did you work together as a team?" "How well did you listen to all the ideas presented?" "What made reaching the goal difficult?" "What were your perceptions/assumptions about the customer requirements?" "How did those perceptions/assumptions hamper your ability to be successful?" "What allowed you to be successful in the end?" "How can we use this experience to improve our ability to work as a team in the future?"

   NOTE: If you had neutral observers, ask them what they observed about the way the group worked together. For example: "How well did the exercise participants listen to everyone's ideas?" "Did everyone offer ideas?" "How did the group decide what to do next?"

Summary

Incrediballs is a technique that challenges a group's paradigms and stimulates teamwork and creative thinking.

Before the Meeting

1. Allow thirty to forty minutes on your agenda for Incrediballs.

2. Purchase three tennis balls and number them 1, 2, and 3 with markers.

During the Meeting

1. Set up the Incrediballs exercise. Explain the purpose and details to participants.

2. Give one ball to Mr. or Ms. X, preferably someone who is not a leader within the organization. This person begins and ends the exercise.

3. After a practice run with one ball, explain that increased production requires that they triple their output by using three balls and that their efforts will be timed. Also explain the three requirements of the exercise.
   • You must maintain the same person-to-person sequence
   • People must contact the balls in the order the balls are put into play
   • The process begins and ends with Mr. or Ms. X

4. Explain that because the competition has cut its production time in half, this group must cut their time at least in half.

5. Repeat step 4 a few times, each time requiring the time to be cut in half. This continues until the group has cut its time to under one second.

6. When the group members achieve the goal, have them take their seats.

7. Debrief the Incrediballs experience as a group.

Source

Organizational Development Department. Boeing Commercial Airplane Group. 1990

"Our own old habits, opinions, and experiences limit our group, but the challenges facing us call for a fuller understanding and broader perspective. We joke that we all need to go back to college to get some new ideas, but, of course, there's no time for that now. Do you have any suggestions?"

24. Team Learning

What Is Team Learning?

Team Learning is a technique that provides a work team or meeting group with the resources to learn new information. Teams often become so busy accomplishing tasks and making decisions that they don't take any time for the reflection, learning, and dialogue needed to stimulate new perspectives, insights, and wisdom. In addition to providing the team with new knowledge, Team Learning can also provide a forum for the group to share ideas and opinions.

Team Learning information can come from people, films, articles, or other resources.

When to Use Team Learning

- When your group needs new skills, ideas, and perspectives to be successful
- When it is necessary to introduce new and/or controversial information
- When you want to build a sense of team as a byproduct of learning

How to Use Team Learning

1. Introduce the technique and discuss the need for Team Learning with the group. You might start the conversation by saying, "In order for us to work as effectively as we need to, we must make a commitment to continuous learning. What do you think?"

2. Determine, with the help of the group, what Team Learning is needed and what methods should be used.

   OPTION A: Find films that will provide useful information. Look for films on topics pertinent to the group's work, industry, or areas for skill development.

   OPTION B: Books or articles from newspapers, professional journals, or other publications can also serve this same purpose. Have your group read a periodical or book together, perhaps one chapter a week, and discuss it as an agenda item at your meetings. Some groups opt for weekly or monthly brown-bag lunch discussions.

OPTION C: Using outside experts or other people outside the group is another idea. These people could come from a local university, another organization, or another department or division within your own organization. Remember to consider those inside the group with special expertise as well.

NOTE: Experts do not necessarily come from high levels within their organization. For example, the best experts may be those directly involved with the manufacture of a specific item. See Content Experts, technique 45, for details on briefing outside experts.

OPTION D: Tours or field trips can also be very insightful. Consider touring the facilities of customers using your products. Visit a noncompeting firm to view their manufacturing facilities, office setup, or specific services. The group can use these tours to gather new information, better understand customer needs, or benchmark best practices.

3. Gain agreement on the purpose, methods, and scheduling of Team Learning. Ask for one or more volunteers to be responsible for coordinating activities. This responsibility could rotate. Document your agreements on a chart paper and distribute the information as part of the minutes of your meeting.

4. Carry out the Team Learning as planned.

5. As part of each learning session, debrief or summarize the Team Learning information. Examples of debriefing questions include: "What were the key points of what we learned?" "What was your reaction to what we heard today?" "What would be the positives for us?" "And the negatives?" "What alternatives to our present methods of working do we have?" "What action shall we take?" Use Shredded Questions, technique 9, for additional ideas for your own situation.

NOTE: Debriefing the Team Learning information is critical. Without this important step, much of the energy and potential from the acquisition of this new information will be wasted.

Summary

Team Learning is a technique to spark creativity and better analysis by providing new information from outside the participant group. Sources for this type of continuous learning can come from films, books, and periodicals and people outside the meeting group.

1. Discuss the need for Team Learning with your meeting group.

2. Determine which Team Learning resources or methods can best provide the information you are seeking.

3. Gain agreement on the purpose, methods, and scheduling of Team Learning.

4. Carry out the Team Learning as planned.

5. Debrief or summarize each learning session.

"Even though we've worked together for a while, no one seems to know very much about the other people in the group. Is there a fun and simple technique that will help us learn more about our fellow participants?"

25. Two Truths and a Lie

What Is Two Truths and a Lie?

Two Truths and a Lie is a team-building exercise that provides your meeting participants with personal information that reveals more about the other team members as individuals. By having fun and revealing pieces of trivia about themselves, people expose parts of their background and interests that other group members didn't know before. This information can help build a more intimate and productive relationship among people within your group.

When to Use Two Truths and a Lie

- When you want a quick, fun exercise to help build relationships among meeting participants
- When you want to use a different form of introduction (see Introductions, technique 1) with a group that has already worked together in the past

How to Use Two Truths and a Lie

Before the Meeting

1. Put Two Truths and a Lie on your agenda.

   OPTION: Depending on the size of your group, this can be used as a large or small group exercise.

   NOTE: If you choose to use this technique in small groups, decide how to break up the groups ahead of time (see Small Groups, technique 20, for options). Ask small groups to nominate one favorite example to share with the larger group.

2. Prepare a chart explaining the exercise, such as in figure 4-3.

TWO TRUTHS AND A LIE

1. Take a few minutes to silently think of Two Truths and a Lie about yourself.
2. Share your Two Truths and a Lie with the others in the group.
3. Let others guess which statement is the lie.
4. Confirm with the group which one is the real lie.

Figure 4-3. Introductions for Two Truths and a Lie.

During the Meeting

1. Introduce Two Truths and a Lie to the group and explain to the group how to prepare for the exercise using a chart or overhead similar to figure 4-3 to reinforce the explanation.

   Consider using yourself as an example. You might say, for example, "I grew up on a farm with nine brothers and sisters; I was fired twice as a waitress; and I'm an avid downhill skier. Guess which one isn't true."

2. Complete the exercise, giving each participant time to share his or her Two Truths and a Lie. After a participant has shared his or her three personal statements, ask the group to guess which is the lie. After a few moments of guessing, ask the participant to share which of the three statements was the lie. Then move on, until you have heard from each participant.

Summary

Two Truths and a Lie helps the group build rapport and know each other better as individuals.

Before the Meeting

1. Include Two Truths and a Lie on your agenda.

2. Prepare the instructions on a chart or overhead.

During the Meeting

1. Introduce Two Truths and a Lie to the group and explain to the group how to prepare for the exercise.

2. Complete the exercise.

"I want a technique for helping our group understand and appreciate the diversity of experience and backgrounds in the room but in an informal and interesting way. Do you have any ideas?"

26. Milestones

What Are Milestones?

The Milestones technique allows participants to learn more about the members of their meeting group, thereby building a stronger sense of team. By focusing on Milestones in each participant's life, the exercise promotes learning more about each other, both on a personal and professional level, which ultimately helps people work together more effectively.

An underlying goal of many meetings is for participants to have the opportunity to get to know each other better. Milestones quickly and informally provides this type of experience.

When to Use Milestones

- When you want to build a stronger sense of team
- When you want your participants to learn more about each other's personal history and interests
- When you need a productive break from a long and serious agenda

How to Use Milestones

Before the Meeting

1. Include Milestones on your agenda.

   NOTE: Allow about fifteen minutes total for the exercise and place Milestones on the agenda immediately before a break.

2. Create a Milestones chart using a large piece of butcher paper or a few chart papers taped together. Create the chart with five-year interval markers, similar to the chart illustrated in figure 4-4, and be sure to leave enough room under each year for a number of sticky notes.

MILESTONES

1945 1950 1955 1960 1965 1970 1975 1980 1985 etc....

Figure 4-4. Milestones chart.

NOTE: Decide how far back your Milestones chart should go by estimating the age of the oldest person in the group. If you aren't sure, create your chart based on the maximum age before retirement (i.e., the year of your meeting minus sixty-five years).

3. Prepare an instructions chart for Milestones similar to the one illustrated in figure 4-5.

MILESTONES

A. Think of three personal milestones in your life. Write one per sticky note. Write your milestones in the third person. For example: Amy was born on the first day of the Iraq War.
B. As you leave for the break, place your sticky notes at the appropriate year on the chart provided.
C. During the break, read the Milestones of the others.

Figure 4-5. Milestones instructions.

During the Meeting

1. Introduce the technique and explain the purpose of Milestones. You might say, for example: "The purpose of this exercise is to share important information about ourselves. This will help us all understand more about the backgrounds of the individuals on the team. Let's take the next ten minutes to chart our personal Milestones."

2. Give the following instructions for Milestones and support your explanation with a preprepared chart, as illustrated in figure 4-5.

    a. Have your participants write three personal Milestones in their lives on sticky notes, one Milestone per sticky note. Milestones should be written in the third person and can be funny or serious. Give some examples to your group. You might say, for example, "Helen rode her bike across the country in 1995." "Richard skied for the first time at age forty." "After ten years of not so serious study at the university, Roger finally received his bachelor's degree in 2011."

NOTE: If the group is small (less than ten people), you may choose to have everyone provide four or five Milestones.

b. After they're finished, your participants should place each Milestone sticky note on the Milestone chart under the appropriate year.

NOTE: This exercise can also be used for sharing company, department, or work-area Milestones.

c. Encourage your participants to read the Milestone chart at their leisure, preferably during breaks or at lunch.

OPTION: If your group is small enough, you can ask each participant to come up to read his or her sticky notes to the group.

3. When everyone understands the instructions, complete the exercise.

4. Debrief the exercise. Debrief questions could include "What were the big surprises?" "What information did you learn that could be valuable to our work in the future?"

Summary

Milestones is a team-building technique. Learning important and personal information about others in the group helps create a cohesive bond between the people.

Before the Meeting

1. Place Milestones on your agenda.

2. Create a Milestones chart.

3. Prepare a Milestones instructions chart.

During the Meeting

1. Explain the purpose of Milestones.

2. Give the instructions for Milestones.

3. Complete the exercise.

4. Debrief the exercise.

"Our group has just gone through downsizing and restructuring, and we're having a difficult time letting go of the past. This negatively impacts our ability to concentrate on future demands. What can I do to help the group deal with this type of situation?"

27. The Funeral

What Is the Funeral?

The Funeral is a technique for helping a group put the past aside and prepare for the future. The Funeral acknowledges in a good-natured way that the past had both its good and bad points. However, in order to go forward, the group must now bury the past and embrace the present and future.

The Funeral is exactly what it implies but in obvious symbolic terms. Emotions are strong after a significant change. Allocating some time to acknowledge the grieving of the group can be very healthy. Rituals, such as the Funeral, create a rite of passage and can be a powerful tool in helping a group move forward.

Although the Funeral is not a technique that is used often, it can be very effective when appropriate for your situation or group.

When to Use the Funeral

- When the organization or group is downsizing, being purchased, or is the subject of other significant cultural changes
- When a dysfunctional group has agreed to act differently in the future
- When a group can't seem to go forward because of a perceived loss of any kind

How to Use the Funeral

Variation 1

This version recognizes and addresses a significant change in the organization.

1. Talk with your meeting group about what has happened (i.e., recent or upcoming downsizing, corporate takeover, etc.). Ask for their support in taking a few hours to acknowledge the changes in a ceremonious fashion. Note that the idea may seem a little silly but has been found to help groups work through their emotional energy about a change and feel more prepared to work together in the future. Explain that the Funeral will be a time to remember the good and the bad and to bury the past. At the Funeral, everyone who wants to will have an opportunity to speak. They could

prepare poems or short stories in writing or sing or provide music if they wish. The Funeral will literally be a mock funeral for the past.

2. Agree on a time and place to hold the Funeral.

    NOTE: If planned during the workday, schedule this for the end of the day.

3. Ask for a few volunteers to plan the event.

4. Ask the participants to wear clothes like those they would wear for a funeral. This is an optional step.

5. Together with your planning team, create an agenda for the Funeral.

    Incorporate the cultural traditions of people within your group. Provide a box that can be your coffin. Poems, photographs, articles, and the like can go in the coffin. Find a place to bury your coffin or cremate it and spread the ashes. Provide beverages and food for the group, just as a gathering of friends and family would after the loss of a loved one.

    NOTE: Ensure you are working within all fire codes and other regulations.

6. Hold the Funeral.

7. The next time your group meets after The Funeral, take a few minutes at the meeting to ask them for their reactions and comments.

Variation 2

This option is for a group that has worked together poorly in the past and has agreed to work together differently in the future.

1. Talk to the group to confirm agreement to work together differently in the future. Ask for the members' support in taking some time to ceremoniously let go of the past and prepare for the future.

2. Agree on a time and a place for the Funeral. This should be the only agenda item.

3. Before that meeting, create a little mock coffin or other suitable symbol of passing. Provide paper and pencils for each participant.

4. Ask the participants to write down all the negative things they have thought about each other in the past, all their bad habits, and so on. After they are finished, ask them to shred their papers and put them in the coffin. They need not share any of their comments with the others.

5. When everyone has finished, close the coffin you have created.

6. Take the coffin to a predetermined place for burial or burning. As you are disposing of the coffin, ask for a moment of silence for all old habits and attitudes.

   NOTE: If you choose to burn the coffin, check to be sure there aren't any laws against open-air burning.

   OPTION: Put the coffin in the company shredder or box crusher and keep it somewhere in the department as a reminder that old ways of working together are no longer acceptable.

7. Bring the Funeral to a close with some music or by humming a song known to the group.

8. The next time your group meets, debrief the exercise. Take a few minutes to get their reactions to the Funeral.

Summary

The Funeral is a technique for helping a group put aside the past and prepare for the future.

Variation 1

This version recognizes and addresses a significant change in the organization.

1. Talk to the group about what has happened and obtain everyone's support for the Funeral.

2. Agree on a time and place.

3. Ask for volunteers to plan the event.

4. Ask the participants to dress as they would for a funeral.

5. With the planning team, create an agenda for the Funeral.

6. Hold the Funeral.

7. The next time your group meets after the Funeral, ask the members for their reactions and comments.

Variation 2

This version deals with a commitment from your meeting group to work better together in the future.

1. Talk to the group members about their agreement to work differently together in the future.

2. Agree on a time and place for the Funeral.

3. Create a mock coffin or other suitable symbol of passing.

4. Ask your participants to write down on paper all the negative things they have thought about each other in the past. Have them shred their papers and place them in the coffin.

5. Close the coffin when finished.

6. Remove the coffin and bury, burn, or shred it as planned.

7. End the Funeral with some appropriate music or singing.

8. The next time this group meets, take a few minutes to discuss everyone's reactions to the Funeral.

5

Six Techniques to Brainstorm Ideas

Harold's accounting department held the bottom position on the division's customer satisfaction results for the third time in five years. "We're getting heat from every direction. And it seems like the harder we try, the worse it gets. Our brainstorming sessions fall flat. Maybe we're too quick to criticize our ideas or just too anxious to make a decision and move on. But what can we do?"

Contemporary organizations expect every group within them to provide creative solutions. Groups need to find better ways of doing business as well as expose, analyze, and deal with problems before they even occur.

The best way to find the most effective idea is to first introduce as many ideas as possible. And that means brainstorming. Brainstorming works on the principle that the quantity of ideas increases their quality. The first ideas are typically the most obvious. When brainstormers are fearful of scrutiny and judgment during the brainstorming session, ideas stop flowing before the best ideas come forward. Deferring judgment on ideas improves the volume of participant input and consequently the value.

This chapter provides six brainstorming techniques that are designed to guide the meeting facilitator toward improving the outcome of any organization's brainstorming efforts.

These techniques include:

28. The Old-Fashioned Way
29. Mind Mapping
30. Storyboarding
31. Card Clusters
32. STP
33. Breaking a Stalemate

"Sometimes I need to gather a lot of ideas quickly, especially when a large group of participants is involved. Is there a basic brainstorming technique that will function well under these circumstances?"

28. The Old-Fashioned Way

What Is the Old-Fashioned Way?

The Old-Fashioned Way is the original brainstorming technique. It is tried and true as a technique that enables participants to input significant amounts of information or ideas in a short period of time. The Old-Fashioned Way works well for both small and large groups.

The general rules for the Old-Fashioned Way serve as the basis or foundation for the other brainstorming techniques included in this chapter.

When to Use the Old-Fashioned Way

- When you want to generate a large quantity of information before problem solving, decision making, or planning
- When you want to inspire creativity and gather ideas

How to Use the Old-Fashioned Way

1. Introduce the topic and the purpose of the specific brainstorming session.

   Remind the group of the ground rules for brainstorming and consider posting these ground rules on a chart, as illustrated in figure 5-1.

BRAINSTORMING GROUND RULES

1. All ideas and information are acceptable.
2. No criticism or analysis of ideas or information is permitted.
3. Build on the ideas of others.
4. All ideas and information are charted.

Figure 5-1. Ground rules for Brainstorming.

2. Begin the discussion by asking a specific open-ended question to focus the discussion (see Open-Ended Questions, technique 34). For example: "What should we name

our new product?" "What do we need to accomplish before the conference begins?" "What can we do to capture a larger market share?"

Ask your participants to "popcorn" their ideas. ("Popcorn" means allowing participants to voice their ideas in an unorderly and unrestrained sequence.)

NOTE: The facilitator or designated recorder charts all ideas as they are stated.

OPTION: Collect the ideas using a round-robin approach. (Round-robin means that ideas are collected in an orderly fashion, by sequentially asking each person in the room for his or her ideas.)

OPTION: Use two recorders to keep up with the fast flow of ideas.

NOTE: A lull in ideas may occur before a round of new and even more creative ideas. Don't be afraid of a few minutes of silence. If the group is stuck, take a break or read aloud all the ideas you have collected to that point.

3. When the group feels comfortable that there are no more ideas to add, go through the list of ideas, one by one. Ask the group if anyone needs clarification or further information on what each item means.

4. As appropriate, narrow down the ideas to a few for further discussion and evaluation. Consider using Multivoting, technique 54, or Nominal Prioritization, technique 58, as tools to help the group narrow down the ideas.

Summary

The Old-Fashioned Way is the original brainstorming technique. This technique enables your meeting group to generate a large amount of information or number of ideas in a short period of time.

1. Introduce the subject.

2. Begin the discussion.

3. Go through the ideas or information, one by one, to ensure they don't need any further clarification.

4. As appropriate, narrow down the ideas.

Source

Osborn, A. F. 1963. *Applied Imagination.* New York: Scribner's.

"Sometimes we brainstorm information and ideas that need to be subsequently placed into a specific sequence, order, or outline. But our group likes to brainstorm in a nonsequential manner, much like the process outlined in the Old-Fashioned Way. Is there an efficient way to brainstorm that will allow us to later sequence the information without extra work?"

29. Mind Mapping

What Is Mind Mapping?

Mind Mapping is a brainstorming technique for quickly charting your group's ideas in logical groupings, even when members give ideas in a nonsequential manner.

It is impossible to effectively outline ideas in a traditional, linear format while brainstorming. The Mind Mapping technique allows you to efficiently brainstorm for ideas as well as simultaneously create a skeletal framework for later categorization of the information you collect.

Examples of situations that benefit from Mind Mapping include planning agendas or projects, identifying customer groups, or dealing with any process that contains many components.

When to Use Mind Mapping

- When group members will have to remember many steps or issues
- When you are brainstorming information to be outlined or sequenced instead of brainstorming specific solutions to a problem

   NOTE: Mind Mapping works best when topics have many components and subcomponents or when there are a number of different categories of information. Mind Mapping does not work well when the participants are brainstorming ideas that they will later narrow down to the best one or two ideas.

How to Use Mind Mapping

Before the Meeting

1. Identify specifically what you want to brainstorm. Plan an open-ended question to focus the brainstorming. You might say, for example: "What are the steps in completing this project?" "Which types of customers shall we target for testing our new product?" "What still needs to be done in order to finalize the annual report?" or "What do we need to do to be prepared for the move to the new building next month?"

NOTE: The first time you use Mind Mapping with your meeting group, you will want to create two instructional charts. These charts should vividly illustrate how the Mind Mapping process works and how it later translates into a linear format. Refer to figures 5-2 and 5-3 for examples of these charts.

During the Meeting

1. Introduce the topic, the question, and the Mind Mapping technique. For example: "As you know, our group is moving to the new building next year. I'd like your help in planning for that move. Let's start by mind mapping your answers to the question, 'What do we need to do to be prepared for the move to the new building next year?'"

NOTE: If your group has never used Mind Mapping before, take a few moments at this point to explain the process. You might say, for example, "We've never used the brainstorming technique called Mind Mapping before. Basically, it is a nonlinear way of outlining brainstormed information. This is an example of how it might look when it is finished" (refer to fig. 5-2).

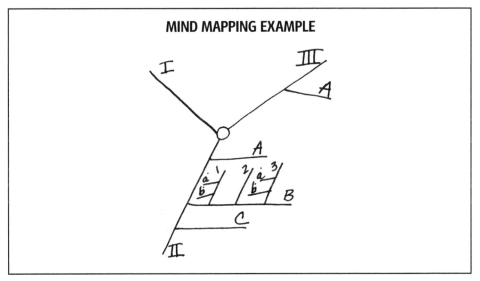

Figure 5-2. Example of Mind Mapping.

"The main arms or branches that emanate from the circle at the center represent the primary ideas or categories that have been brainstormed. The secondary branches represent the subissues of the primary categories, and the smaller branches are the subsets of the secondary categories, and so on. The idea is similar in structure to the old outline form that many of us learned in school, with roman numerals, letters, and numbers. This chart [refer to figure 5-3] is how the Mind Map [figure 5-2] translates into this linear format. I will demonstrate as we go along."

MIND MAPPING EXAMPLE

In Linear Form:
I.
II.
   A.
   B.
      1.
         a.
         b.
      2.
      3.
         a.
         b.
   C.
III.
   A.

Figure 5-3. The same Mind Mapping example in linear format.

2. Prepare your own Mind Mapping chart by drawing a circle in the middle of a clean sheet of chart paper. Write your topic or question (probably in an abbreviated form) within the circle, or at the top of the chart.

3. Begin the brainstorming session, writing all your group's ideas down on the appropriate section of the Mind Map. Brainstorm to an appropriate level of detail given your purpose. Continue to brainstorm until the group has exhausted all pertinent information or ideas.

OPTION: If your Mind Map is getting too complex and cumbersome, consider taking an arm of the Mind Map and using it to create a new, separate, more specific Mind Map.

Figure 5-4 shows a completed Mind Map, one that categorizes the information brainstormed for planning the summer company picnic.

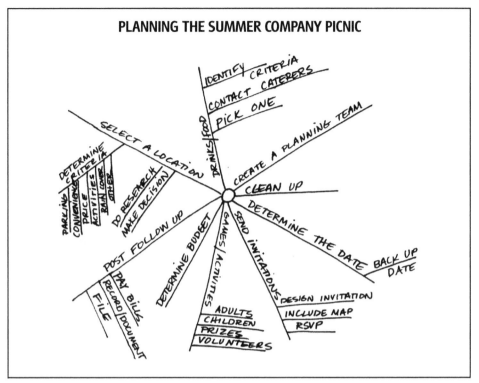

Figure 5-4. Completed Mind Map for planning the summer company picnic.

4. After completing your mind map, have the group sequence the information if appropriate. You might say, for example, "Which of these arms or branches needs to be dealt with first?" "Which is next important?" and so on. Number them as the group dictates and reproduce your outline in linear form if appropriate. Figure 5-5 on the next page is the resulting linearly formatted outline created from the Mind Map illustrated in figure 5-4.

NOTE: You may find you want to move some information to different sections once your Mind Map is developed.

PLANNING THE SUMMER COMPANY PICNIC IN LINEAR FORMAT

I.   Create a planning team
II.   Determine the budget
III.   Determine the date
         A. Select a backup date
IV.   Select a location
         A. Determine criteria for preferred site
                 1. Parking
                 2. Convenience
                 3. Price
                 4. Rain cover
                 5. Possibilities for activities
                 6. Other
         B. Do research
         C. Make a decision
V.   Send invitations
         A. Design the invitation
         B. Include a map
         C. RSVPs
VI.   Order food and drinks
         A. Establish criteria for caterers
         B. Contact possible caterers
         C. Select a caterer
VII.   Plan games and activities
         A. For adults
         B. For children
         C. Determine prizes
         D. Determine need for volunteer coordinators
VIII.   Plan for cleanup
IX.   Post picnic follow-up
         A. Pay bills
         B. Record lessons learned
         C. Create a file for reference next year

Figure 5-5. Mind Map for planning the summer company picnic in linear format.

NOTE: To create a formal project plan from your Mind Map, see Project Plans, technique 72.

Summary

Mind Mapping is a nonlinear way of outlining ideas. It works best when the group is not likely to eliminate information but will need to categorize, sequence, or prioritize the information.

Before the Meeting

Identify specifically what you want to brainstorm. Plan an open-ended question to focus the brainstorming discussion.

During the Meeting

1. Introduce the topic, the question, and the Mind Mapping technique.

2. Prepare your Mind Mapping chart by drawing a circle in the middle of a clean sheet of chart paper. Write your topic or question in the circle or at the top of the chart.

3. Begin brainstorming, writing all ideas down on the Mind Map. Brainstorm to an appropriate level of detail.

4. After completing your Mind Map, have the group sequence the information if appropriate. Prioritize the items as the group dictates and reproduce your outline in linear form if necessary.

Source

Buzan, Tony. 1993. *The Mind Map Book*. New York: Dutton.

"Nonlinear brainstorming techniques seem to suit many of the groups I facilitate. Is there an alternative to Mind Mapping that provides a flexible and visual process for sequencing information?"

30. Storyboarding

What Is Storyboarding?

Storyboarding is a nonlinear brainstorming technique that allows you to later arrange the ideas your group generates into a desired order or linear format. Many brainstorming techniques are designed to seek specific solutions to a given question or problem. Storyboarding differs from these techniques because it provides a process to visually manipulate brainstormed information into the most desirable order or format.

Examples of specific items that benefit from Storyboarding include agendas, presentations and speeches, training programs, and any other project that requires the ability to move items around and look at information simultaneously.

When to Use Storyboarding

- When you want to categorize and sequence ideas at a later time
- When you aren't sure how to structure things from the start
- When brainstorming will identify only primary categories of information (Mind Mapping, technique 29, is a better choice when subcategories need to be identified)

How to Use Storyboarding

Before the Meeting

1. After you select Storyboarding as the appropriate brainstorming technique, be sure that you bring the necessary materials to the meeting. These include markers or felt-tip pens and large cards (five by eight inches or larger) and tape or large sticky notes. If there is not an appropriate wall in the room to attach your cards or sticky notes, bring additional chart paper for this purpose.

During the Meeting

1. Introduce Storyboarding as a brainstorming technique that allows the group to categorize and sequence information at a later time.

2. As the group brainstorms, write each idea on a card or sticky note, and post it randomly on a wall or other predetermined location.

3. When the brainstorming is finished, ask the group to help you sequence the items as appropriate based on the specific goal of the agenda item. See figure 5-6 as a high-level example of Storyboarding, which uses the chapters of this book as its subject.

(1) Introduction: The Foundations	(2) Before the Meeting	(3) Improve Meeting Productivity	(4) Boost Creativity and Teamwork	(5) Brainstorm Ideas
(6) Gather Information	(7) Make Decisions	(8) Implement Decisions	(9) Evaluate Meeting Effectiveness	Conclusion

Figure 5-6. Example of Storyboarding.

NOTE: Storyboarding is similar to Card Clusters, technique 31, in that both use cards or sticky notes to capture information. However, with Storyboarding, a group brainstorms and sequences the information afterward. With Card Clusters individuals brainstorm information, and the group categorizes it later.

4. When the group agrees on a structure or an order, number each of the ideas in the determined sequence for documentation in the minutes.

NOTE: It is a good idea to keep the Storyboard posted in a central location as a visual reminder of sequence. Make alterations if and when necessary.

OPTION: If your Storyboard requires more detail, you may use this same technique again for each category in your Storyboard.

Summary

Storyboarding is a brainstorming technique that provides a specific process for sequencing or ordering information.

Before the Meeting

1. Bring markers or felt-tip pens and large cards (five by eight inches or larger) and tape or large sticky notes to the meeting.

During the Meeting

1. Introduce Storyboarding as a brainstorming technique that will allow the group to categorize the information at a later time.

2. As the group brainstorms, write each idea on a card and post it on the wall, chart, or predetermined area within the room.

3. When the brainstorming is finished, ask the group to help you sequence the items as appropriate based on your agenda item goal.

4. When the group agrees on a sequence, number each of the cards for documentation in the minutes of the meeting.

"I know that sharing ideas is essential to our group's success. But ensuring that everyone's ideas are heard can be a slow and difficult process. Some people don't like to talk in front of a group, some people talk too much, and others continuously judge ideas prematurely. I need a technique that is fast and efficient in gathering maximum input in minimum time. What do you suggest?"

31. Card Clusters

What Are Card Clusters?

The Card Clusters technique gathers ideas and information quickly and efficiently, while eliminating common brainstorming problems.

For this technique individuals silently write ideas on cards (usually sticky notes), then the group categorizes the cards together. The Card Clusters technique has been around for some time, and different professional groups call it by different names. The technique is effective in any meeting where it is necessary to gather information quickly.

When to Use Card Clusters

- When you want to get everyone's ideas but don't have much time
- When some participants are not very verbal or like quiet time to think
- When some participants tend to talk too much
- When the group must categorize brainstormed information

How to Use Card Clusters

Before the Meeting

1. Identify the topic for discussion. Determine a specific Open-Ended Question that will elicit the information you need. (See technique 34 for details.) You might plan to ask, for example, "What are the characteristics we desire in a new department manager?" "What issues do we need to address to decrease our turnaround time?" "What is our vision for the future of our company?"

2. Plan how you will use the gathered information. Relative to the topics suggested above, you might plan to say, for example, "This information will help us create a job description for the new department manager," or "We will use this information to determine which issues to address first," or "This information will serve as the foundation for writing our group's vision statement."

NOTE: You can use information from Card Clusters for many purposes. Other examples include establishing goal areas and creating a shared understanding of a problem.

3. Plan how you will introduce the topic at the meeting. Determine what background information to share.

4. Prepare the visual aids you will need to support the discussion. Charts or overheads of instructions are usually enough.

5. Acquire the necessary materials: sticky notes and felt-tip pens for all participants.

   NOTE: Bring at least thirty sticky notes per person. Use felt-tip pens so that writing can be seen from a distance.

6. Identify a space within the meeting room to place the sticky notes that the group will generate. Put chart paper or butcher paper over part of a wall.

   NOTE: Some sticky notes aren't very sticky at all! Use high-quality sticky notes to ensure they do not fall down while your group(s) are working. Take photos of the card clusters before moving the charts, so you don't get confused if some fall off in transport.

In the Meeting

1. Introduce the agenda topic and your open-ended discussion question. Share how the gathered information will be used. Use an instruction chart like the example illustrated in figure 5-7 for support.

INDIVIDUAL EXERCISE

Please brainstorm your ideas to this question: (Your question here.)

- Write all your ideas on sticky notes.
- One idea per sticky note.
- Write in short phrases. Use verbs followed by nouns to help ensure clarity.
- Write as large as possible.

10 minutes

Figure 5-7. Card Cluster guidelines.

2. Ask everyone to silently and individually brainstorm their ideas about the specific question you asked. Ask them to write all their ideas on sticky notes, one idea per sticky note.

   NOTE: Participate in the brainstorming unless you are a neutral facilitator.

3. Collect all written ideas and categorize them with other similar ideas.

   OPTION A: Ask everyone to bring his or her sticky notes up to the front of the room and place them on the wall or designated chart papers. As a group, ask participants to read each other's sticky notes and start to cluster them into themes. Once themes emerge, ask participants to give the clusters a heading.

   Use a prepared chart similar to figure 5-8 to help you explain the process.

WHEN YOU ARE FINISHED

- Put your sticky note ideas up on the wall
- Silently read others' sticky notes
- Cluster your ideas with other similar ideas
- Give each cluster a name or headline to describe its theme

15 minutes

Figure 5-8. Card Cluster instructions.

NOTE: It's common to have more than one response that is the same. This shows any overlaps in thinking.

NOTE: Headings should be short phrases, such as "Improved Communication" or "Mechanical Difficulties."

NOTE: If your clusters are messy, draw lines around each cluster in order to make it easy to see what goes where.

OPTION B: If there are more than ten to twelve people in the meeting, it is impractical for all participants to participate in the clustering. Instead, ask a smaller group of volunteers to cluster the ideas. (Use the other participants' time wisely during this period. Have them work on something else or take a ten-minute break.) When the small group has finished, ask them to read aloud what they have put into each category, along with the headings their group has given each cluster. Gain agreement on what is in each category and its heading before moving on.

NOTE: If you have asked the group more than one question, you can break into Small Groups (see Small Groups, technique 20) to complete the exercise.

OPTION C: Ask each participant to choose his or her favorite idea and send it forward to you. After posting all these ideas up on the wall, read each idea aloud and ask what ideas are similar to others. Begin to cluster ideas and give each cluster a heading as appropriate. (Many ideas may not have clusters at this point.)

Next, ask participants to send up another favorite idea that is not already represented. With the group's help, cluster those new cards with other posted cards. Finally, ask participants to bring forward any other new ideas. Put them into the categories that the group thinks are most appropriate, and create a heading for each of them.

4. Use the accumulated Card Cluster information as planned.

Summary

Card Clusters involves individually and silently writing ideas on cards and then categorizing the cards together as a group.

Before the Meeting

1. Identify your topic and an appropriate Open-Ended Question.

2. Plan how you will use the gathered information.

3. Plan how you will introduce the topic at the meeting.

4. Prepare the visual aids you need to support the discussion.

5. Acquire sticky notes and felt-tip pens for all participants.

6. Identify a space within the meeting room to put the sticky notes.

During the Meeting

1. Introduce the agenda topic. Share how the information will be used.

2. Ask all participants to write their ideas on sticky notes.

3. Collect all written ideas and categorize them with other similar ideas. Create headings for each cluster.

4. Use the accumulated Card Cluster information as planned.

"Often our discussions ramble from problem to solution and back again. Sometimes we even look for solutions before agreeing on what we want as an end result. What can we do to focus on one thing at a time without over-structuring ourselves?"

32. STP

What Is STP?

STP (Situation, Target, Proposal) is a brainstorming technique designed to clarify a situation, define a target, and articulate a proposed solution. *Situation* refers to the current, undesirable state. *Target* refers to a future, desired state. The *Proposal* portion of the equation is the proposed action(s) to move from the current situation to the desired target.

Some people have the ability to jump from one category to another without problem or confusion. But this is not true for all individuals, and it's certainly not true for groups of people. Focusing on one aspect of the process at a time avoids confusion and improves results.

When to Use STP

- When an issue is multifaceted
- When the group members needs to determine where they are, where they want to be, and how best to get there
- When you want to clarify issues for a presentation
- When discussions seem to be unfocused and without direction

How to Use STP

1. Write Situation, Target, and Proposal on a white board or chart papers in three sections (refer to figure 5-9 as an example).

SITUATION	TARGET	PROPOSAL

Figure 5-9. Template example for STP.

2. Brainstorming as a group, start with the first category on the chart, Situation. Ask the question: "What do you see as the current situation?"

NOTE: Review the ground rules for your meeting and the guidelines for brainstorming if necessary. See the Old-Fashioned Way, technique 28, for brainstorming guidelines.

Chart the group's responses.

NOTE: If ideas emerge from the discussion that belong in the Target or Proposal categories, chart them accordingly with permission from the person submitting the idea. If you find that the group is jumping all over the place, remind them to focus on the Situation category first.

3. After all ideas are charted, go back and obtain agreement from the group on each of the brainstormed items.

    NOTE: It is important that the analysis of ideas follows the process of brainstorming. Do not analyze the ideas during the brainstorming portion of the process.

    a. Read all of the brainstormed comments. Ask, "Which comments need clarification?"

    b. Ask, "Is there anything written here that you cannot agree with?" Where disagreements exist, look for the cause of the disagreement, and modify or clarify the statement as necessary.

        NOTE: If there is a controversy or disagreement about any particular point and the conversation is bogging down, ask the group, "How shall we handle this?" You will want to compromise between having complete agreement and not getting bogged down. It may be a good idea to come back to a point of disagreement later, after the rest of the work in that section is complete.

        NOTE: Be sure that the group is not stating the Situation as a Proposal. For example: "We don't have money for a new building" presumes that a new building is a proposed solution to some problem. A better way to address the situation would be to describe the current situation without bias about the solution. For example, "There are not enough desks, phones, and computers for everyone during peak periods of use." Look for Open-Ended Questions, technique 34, to support you when this problem occurs. For example: "What specifically is causing you to conclude that we need a new building?"

4. Once the Situation area is completed, move to the next category, Target. Target refers to defining your preferred future or the way the situation would be if it were perfect or at least satisfactory. Ask the question, "What would it be like if it were perfect, or at least satisfactory?"

   a. Brainstorm as before. Chart all responses.

   b. Seek consensus, modifying the ideas as necessary.

   > OPTION: Before defining your Target, create a list of consequences that result from the current Situation. This reinforces why change is important.

5. Use the same process for Proposal.

   This may include brainstorming several solutions and picking one, or creating an action plan. See Chart Actions, technique 63, for details. Ask the question, "How can we move from our current situation to our preferred target?"

   a. Brainstorm as before. Chart all responses.

   b. Seek consensus, modifying the ideas as necessary.

6. Document and send out your summary for participant approval. Use this resulting information to start action or to obtain approval to start action.

Summary

STP (Situation, Target, Proposal) is a brainstorming technique designed to clarify the situation, define the target, and articulate a solution. Situation refers to the current, undesirable state. The Target refers to a future, desired state. The Proposal refers to the proposed action that moves the situation from the Proposal to the Target.

1. Write Situation, Target, and Proposal on a large board or three pages of chart paper.

2. Brainstorm the Situation portion of the equation. "What do you see as the current situation?"

3. Seek agreement on the brainstorming ideas developed in step 2.

4. Use the same process for Target that you used for Situation in steps 2 and 3. "What would our situation be like if it were perfect or at least satisfactory?"

5. Use the same process for Proposal that you used for Situation and Target. "How can we move from our current situation to our preferred target?"

6. Use the resulting information to start action or to obtain approval to start action.

"Sometimes when we need to be the most creative, my participants seem to be restricted by their assumptions. I need to find a way to help them challenge those assumptions so we can generate a new level of thinking and creativity. What do you suggest?"

33. Breaking a Stalemate

What Is Breaking a Stalemate?

Breaking a Stalemate is a brainstorming technique designed to challenge the paradigms and assumptions of your participants that seem to get in the way of their creative energy.

Instead of brainstorming solutions to a stated question or problem like other brainstorming techniques, Breaking a Stalemate brainstorms the assumptions upon which a given issue, product, or service is based and then brainstorms creative alternatives that challenge or overturn these assumptions.

Breaking a Stalemate demands that your group look at doing business outside the accepted norms of that business.

When to Use Breaking a Stalemate

- When your group is looking for a method to get ahead of the competition
- When your group is stuck in old ways of doing business and you are afraid that this thinking will hamper the group's success in the future

How to Use Breaking a Stalemate

1. Introduce Breaking a Stalemate and why you are choosing to use the technique. You might say, for example: "As you know, our primary competition, X Corporation, is gaining on us fast. If we don't come up with a new way of addressing this, we'll lose significant market share. And to make matters worse, X Corporation is owned by a multinational that traditionally throws money at marketing as a method to capture more market share. We can't win this battle fighting fire with fire, so let's look for a more ingenious and creative way to compete."

2. Have your participants brainstorm an exhaustive list of all the assumptions that their industry accepts as common sense. For example, Corporation X will always be better at marketing than we are. Petroleum is needed to run the engines in our factories. We need to lay off people and cut costs to survive. Chart the group's responses.

3. Brainstorm ways to overturn these assumptions.

NOTE: The Old-Fashioned Way, technique 28, will probably work best.

4. Decide how best to proceed, usually in terms of research or other actions.

Summary

Breaking a Stalemate is a brainstorming technique designed to challenge the assumptions and paradigms that seem to restrict creative problem solving. It differs from other brainstorming techniques because it brainstorms the assumptions upon which a given issue, product, or service is based and then brainstorms creative alternatives that challenge these assumptions.

1. Introduce Breaking a Stalemate and why you are choosing to use the technique.

2. Have your group members brainstorm an exhaustive list of all assumptions that their industry or profession accepts as common sense. Chart the group's responses.

3. Brainstorm ways to overturn or change these assumptions.

4. Decide how best to proceed, usually in terms of research or other actions.

Source

Ohmae, Kenichi. 1982. *Mind of the Strategist: The Art of Japanese Business*. New York: McGraw Hill.

6

Nineteen Techniques to
Gather Information

Tameron's management team just spent the last hour reviewing the previous quarter's sales figures. "We can't afford to lose any more business. We've been pummeled in the marketplace over the past few years, and we just can't survive any more false starts. Why aren't we getting the same quality of information as other organizations seem to be?"

Organizations need to gather and analyze information in order to make intelligent decisions. This can be an arduous and daunting task. Because the quality of decisions inevitably suffers when based on incomplete and therefore inferior data, comprehensive information is absolutely essential. Today, this information comes from both inside and outside the organization and often from nontraditional sources.

This chapter gives the meeting facilitator nineteen options for accumulating maximum information in record time. Some of these techniques can be used to gather information before meetings; others are designed for use within meetings; and one technique, the Delphi Technique, is designed specifically for use in place of a meeting. The broad range of these techniques ensures that they cover almost every potential situation.

Techniques include:

34. Open-Ended Questions
35. Individual Interviews
36. Focus Groups
37. Questionnaires
38. The Delphi Technique
39. Expectations Survey
40. Passing Notes
41. Skits
42. Is/Is Not
43. Nominal Group Process
44. Process Flowcharting
45. Content Experts
46. Prouds and Sorries
47. Keep/Throw
48. Working Break
49. New Shoes
50. Five Whys
51. SWOTs
52. Road Shows

"Sometimes when I ask a question, people just sit there and shrug their shoulders or blandly say yes or no. What can I do to stimulate more conversation?"

34. Open-Ended Questions

What Are Open-Ended Questions?

The Open-Ended Questions technique gathers information in a manner that invites the greatest response.

The way you form your questions determines the type of response you will receive. Open-Ended Questions are questions that cannot be answered yes or no. "What are your ideas?" is an open-ended question. "Do you have any ideas?" is a closed-ended question because it can be answered with a simple yes or no response. Other examples of Open-Ended Questions include: "What ideas do you have?" as opposed to "Do you have any ideas?" and "What are your reactions to this plan?" as opposed to "Do you like this plan?"

The use of Open-Ended Questions presumes that participants have ideas or questions and that you are interested in hearing them. It is essential to use Open-Ended Questions in order to ensure maximum participation. It is a core facilitation technique.

When to Use Open-Ended Questions
- When you want to gather information
- When you are interested in hearing the opinions of others
- When your group tends to be silent

How to Use Open-Ended Questions

Before the Meeting

1. As you plan for each agenda item, determine specific Open-Ended Questions that will elicit the type of information you need. Decide how broad or narrow the focus of your question should be. For example: "What is causing this increased error rate?" or "What is causing this increased error rate on the third-shift production line?" or "What is causing this increased error rate on the third-shift production line over the weekends?"

   NOTE: Sometimes proposed solutions are disguised as Open-Ended Questions. For example: "How can we get the funding to hire another administrative assistant?" is really a proposed solution. "How can we resolve our paperwork backlog?" would be a better question to solve the underlying problem.

2. Plan how you will state the purpose for the Open-Ended Question. It is necessary to use a lead-in to the Open-Ended Question, stating the purpose for the discussion. When participants hear a question without knowing its purpose, they are often reluctant to respond. For example: "We need to determine the best way to fix this problem. What have you heard about what's happening out on the shop floor?"

NOTE: Most people ask closed-ended questions out of habit. To change your habits, consider recording your meeting or ask a participant to record the questions you ask throughout the meeting.

During the Meeting

1. State the purpose for your question to the group and ask your Open-Ended Question(s). Consider posting the Open-Ended Question(s) on a chart or overhead.

NOTE: Be patient and wait for responses. And be careful. Meeting facilitators will often give some examples of right answers, which can inadvertently turn their Open-Ended Question into a closed-ended question. For example: "What do you think is causing the increased error rate?" (open-ended question) versus "Is it the employees we hire?" (closed-ended question).

NOTE: If you think you are getting responses that are too broad or too narrow, expand or contract your question.

2. Chart the responses to your Open-Ended Question.

NOTE: Open-Ended Questions are an important tool and should be used in virtually every technique when asking questions. See Shredded Questions, technique 9, and Five Whys, technique 50, for two specific examples.

NOTE: Closed-ended questions have their place. They are used to verify consensus or understanding of an issue. For example: "Do we all agree?" "We're meeting next Thursday, is that correct?"

Summary

Open-Ended Questions is a technique for gathering information in a manner that ensures the greatest response and participation. Open-Ended Questions are questions that cannot be answered with a simple yes or no.

Before the Meeting

1. Plan the specific Open-Ended Question(s) you are going to ask.

2. Plan how you will state the purpose for the Open-Ended Question(s).

During the Meeting

1. State the purpose for your question and pose your Open-Ended Question(s).

2. Chart the responses to your Open-Ended Question(s).

"Sometimes we need to gather information from people other than those attending our meetings. On other occasions, we need to spend our limited meeting time making decisions instead of collecting information. Is there a technique you can suggest for these situations?"

35. Individual Interviews

What Are Individual Interviews?

The Individual Interviews technique is designed to gather information and ideas from specific stakeholders before a particular meeting takes place. Stakeholders are those people who have any vested interest, share, or stake in a given outcome. This information is generally collected and categorized for use in a specific meeting, but there are also times when Individual Interviews can take the place of a group meeting.

Individual Interviews ensure input, increase ownership, and help guarantee that the processes used and the decisions made in your meeting(s) will have the highest return on investment.

When to Use Individual Interviews

- When information is needed from people other than those attending your meeting
- When ideas and information can be gathered more efficiently on a one-to-one basis
- When 100 percent meeting attendance is not possible
- When the planned meeting time is too short for the quantity of information anticipated from the proposed agenda
- When you want input from your stakeholders before an upcoming decision

How to Use Individual Interviews

1. As you plan your agenda, determine what type of information or ideas need to be gathered before the meeting and how best to gather the information. Individual Interviews are most often face-to-face, verbal exchanges.

   OPTION: Alternatives to Individual Interviews include telephone and video conference interviews, small-group interviews (see Focus Groups, technique 36), and written questionnaires (see Questionnaires, technique 37).

2. Decide who should be interviewed and who should send the interview invitation.

NOTE: Be sure to schedule interview times well before the actual meeting. Ensure that the interview invitations come from an appropriate person of authority and include an explanation of the purpose of the interview, time requirements, and how the interview results will be used.

3. Plan the specific questions to ask during your interviews.

   NOTE: Refer to Open-Ended Questions, technique 34, and Shredded Questions, technique 9, for support.

   Unless you are the leader, ensure that the appropriate person of authority signs off on your questions in advance.

   The type of information or ideas requested obviously will depend on the nature of your group, the meeting, and its agenda.

   • If you want to interview participants about their expectations for the meeting, you might ask, for example, "What do you think are the most important issues for our group to address at our next meeting?" or "How do you think we are doing at working together as a group?"
   • If it is appropriate to interview employees about a specific process, product, service, or problem, you might ask, "Where do you see the biggest opportunities for improvement?" or "How do you feel this specific problem should be addressed?"
   • If you want to question customers or suppliers about a specific issue, you might ask, "What can we do to simplify our interactions with you?" or "Where do you see our biggest opportunities for improvement?" or "How do our products/services compare to our competitors?"
   • If you choose to interview upper management about their perspective or considerations for your group planning session, you could ask, "What information do we need from you before our planning discussions begin?" or "What do you specifically expect from our department in the next three years?" or "What do you think we are currently doing well?" or "Where do you see our biggest areas for improvement?"

4. Determine who should ask the questions. Be sure that the person(s) that you choose are credible and perceived as neutral.

NOTE: Ensure that external consultants or anyone new have the proper introductions in advance.

5. Decide how the information should be documented during the interviews.

    OPTION: Consider recording your interviews. This can avoid confusion about what was actually said when preparing documentation. Be sure to get permission from the interviewees beforehand.

    NOTE: If you use more than one person to conduct interviews, consider quality control measures to ensure consistency. Make sure there is congruity between interview questions and summarization techniques. Agree ahead of time on a system of documenting and compiling the information. Let participants know if their comments will be anonymous or on the record and credited to them.

6. Decide how the information and ideas collected will be summarized and presented at the meeting group.

    NOTE: Consider summarizing information into clustered categories, for example, by response type or group or level within the organization. Determine which categories to use based on what you feel will reveal the best quality and most relevant information. Then determine how to present the information, that is, in narrative format, with graphs, and so on.

    NOTE: Be sure to get permission from interviewees if you quote them by name in your interview summaries. Also inform interviewees if, how, and when they will see the results of the interviews.

7. Conduct your Individual Interviews.

8. Use the information as planned.

Summary

The Individual Interviews technique gathers information or ideas before a specific meeting takes place.

1. Determine what type of information or ideas you need to gather before the meeting.

2. Decide who should be interviewed and who should send the invitations. Schedule appointments well ahead of time.

3. Plan what open-ended questions to ask.

4. Determine who should conduct the interviews.

5. Decide how the information should be documented during the interviews.

6. Determine how the ideas and information collected will be summarized and presented.

7. Conduct your Individual Interviews.

8. Use the information as planned.

"We need to collect a lot of information from a large number of people in a short period of time. Face-to-face input is important, but our group doesn't have the time or the resources to gather this information through individual interviews. What do you suggest?"

36. Focus Groups

What Are Focus Groups?

Focus Groups are designed to gather information from groups of people. The need for this technique can be motivated by time constraints or the belief that the synergy of group discussions can create more input and ideas than one-on-one discussions.

Focus Groups are not recommended when you want quantitative or statistical types of information but are excellent at providing qualitative information. Focus Groups can also be extremely effective when used in combination with Individual Interviews, technique 35, and Questionnaires, technique 37.

Focus Groups are usually discussions with groups of eight to twelve people, and these groups generally contain a homogeneous selection of participants, that is, a group of suppliers, customers, or employees from a specific department or level within an organization. Discussions usually last from one and a half to two hours and are facilitated by an interviewer or moderator. Data collected from a Focus Group is generally used outside the Focus Group itself. The data provides information that the organization can use to improve its competitive position, its existing or future products or services, its work processes, or its organizational culture.

When to Use Focus Groups

- When you want to gather information from a large number of people in a short amount of time
- When you want to determine how specific decisions and/or actions are perceived within the organization
- When you want to test the clarity of communication
- When you want to generate hypotheses or new ideas
- When you want to plan an organization-wide questionnaire
- When you want to evaluate another group's ideas
- When you are unfamiliar with opinions of specific groups and want a broad view quickly

How to Use Focus Groups

1. Clarify the information needed, why it is needed, and how it will be used. Agree that Focus Groups (or another technique) are the best process to gather the necessary information.

2. Determine who you will include in your Focus Groups(s). Examples include specific teams or departments; groups of suppliers or customers; groups of executives, managers, or board members; community members; and special-interest group members.

   NOTE: Homogenous groups where group members have something in common with each other work best.

   OPTION: Consider using Mind Mapping, technique 29, to help identify groups or specific participants within groups.

3. Determine the questions you will ask as well as the format of those questions.

   NOTE: Use Introductions, technique 1, as a technique to help participants become comfortable with each other. It is difficult for participants to be open without knowing who else is in the room. Food and beverages also give the meeting a more comfortable feel.

   Review Shredded Questions, technique 9, and Open-Ended Questions, technique 34, for ideas. Prepare an agenda for each Focus Group, like the one in figure 6-1.

SAMPLE AGENDA

Introduction   10 minutes

Review the purpose of meeting.
Outline the structure of the meeting and how information will be used.
Participant introductions.

Questions   75 minutes

What do you like best about our product/service?
What do you like least about our product/service?
What ideas for improvement do you have?

Summary   5 minutes

Plans for follow-up with participants.
Thank you.

Figure 6-1. Sample agenda for Focus Groups.

4. Determine who will facilitate or moderate each Focus Group. To ensure neutrality, consider using an external facilitator or a combination of internal and external persons.

5. Determine how to document the information collected in the Focus Groups.

   Chart responses, video or audio record responses, have a second person take notes during the meeting, or use a combination of these.

6. Decide how information will be summarized. For instance, cluster in categories of information, categorize by focus group, or categorize by question asked.

7. Prepare invitations for Focus Group attendees that include the following information:
   • Purpose of the Focus Group
   • Who will be attending
   • Why and how participants were selected
   • Time and place

- Duration of the meeting
- Who will moderate/facilitate the Focus Group
- Incentives for attendance—i.e., food, gifts, and so on
- Request for confirmation of attendance

NOTE: Ensure that invitations are sent by a person who will be able to influence participants to attend—i.e., a line manager, an executive, or another person of influence.

8. Prepare the logistics for the meeting.

   NOTE: See chapter 2 for ideas.

9. Conduct the Focus Group.

10. Use the information as planned.

    NOTE: In addition to entire books on the subject of Focus Groups, a number of professional organizations provide expertise in conducting Focus Groups. The information provided here is designed to provide the fundamentals for facilitating Focus Groups.

Summary

Focus Groups help gather qualitative information from large groups of people in a minimum amount of time. Although not recommended for quantitative, very negative, or controversial information, Focus Groups can create a synergy that stimulates more input and ideas than one-on-one discussions.

1. Determine what information is needed and agree that Focus Groups are the best technique for gathering that information.

2. Determine who will be included in the Focus Group or groups and who will send the invitation to attend.

3. Determine the questions you will ask.

4. Determine who will moderate the Focus Group.

5. Determine how to document the collected information.

6. Decide how the information will be summarized.

7. Prepare invitations.

8. Prepare the logistics.

9. Conduct the Focus Group.

10. Use the information as planned.

"I know that a number of organizations and facilitators use Questionnaires to gather information. What can you tell me about this technique?"

37. Questionnaires

What Are Questionnaires?

Questionnaires gather written information from individuals that can be quantitative, qualitative, or a combination of both. It is a relatively inexpensive technique that allows you to gather information from large numbers of people in a short period of time.

This technique does, however, have limitations. Because it is one-way communication, sometimes the data collected can be difficult to interpret. Some people will give you less information in writing than in person and you can receive lower response rates. But if utilized under the proper circumstances, Questionnaires can be a valuable technique for gathering information.

There are five techniques described in this book that are designed to gather information outside actual meetings. Questionnaires tend to be the least time-consuming of these techniques. The more time-consuming techniques, Individual Interviews, technique 35, and Focus Groups, technique 36, have already been described, and the Delphi Technique, technique 38, and Expectations Survey, technique 39, follow.

When to Use Questionnaires

- When you want to gather information from large groups of people
- When gathering information in writing will meet the needs of your group
- When you want to gather information from meeting participants before the meeting

How to Use Questionnaires

1. Determine the purpose and scope of the Questionnaire you are developing by asking yourself the following questions:
   - What is the purpose of your Questionnaire?
   - Who is the audience for your Questionnaire?
   - How will the information be used?
   - Who will use the results?
   - How will results be communicated?

2. Develop your Questionnaire, choosing whether to structure your questions as open-ended or closed-ended. The following three samples show how to design the same

basic question. The first two are closed-ended examples and the last is open-ended. Note that questions can be expressed as both questions and statements.

(A) My manager listens to my ideas.
   Strongly Agree ( )
   Agree ( )
   Neither agree nor disagree ( )
   Disagree ( )
   Strongly Disagree ( )
(B) How frequently does your manager listen to your ideas?
   Always ( )
   Almost always ( )
   Sometimes ( )
   Rarely ( )
   Never ( )
(C) Describe the way your manager listens to your ideas.

NOTE: Effective closed-ended questions are very difficult to develop. Respondents can easily omit important information, and this can skew the validity of your Questionnaire.

Open-ended questions gather a much wider breadth of information than closed-ended questions but are much more difficult to summarize and statistically analyze. Choose the method that will work best for your purposes. You might also consider using both open- and closed-ended questions for different parts of your Questionnaire.

When developing your Questionnaire, consider following the following basic guidelines:

- Be sure questions focus on one topic at a time
- Use language that is easy to understand
- Ask questions that are applicable to all who receive the Questionnaire or note exceptions clearly
- Avoid asking leading or loaded questions and questions where only partial alternatives are provided
- Start with the least difficult and controversial questions
- Cluster questions in relevant categories, unless you have a specific reason not to

- Make the Questionnaire look approachable. Crowded pages with small print are intimidating and look like they will take too much time to complete
- When you have the choice, shorter is better
- With forced-choice responses, be sure that there are the same number of positive and negative responses
- Test your Questionnaire for clarity and accuracy with a small sample of participants before sending out to large groups of people. Consider using a Focus Group, technique 36, to help plan the Questionnaire
- Include a cover letter clearly outlining the purpose of the Questionnaire, who is receiving the Questionnaire, a deadline, and who to contact with problems or questions

3. Determine the logistics of your Questionnaire by answering the following questions:
   - Who will the Questionnaires be returned to?
   - When do they need to be returned?
   - How will the Questionnaires be distributed?
   - Who will write and who will sign the cover letter to accompany the Questionnaire?
   - What publicity, if any, is appropriate?
   - How will the responses be compiled and by whom?
   - How will the results be summarized and presented?
   - How, when, and by whom will the results of the Questionnaire be communicated?

NOTE: Many online services, for example, Survey Monkey, exist and provide excellent results. However, the quality of your Questionnaire and its summary will still require your attention. This cannot be fully outsourced.

OPTION: For large efforts, such as company-wide surveys, or if you have little experience with Questionnaires, consider hiring a professional firm to help you.

4. Administer the Questionnaire.

5. Use the information as planned.

Summary

Questionnaires are designed to gather information from individuals in writing. It is a relatively inexpensive technique that allows you to collect large amounts of information from large numbers of people in a relatively short period of time.

1. Determine the purpose and scope of the Questionnaire.

2. Develop your Questionnaire.

3. Determine the logistics of your Questionnaire.

4. Administer the Questionnaire.

5. Use the information as planned.

"I need to gather information from a range of people in different locations. The information I require is relatively straightforward, but getting these people together is impossible. Help!"

38. The Delphi Technique

What Is the Delphi Technique?

The Delphi Technique is used to gather information and opinions from the members of a group without any face-to-face discussion. This occurs most often when it is logistically difficult for the group participants to get together. The process is carried out through a series of Questionnaires and ends with a written summary given to each participant. Because the group using this technique will never meet, the entire process is executed through e-mail or some other online media.

The Delphi Technique takes the place of a meeting, allowing participants the benefits of others' insights without physically interacting with them. However, sometimes the information gathered from this technique is later used in a meeting composed of a smaller or different group of people.

Among its obvious limitations, the Delphi Technique requires much more time for the facilitator to prepare and, because there is no direct contact, it is difficult for participants to create a sense of team. Additionally, the success of the process depends significantly upon the analytical and reporting skills of the facilitator.

When to Use the Delphi Technique
- When it is very difficult for participants to get together
- When the focus is on one primary question or concern
- When the contents of the discussion can be easily categorized and summarized for review

How to Use the Delphi Technique
1. Determine if the Delphi Technique is appropriate for your purposes. If it is, take the time to write a clear letter of introduction outlining the purpose and process you will use. Refer to Three P Statements, technique 8, for support.

2. Ask group members one or more questions as an initial inquiry that starts the process. Question(s) should be Open-Ended Questions, such as "What are the problems in meeting holiday season customer demand?" Be sure to explain the purpose of the

question and how the information will be used. Consider providing a Questionnaire form that members complete online by a specified date.

3. Tabulate the responses and include them on a second Questionnaire that asks participants to vote for or rate the importance of various responses. See Multivoting, technique 54, or Nominal Prioritization, technique 58, for ideas. In some cases, ask participants to write arguments or position papers justifying their reactions and reasoning.

4. Tabulate the ratings and summarize the arguments. Send the information back to group members and request that they evaluate their selected choices. Continue this process until no new information is forthcoming and a consensus is reached.

5. Use the information as planned.

Summary

The Delphi Technique is used to gather information and opinions from the members of a group without any face-to-face discussion among group members.

1. If the Delphi Technique is appropriate for your purposes, prepare the necessary introductory correspondence.

2. Ask group members one or more open-ended questions as an initial inquiry that starts the process.

3. Tabulate the responses and include them on a second questionnaire that asks participants to vote for or rate the importance of various responses.

4. Tabulate the ratings and summarize the arguments. Send the information back to group members and request that they evaluate their selected choices. Continue this process as needed.

5. Use the information as planned.

"Our group is planning where to focus our improvement efforts for the next few years. We want input from our customers and employees but don't really know how to organize ourselves to get this input. What do you suggest?"

39. Expectations Survey

What Is an Expectations Survey?

The Expectations Survey is a technique designed to gather quantifiable information from customers of a specific group. In this case, a group can mean a company, division, department, or team within any organization. An Expectations Survey measures the expectations for a group from a wide variety of customers. This information then provides a basis for examining priorities and setting goals.

The term *customer* not only refers to the traditional concept of the customer, who is typically the end user or purchaser of an organization's products or services. A customer can also be defined as anyone who is impacted by a group's products or services. This includes the traditional customer noted above, as well as employees, management, stockholders, suppliers, lenders, and others.

Without input from its customers, no group will ever have a complete picture of its top priorities. Understanding the needs and priorities of customers has become commonplace because it makes good business sense. Any group or organization that neglects to do so will likely experience rework, loss of market share, and unnecessary conflict over priorities.

When to Use an Expectations Survey
- When preparing to agree on group or team goals
- When you want to establish priorities for improvement
- When you want feedback from your customers

How to Use an Expectations Survey
1. Present the purpose of the Expectations Survey to your meeting group. For example: "An Expectations Survey gathers information and feedback from all the customers of a group, both inside and outside the organization. This information measures the perceived expectations of these customers and provides a basis for decision making and goal setting." To support your efforts, you might ask the group, "What would you see as the advantages of asking customers for their expectations?" "What would be the disadvantages?" "How could we use this information to help us plan our improvement efforts?"

2. Determine which customer groups to ask for feedback. Be sure to include all customers that are impacted by the activities of your specific meeting group. Consider Mind Mapping, technique 29, as a tool for brainstorming and categorizing information.

3. Make logistical decisions. You might ask the group, for example, "Will the survey be executed in person or in writing?" "Who will conduct the survey and coordinate gathering the responses?" "What are the time frames involved?" "Who will send the invitation to participate?"

4. Agree on how to prepare the information for analysis at your next meeting. Determine the specifics by asking, "Who will do what by when?" See Chart Actions, technique 63, for a template.

5. Agree on an appropriate amount of time to follow up with your customers. This follow-up will test your group's progress toward the improvements identified by your customers.

6. Plan how to communicate to your customers about the Expectations Survey. Agree on any written communication to each customer group. Be sure to clearly communicate the purpose of the survey when communicating with your customers. For example: "We are currently planning how to better serve you in the future. Please help us plan appropriately by sharing your expectations of our group, how important each of these expectations is to you, and how well we are currently meeting those expectations."

7. Prepare Expectations Survey sheets, an example of which is shown in figure 6-2.

CUSTOMER EXPECTATIONS	LEVEL OF IMPORTANCE	LEVEL OF CURRENT SATISFACTION
LIST YOUR EXPECTATIONS OF OUR GROUP. PLEASE BE AS SPECIFIC AS POSSIBLE.	1 LOW 5 HIGH	1 LOW 5 HIGH

Figure 6-2. Sample template for Expectations Survey.

8. Conduct the Expectations Survey.

   NOTE: Be sure to coach any interviewers to remain neutral and nondefensive. Issues will surface that might surprise the interviewers, and their reactions may impact the quality of responses. Remind them that all feedback is valuable feedback, even if it exposes a misunderstanding between the customer and the group. While on-the-spot solving of little problems is sometimes acceptable, the goal of the Expectations Survey meeting is information gathering, not problem solving.

9. Collect and tabulate all the information. Cluster information together where appropriate and possible. It may be helpful to sort the information by different types of customer.

   NOTE: Look for the biggest gaps—for instance, where the level of importance is very high and the level of current satisfaction is very low. These are the areas where you have the biggest opportunities for improvement and where your clients will take notice. Figure 6-3 provides an illustration.

CUSTOMER EXPECTATIONS	LEVEL OF IMPORTANCE	LEVEL OF CURRENT SATISFACTION
LIST YOUR EXPECTATIONS OF OUR GROUP. PLEASE BE AS SPECIFIC AS POSSIBLE.	1 LOW 5 HIGH	1 LOW 5 HIGH
Return phone calls within half a day.	4	4
Provide accurate reports.	5	2
Give us advance warning about changes that will affect the way we work.	5	1
Communicate to our support staff in a professional manner.	4	3

Figure 6-3. Sample of a completed Expectations Survey.

As you can see from the example, giving advance warning about upcoming changes and providing accurate reports are the most important opportunities for improvement in this Expectation Survey.

10. Use this information in planning goals for the next period. This period could be six months, one year, two years, or whatever period is practical given the nature of the information collected. (See SMART Goals, technique 64, for support.)

11. Communicate to your customers involved in the Expectations Survey what you found and what your group intends to do with the information. Share the specific goals you have set in response to the information.

12. After the agreed-upon time frame, return to your customers for additional feedback. Ask them once again for their expectations of your group, their ranking of these expectations, and their current level of satisfaction. Benchmark the progress of your efforts from one year to the next.

    NOTE: This is a process that your group could continue or modify on an annual or otherwise regular basis.

Summary

Expectations Survey is a technique for gathering information and feedback from all the customers of a group, both inside and outside the organization. This information measures the expectations of these customers along with current levels of satisfaction and provides a basis for decision making and goal setting.

1. Introduce the concept and purpose of an Expectations Survey.

2. Determine which customer groups to ask for feedback.

3. Make the necessary logistical decisions.

4. Agree how to specifically prepare the returned information for analysis at your next meeting with this group.

5. Agree on an appropriate amount of time to follow up with your customers.

6. Plan how to communicate to your customer groups about the Expectations Survey.

7. Prepare the Expectations Survey sheets.

8. Conduct the Expectations Survey.

9. Collect and analyze the information.

10. Use this information with your group in planning goals for the next period.

11. Communicate the results to the customer groups involved in the Expectations Survey.

12. After an agreed-upon time frame, return to the customer groups for feedback on any improvements, changes, or additional concerns.

"Several of the groups within our organization are interdependent. Productivity suffers because none of the groups seems to understand exactly how their own work impacts the other group. Also, the atmosphere that has developed is more competitive than collaborative. We want to find an effective way to give each other feedback, but we need to learn a technique that is not heavy handed. Do you have any ideas?"

40. Passing Notes

What Are Passing Notes?

The Passing Notes technique is used for giving and receiving specific feedback to and from other divisions, departments, groups, work shifts, or even individuals within an organization. The purpose and goals of Passing Notes are very serious, but the process is achieved in a light-hearted manner.

The ultimate objective of the Passing Notes exercise is to help specific, interdependent groups or even individuals understand what other groups or people need from them in order to do their jobs more effectively.

Passing Notes is not an appropriate tool in highly contentious situations. In those cases, consider a more controlled technique such as Individual Interviews, technique 35.

When to Use Passing Notes

- When you have groups or individuals that are dependent on each other but have not communicated very well in the past
- When you want to prepare for a goal-setting session by sharing feedback and information first
- When you want to help groups, or individuals within a group, understand their interdependence and what the others need to work more effectively with them

How to Use Passing Notes

Before the Meeting

1. Plan how you will use Passing Notes in the meeting.

   NOTE: This exercise is generally done in a large-group session with smaller intact work group breakouts. It can also be done between individuals within a group.

   NOTE: You will need to allot approximately ninety minutes for this exercise.

2. Create the four instructional charts or slides you will use (see figures 6-4 through 6-7 for examples).

During the Meeting

1. Present the purpose of Passing Notes. You might say, for example: "We are a group of people who are dependent upon each other for success, but we haven't taken much time to communicate what we need from each other to be successful. We will take the next hour and a half to exchange information and then use that information to make plans to help support each other's efforts better."

2. Break the group into specific work groups. Ask each group to write notes to all of the groups that they are dependent on to get their own work done. These notes need to be specific. Examples of how to introduce such a note include: "In order for us to meet our goals, we need you to ... " or "In order for us to work more effectively, we need you to ... " Be sure to include positive feedback too—for example, "It is very helpful when you ... " Display the Passing Notes guidelines chart or overhead you prepared before the meeting, an example of which is illustrated in figure 6-4.

PASSING NOTES

Answer this question for each of the other groups you work with: "In order for us to meet our goals (or work more effectively) with you, we wish you would...

Be sure to:

- Share what is going well in addition to opportunities for improvement
- Honor the self esteem of others
- State the rationale of your request
- Make your request in concrete, specific, and measurable terms

20 minutes

Figure 6-4. Guidelines for Passing Notes chart.

Coach your groups on how to give constructive feedback and provide specific guidelines on how to respond to Passing Notes in positive terms. All feedback must honor the self-esteem of others, state the purpose of the request, and make the request in concrete, specific, and measurable terms. For example, one note might read: "We need more lead time in order to get you the materials you need when you need them.

We would appreciate your communicating with us as soon as you hear from your customers with even an estimate of your needs." An inappropriate note would read "If you jerks can't get your act together to pick up the phone, don't blame us."

NOTE: Unless you are a neutral facilitator, participate with your group.

3. When everyone has finished writing, ask each group or individual to give the other groups their notes.

4. Ask each group to read all their notes. They are allowed to ask for clarification, but rebuttals or excuses are not allowed. Post the instructional chart or overhead you have prepared for this section, similar to figure 6-5.

READ YOUR NOTES

Read all your notes. Formulate any questions for clarification.	10 minutes
If needed, send representatives to different groups to get clarification. No rebuttals or excuses. Just listen. Representatives take notes and summarize what they heard before returning to their own group.	10 minutes
Representatives report back to their own group what they learned.	10 minutes
	30 minutes total

Figure 6-5. Instructions chart for Passing Notes.

5. When everyone is finished reading, ask each group to start problem solving the issues expressed in the notes. This will result in a list of corrective action items that they can commit to. (See the Old-Fashioned Way, technique 28, for details.) Post a chart or overhead similar to figure 6-6 for clarification.

GROUP COMMITMENTS

- Pick a recorder, reporter, and timekeeper.
- Respond to each Note, one at a time. Brainstorm as necessary.
- Agree on corrective actions, document on charts. Include a contact or coordinator name for each action.

20 minutes

Figure 6-6. Problem-solving chart for Passing Notes.

6. Next, ask each group to report their action plans for all the notes they received. The group sending each note then responds to the action plans with a thumbs-up (affirmative) or thumbs-down (negative) signal. Coach the groups giving negative signals to also briefly explain why they don't accept the action plan. Plan about ten minutes for every group reporting back. Post an instructional chart similar to figure 6-7 during this section.

PASSING NOTES: ACTION REPORTS

- Report your action plans for each Note received.
- Pause to get a "Thumbs-Up" or "Thumbs-Down" reply from the sender group. Any "Thumbs-Down" are noted on a chart paper for later discussion.

10 minutes per group

Figure 6-7. Action plan instructional chart for Passing Notes.

OPTION: If you have more than three to four groups, or if your notes came from individuals instead of groups, consider having representatives go back to each group to get one-on-one feedback instead of a group report.

7. If necessary, ask groups to plan another meeting to work on issues left unresolved between themselves and other groups. If possible, have this unresolved-issues meeting immediately after step 8. Dismiss all groups who have no unresolved issues and ask those remaining to make necessary changes to get approval.

NOTE: The unresolved issues meeting would follow steps 4, 5, and 6 outlined above.

8. Plan a follow-up session/progress report, including a specific date and time whenever possible.

Summary

Passing Notes is a technique for giving and receiving specific feedback from interdependent groups or individuals within the same organization. The purpose is to help groups or individuals better understand what other groups or individuals need from them in order to do their jobs more effectively. This information is used to plan improvements in work processes and communication.

Before the Meeting

1. Plan how you will use Passing Notes in your meeting.

2. Create the charts or overheads you will need.

During the Meeting

1. Introduce Passing Notes.

2. Break participants into their specific, intact work groups. Ask each group to write notes to all of the groups they are dependent upon to get their own work done.

3. Ask each group to distribute their notes to the appropriate recipients.

4. Groups read their notes and ask for clarification as needed.

5. Groups then start problem solving, making a list of corrective action items they can all agree to.

6. Ask each group to report their action plans for each note they received.

7. If necessary, plan another meeting to work on unresolved issues between specific groups.

8. Plan a follow-up session/progress report.

"We are constantly trying to maximize the efforts of our organization. But it's difficult to know how to help work teams without knowing exactly what they do or the problems they face. How can I lead work groups to share this kind of information without being boring?"

41. Skits

What Are Skits?

Skits allow groups to share information about their responsibilities and work situation with other groups in their organization. In this way they can help others better understand the reality of their situation.

Skits use the power of example to illustrate a position, depict a problem, or illuminate a typical work situation. In addition to being a fun and creative group exercise, Skits can be an extremely effective technique that exposes emotional, difficult, and frustrating work situations in memorable, profound, and powerful ways. Skits can also be used in many other ways, such as to celebrate the end of a project or as an alternative to presentations in a large conference.

When to Use Skits

- When it is important to share job information with other departments
- When you want to illustrate a feeling or point that is not well explained in words alone
- When you want to get a point across in an interesting, memorable way

How to Use Skits

1. Ask participants from each group represented in the meeting to create a Skit that describes what it is like to work in their department. Include as much information as possible, such as the atmosphere, roles, and responsibilities as well as frustrations they might feel.

   a. Have each group first agree on the key points they would like to make in their Skit.

   b. Next ask them to plan the best way to portray those points in their Skits. This information is best presented on a chart, as in figure 6-8.

PLAN YOUR SKITS

Plan a Skit that describes what it is like to work in your department. Include information on atmosphere, frustrations, roles, and responsibilities.

1. Agree on the key points you would like to make in your Skit.

2. Plan the best way to portray those points. You may be literal, or use metaphors, analogies, or other creative ways to make your points.

20 minutes

Figure 6-8. Instructional chart for Skits.

In addition, establish clear ground rules for the exercise by posting a chart as illustrated in figure 6-9.

SKITS GROUND RULES

- Do your best to provide an unbiased view
- Be as clear as possible
- Honor the self esteem of others
- Skits between 3–10 minutes in length
- Your Skits can be funny or serious, real or abstract
- Professional acting and directing experience are not required or expected

---

Figure 6-9. Ground rules for Skits.

c. Allow approximately twenty to thirty minutes for preparation.

NOTE: To begin, it is a good idea to allow twenty minutes for the preparation. About fifteen minutes into the exercise, ask each group how they are doing and allow them to negotiate for more time if necessary.

OPTION: Groups could come to the meeting already prepared to do this.

2. Have each group present its Skits.

3. Debrief the Skits. The debriefing exercise should take place in small, intact work groups. Use the same debriefing questions for each Skit, as shown in figure 6-10. The group that presented the Skit does not debrief its own Skit.

SKITS DEBRIEF QUESTIONS

- What were the key points you observed?
- What points need clarification?
- What were your reactions?
- What can your department/you do to diminish the frustrations you observed in this Skit?

15 minutes debrief for each skit presented

Figure 6-10. Debriefing chart for Skits.

4. Have each group report back the summary of its discussions.

   NOTE: If you have more than one group debriefing the same Skit, have each of those groups share their debriefing information for that same Skit before moving on to debrief other Skits.

5. Ask each group to take up to twenty minutes to create an action plan based on the information in the summaries. You might introduce this section by asking, for example, "What can your department/you do to improve communication and diminish the frustrations you observed in this skit?" The action plan should be typed and distributed as soon as possible after the meeting.

6. Ask the group to define when and how to best follow up. Take responsibility to make sure that the follow-up occurs in the manner and time frame that the group agrees to.

Summary

Skits is a technique for sharing information across departments or groups. It is especially effective at educating people or groups about another group's roles and responsibilities and describing frustrations in working effectively with those groups or individuals.

1. Introduce Skits and ask each group that is represented to create and prepare a Skit that describes what it is like to work in their department.

2. Have each group present its Skit.

3. Debrief the Skits in small groups.

4. Report back a summary of all discussions.

5. Ask groups to create an action plan for improvement. Distribute agreements to other pertinent groups.

6. Ask the group how and when it would be best to follow up on their actions. Follow up as appropriate.

"We have a demanding problem to solve, and we're finding it difficult to get a grip on it. Is there a simple technique that will focus our efforts in the right direction?"

42. Is/Is Not

What Is Is/Is Not?

Is/Is Not is a technique for specifically identifying a problem. "A problem well stated is a problem half solved" goes the old adage, revealing that you can't solve a problem until you clearly and accurately identify it. Is/Is Not defines exactly what a problem is and what a problem is not.

Sometimes the process of isolating a problem is quite simple. For instance: "The problem is not that the order is a week late. The problem is that you didn't communicate with us." Sometimes a problem is so ambiguous or complex that it demands a lengthy process of questioning and analysis. For example, the question "What is causing our company to lose money?" may be too complicated to correctly diagnose with only Is/Is Not. This technique will, however, appropriately steer a group to further in-depth analysis.

The Is/Is Not technique surrounds a problem like a net surrounds a school of fish. As the net gradually tightens, some fish escape while others are trapped and can't find their way out. Once the net is finally pulled in, the true nature and size of the catch are revealed. The fishermen then analyze their catch, throwing out what is not useful to keep and keeping only that which will benefit them.

When to Use Is/Is Not
- When your group is not sure about the cause of a problem
- When a problem needs to be isolated
- When the true nature of a conflict between groups or individuals is not clear

How to Use Is/Is Not
1. Explain Is/Is Not and how your group will use it to define the nature of the problem you are addressing. For example: "Is/Is Not is a technique for helping us isolate the problem we face. By asking a series of questions about what the problem is and what the problem is not, we will be able to clearly articulate our problem. Then we can work on how to solve the problem."

2. Ask your meeting group a series of questions pertinent to their own situation.

a. You might ask, for example, "Where does the problem happen?" "When does the problem happen?" "How does it happen?" "What processes and people are involved?"

b. And then you might ask, "Where else could the problem occur but does not?" "When could the problem occur but does not?" "Where are the same people, processes, and materials being used but without this problem?"

OPTION: Make two columns on a chart or overhead, one for what you know the problem *is* and one for what you know the problem *is not*. Record the group's answers appropriately.

NOTE: Depending on the nature of the problem, groups may need to go out to find information and discuss their findings at a later meeting.

3. Review your Is/Is Not data.

4. Agree on the focus of the problem.

5. Plan to test the cause of the problem as necessary.

6. Plan how to address and solve the problem.

Summary

Is/Is Not is a technique for identifying what a problem is and what a problem is not. This allows a group to get beyond assumptions and focus on the core issues that need to be addressed.

1. Set up the exercise and explain the technique.

2. Ask your group a series of Is/Is Not questions.

3. Review your Is/Is Not data.

4. Agree on the focus of the problem.

5. Plan to test the cause of the problem as necessary.

6. Plan how to address and solve the problem.

Source

Kepner, Charles H., and Benjamin B. Tragoe. 1965. *The Rational Manager*. New York: McGraw-Hill.

"Our group needs some discipline. A few outspoken people seem to be influencing the thinking of the other meeting participants. If we are to truly benefit from everyone's ideas, we need to find a way to eliminate this type of pressure. Do you have any ideas?"

43. Nominal Group Process

What Is Nominal Group Process?

Nominal Group Process is a technique that allows meeting participants to express themselves without immediate outside influence. The process involves having each group member individually think and write down his or her thoughts about an issue or problem before presenting them to the group verbally.

Nominal Group Process provides the time for participants to collect and articulate their own thoughts before they hear other perspectives. This creates fuller participation and assures that the most persuasive individuals in the group do not impact and alter the valuable input of the whole group.

When to Use Nominal Group Process
- When you want to make sure individuals are doing their own thinking
- When you want to be sure that you hear from everyone in the meeting group
- When you need a method to collect maximum ideas in minimal time

How to Use Nominal Group Process
1. Introduce the issue or problem under consideration and the Nominal Group Process technique. You might say, for example, "Before we can solve this problem, we need to clearly understand it. Each of you has a slightly different perspective of the problem because of your different experiences and areas of expertise. In order to fully understand everyone's point of view, let's use a technique called Nominal Group Process. This technique will allow us to each spend a few minutes thinking quietly and individually about the problem. We will then share our perspectives with each other so that we will have a more complete picture to consider."

2. Ask each member to write down his or her ideas about the specific problem under consideration. Present the issue as a specific question or set of open-ended questions (see Open-Ended Questions, technique 34) and post your questions on chart paper or an overhead. For example: "We're having a problem delivering our goods on time. When does it happen?" "What is the cause of the problem?"

OPTION: Ask meeting participants to come to the meeting already prepared to share this information.

NOTE: Do not ask more than two questions or the process will be too slow. Do not use this method with large groups. Consider Card Clusters, technique 31, instead.

3. Ask each participant to concisely share his or her thoughts, facts, or ideas with the group.

   a. Chart each person's comments, and use one chart for each question asked.

      NOTE: Post all charts around the room when the pages are full. (The participants will need them as visual aids later on.)

   b. Allow other participants to ask questions for clarification, but they may not evaluate or elaborate further at this time.

      OPTION: Hold off on all questions for clarification until after all ideas from all participants have been documented.

4. Review all the shared information.

   OPTION A: With input from the group, make a summary list that includes all information while eliminating duplications.

   OPTION B: Review all information, and select three or four items that are most worthy of further exploration. Consider using Multivoting, technique 54.

   OPTION C: Ask the group members for their reactions and conclusions. For example: "What patterns do you see? In what areas do we have general agreement? In what areas are there significant disagreements? What conclusions can we draw from this information? What additional information do we need to gather?" Chart the group's responses.

5. Summarize your findings, and determine how to proceed to address the uncovered issues and the problem overall.

OPTION: Define the problem with one statement that deals comprehensively with all the information gathered. Use that statement as a basis for problem solving.

Summary

Nominal Group Process is a technique for gathering problem-solving information from all meeting participants individually and later evaluating and prioritizing that information as a group.

1. Introduce the issue or problem under consideration and the Nominal Group Process technique.

2. Ask each person to write his or her ideas to the question(s) you have posed.

3. Ask each participant to share his or her responses to the questions. Chart their responses.

4. Review the information as a group.

5. Summarize your findings, and determine how to proceed.

Source

Debecq, A. L., and A. H. Van de Ven. 1971. "A Group Process Model for Problem Identification and Program Planning." *Journal of Applied Behavioral Science* 7: 466–92.

"We want to make improvements to our processes, but we don't know where to begin. How can we gather information about what is happening with a process that goes through many hands and even many departments?"

44. Process Flowcharting

What Is Process Flowcharting?

Process Flowcharting is a technique for identifying, documenting, and analyzing all the steps in an existing process and then looking for methods to improve that process. *Process* in this situation is defined as any series of progressive and interdependent steps to achieve an end result.

People often don't recognize all the steps involved in a process. Because of this lack of awareness, people can be critical and intolerant of the concerns and perspectives of others. When they understand specifically how a current process works, they can more easily look for opportunities to improve and streamline it. Process Flowcharting can be an eye-opener for groups that are unaware of all that must be done to accomplish a specific task and thus serves as an effective approach to analyzing and improving existing processes.

When to Use Process Flowcharting

- When you need to analyze a process or problem that involves many steps and many people
- When people disagree on what is happening, should happen, or why things need to happen
- When you need to save time, money, and/or resources by improving efficiency
- When part(s) of a process are causing problems, but you cannot easily identify the best methods for fixing the problem
- When creating a job aid or formalizing a new or existing procedure
- When introducing new technology

How to Use Process Flowcharting

Before the Meeting

1. Determine what process will be analyzed.

2. Determine where in the process to begin your analysis, where to end, and at what level of detail. You might plan to say, for example: "We will examine the billing pro-

cess from the time an invoice is received in our office until the time that it is paid. We will look at the process in sufficient detail that we can all understand how much time is needed for each specific step."

3. Determine who needs to be involved. Be sure to include all people who are involved in the process.

   NOTE: With processes involving large numbers of people, include representatives of each group or department.

4. Assemble necessary materials: enough sticky notes, felt-tip pens, and chart paper for the meeting.

   NOTE: Most processes involve many steps and will require several sheets of chart paper taped together, so instead you might consider using large sheets of brown paper, which are available at most office supply stores.

During the Meeting

1. Explain the purpose of Process Flowcharting. You might introduce the topic by saying, for example, "Process flowcharting is a technique for identifying all the steps in an existing process and looking for ways to improve that process."

2. As a group, list the steps involved between the beginning and end of the process.

   NOTE: Ask those who actually perform any specific step to give you the information on what that step involves. If your process is very complex, start with high-level steps first and move to the details in a second round.

   Use a sticky note for each step in the process. (This way you can move things around if you have forgotten anything or put it in the wrong order.) Place each sticky note on your chart paper, one after another.

   NOTE: If you encounter a portion of the process that no one in the room is familiar with, make a note of it, and keep moving forward.

   When the process comes to a decision point, split your flowchart in as many directions as there are options for that decision point. Follow each new direction when appropriate, or make a note to see another flowchart for details. A decision point is revealed by a closed-ended question, one that can only be answered by yes or no. If yes, one activity happens. If no, another activity happens. You might express this situation as follows: "Is the form completed correctly? If the form has all the information on it, the order is filled. If the form doesn't have all the necessary information, it is put in a box labeled incomplete."

3. When the Process Flowchart is finished, review the completed chart for possible gaps or inconsistencies. Plan to show the chart to others familiar with the process to help you identify any missing areas, increase understanding of current processes, and verify the accuracy of the chart.

4. If necessary, assign symbols and redraw the resulting chart. A sample of potential symbols is illustrated in figure 6-11.

PROCESS FLOWCHARTING SYMBOLS

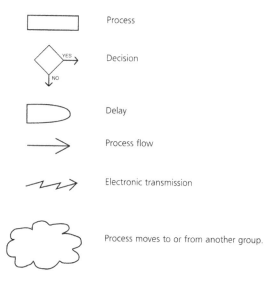

Figure 6-11. Sample symbols for Process Flowcharting.

5. With the group, analyze the current process illustrated on the Process Flowchart. Figure 6-12 illustrates an example of what an invoicing Process Flowchart might look like.

SAMPLE INVOICING PROCESS

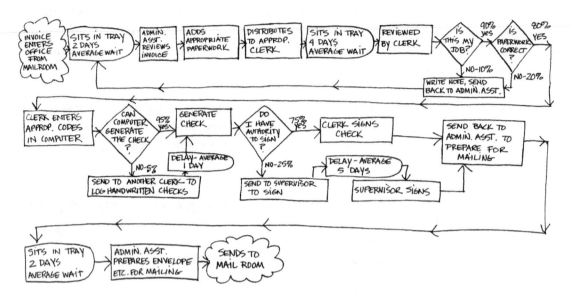

Figure 6-12. Sample of an invoicing Process Flowchart.

Identify problems, unnecessary steps, and methods for improvement.

With help from all involved, look for waste, redundancy, and steps that do not add value.

6. Brainstorm and agree on changes to improve the process. Create a new Process Flowchart as a tool for documenting these changes.

   NOTE: Consider documenting the anticipated time and cost savings from these changes.

7. Test the new process. Plan how to communicate the changes to others involved in the process and establish a specific follow-up time to measure how well the changes are working.

8. Meet again at a predesignated time to review how well the changes are working. Make any required modifications at that time, and look for additional ways to make the process more effective.

NOTE: Process Flowcharting software exists and is a helpful way of documenting agreed-upon processes.

Summary

Process Flowcharting is a technique for identifying, documenting, and analyzing all the steps in an existing process and then looking for opportunities and methods to improve the process.

Before the Meeting

1. Determine the process to be analyzed.

2. Determine where in the process to begin your analysis, where to end it, and at what level of detail.

3. Determine who needs to be involved.

4. Assemble enough sticky notes, felt-tip pens, and chart paper for the meeting.

During the Meeting

1. Introduce and explain the purpose of Process Flowcharting.

2. As a group, list the steps involved in the process.

3. When your Process Flowcharting is finished, review the chart for gaps and inconsistencies.

4. If necessary, assign symbols and redraw the resulting Process Flowchart.

5. As a group, analyze the process revealed by the Process Flowchart, identifying problems, unnecessary steps, and methods for improvement.

6. Brainstorm and agree on changes to improve the process.

7. Test the new process for effectiveness.

8. Meet again at a predesignated time to review how the changes are working. Make modifications to the process as required.

"Sometimes our group needs to hear from experts in various fields in order to understand more about a technical issue. But whenever we have an expert come in to talk, things never go as planned. They either talk over our heads, talk too long, or totally miss the point we are seeking. How can I work more effectively with these people?"

45. Content Experts

What Are Content Experts?

Content Experts allow you to gather information on a specific subject from someone who does it for a living, studies it for a living, or uses it for a living. These people can come from both inside or outside the organization, and they may be persons several levels above or below you in the organization.

Content Experts can only be successful when they clearly understand the purpose for talking to your group, the current level of understanding of the group, and the parameters of the discussion. These parameters can include time, the amount of two-way communication expected, and any anticipated questions.

It is the responsibility of the meeting facilitator to strictly control these Content Experts in order to provide the meeting group with a relevant, clear message and helpful basis upon which to move forward.

When to Use Content Experts
- When you need to get information or an opinion based on expert knowledge
- When an outsider can best address a controversial issue
- When the group is interested in learning new skills or perspectives

How to Use Content Experts

Before the Meeting

1. After defining the purpose of this part of your meeting, brainstorm the best methods to gather information. You might ask yourself, for example: "Who would know the answers to our questions?" "Who could we invite to our next meeting to shed some light on this issue for us? Is having a person come to speak to us the best way for us to gather the information we need?"

   OPTION: Consider films, articles, panel discussions, and field trips as possible alternatives.

If you choose to use a Content Expert, question people within your organization, colleagues, or professional organizations to find out who is the best person for your purposes.

NOTE: Be sure not to overlook the Content Expert(s) working within your organization. For example, the best people to discuss a certain type of machinery are members of the crew that uses that machinery. To better understand industry issues or customer perspectives, tap a person from a competitor's company who has recently joined your firm.

2. When you contact the Content Expert(s) whose services you desire, clearly state the purpose of your request. If they agree to participate, tell them how to best prepare for your meeting. For example, you might want to share answers to the following questions:

- Who is the audience?
- What does the audience want to know?
- What level of current knowledge do the meeting participants have?
- What level of detail would the group like the expert to provide?
- What type of presentation do participants expect?
- Will the presentation be formal or informal?
- Will questions and answers be encouraged during the presentation or held to the end?
- How much time will the expert have to speak?

    NOTE: Tell the Content Expert(s) that your group is committed to staying within time frames and that you will use a timekeeper to help you keep on track.

- What visual aids will be available for use?
- What compensation can the group provide?

    NOTE: External experts will likely want to be compensated for their time. Letters of recognition to supervisors are appropriate for internal experts, and sometimes this is even adequate for external people.

3. Follow up your conversation with written confirmation. Follow up again a day or two before the meeting to confirm all the details.

4. Schedule the Content Expert(s) at the beginning of the agenda. That way, if your agenda slides, you do not have to keep the expert(s) waiting.

During the Meeting

1. Introduce your guest. Give your group some guidelines for the presentation. Negotiate these guidelines with both the Content Expert(s) and your group. Ask for a timekeeper or act as the timekeeper yourself.

2. Listen to the presentation of the Content Expert(s).

3. After the presentation, take at least a few minutes to debrief and plan appropriate follow-up. Depending on the size of your group, consider either one large group discussion or several small group discussions. See Small Groups, technique 20, for details. Post the debrief questions, a sample of which is illustrated in figure 6-13.

DEBRIEF QUESTIONS

1. Choose a recorder/reporter and timekeeper
2. Answer these questions:
   - What conclusions can we draw from listening to this expert?
   - What actions should we consider?
   - What recommendations do we have as a group?

                                                                15 minutes

---

Figure 6-13. Debriefing chart for Content Experts.

NOTE: You may want to ask the Content Expert to stay during this discussion to answer any remaining questions or concerns.

4. Based on the answers to the debrief questions, make decisions for action or follow-up as is appropriate for your group.

After the Meeting

1. Send a thank-you note to your guest. Include a copy for the person's supervisor if appropriate.

2. When appropriate, pay the Content Expert in a timely manner. Follow up on any other commitments made as soon as possible.

Summary

The Content Experts technique involves utilizing experts to provide technical or complex information not readily available from within your meeting group.

Before the Meeting

1. Define specifically what the group needs or wants to learn.

2. Once you locate the Content Expert, inform him or her how to prepare for the meeting.

3. Follow up your conversation with written confirmation.

4. If possible, schedule the Content Expert(s) at the beginning of the agenda.

During the Meeting

1. Introduce your Content Expert(s) and provide any guidelines for the presentation.

2. Listen to the presentation as planned.

3. After the presentation, debrief the information and plan appropriate follow-up.

4. Make decisions for action.

After the Meeting

1. Send a thank-you note to your Content Expert(s).

2. Follow up with any agreements in a timely manner.

"Our group has been through a lot together, and we've developed some serious emotional energy about how we worked with each other in the past. It's difficult to articulate exactly what all the issues are, but I want to use this energy and past experience to help us in the future. What do you suggest?"

46. Prouds and Sorries

What Are Prouds and Sorries?

The Prouds and Sorries technique constructively addresses both the positive and potentially negative emotional issues facing your meeting group. Because emotional issues can heavily impact the effectiveness of any group, it is imperative for you to have a technique in your arsenal to help effectively deal with these types of problems. Overlooking these emotional issues or pretending that they don't exist can be disastrous.

Conveying Prouds and Sorries helps a group come to terms with its past. The technique analyzes, in a methodical way, what the group's participants feel proud about and what they feel sorry about. This information is used to clear the air as well as to initiate discussions to establish norms, goals, and objectives for the future.

Emotional energy is common within work groups. It is especially strong in organizations that are downsizing and going through dramatic change, in groups where a project has ended negatively, and in organizations that have been purchased or taken over by another group. Prouds and Sorries allow people to own up and move on.

When to Use Prouds and Sorries
- When you want to reflect on the past in order to make the future even better
- When there are many hard feelings among a group
- When you want to allow people to share feelings about a project in a constructive, focused manner
- When you want to use the past to build on the future

How to Use Prouds and Sorries

Before the Meeting

1. Assemble the necessary materials: enough sticky notes, marking pens, and chart paper.

2. Create the charts you will use. (See figures 6-14 through 6-16.)

During the Meeting

1. Explain the purpose of the exercise, and introduce the Prouds and Sorries technique. Consider using a Three P Statement, technique 8, in your introduction as charted in figure 6-14.

PROUDS AND SORRIES

Purpose:

To articulate and learn from the best and the worst, the highs and lows of the past year.

Process:

We will look first individually and then as a group at your Prouds and Sorries. Then we will use this information to analyze what we want to keep in the future and what we want to discard.

Payoff:

Insights to build a stronger team.
Information to establish realistic goals and norms for the next year.

Figure 6-14. Three P statement for Prouds and Sorries.

2. Ask the group to answer these questions: "What are you proud about?" "What are you sorry about?" Display these questions on a chart similar to figure 6-15.

PROUDS AND SORRIES

As you look back on xxx (the last year, this project, etc):

- What are you proud about?
- What are you sorry about?
- Write your ideas on sticky notes, one idea per sticky note. Please use verbs before nouns to ensure we understand your points clearly.

10 minutes

Figure 6-15. Instructional chart for Prouds and Sorries.

Then explain the ground rules for answering the questions you have posed in figure 6-15, exhibiting a Prouds and Sorries ground rules chart. An example of this chart is illustrated in figure 6-16.

PROUDS AND SORRIES GROUND RULES

1. It's OK to say what you're proud about that others did.
2. It's not OK to say that you're sorry about what others did, except for your reactions or responses to what others did, or your part in what happened.

For example: "I am sorry you were a jerk." (not OK) versus "I am sorry that we didn't work better together under pressure" (OK).

Figure 6-16. Ground rules chart for Prouds and Sorries.

NOTE: Unless you are an outside facilitator, remember to write your own Prouds and Sorries, too. If you think you will be too rushed to do them during the meeting and facilitate the meeting as well, write them down ahead of time.

3. When everyone is finished, ask the participants to bring their ideas forward and attach them to the appropriate charts you have prelabeled Prouds and Sorries.

4. Ask the group to cluster their ideas with similar ideas. Split the group in two, one to cluster Prouds and one to cluster the Sorries. Allow ten to fifteen minutes for clustering. Ask the two groups to put a heading on each cluster. (See Card Clusters, technique 31, for more information on how to cluster information.)

OPTION: If your group has more than twenty people, consider asking for volunteers to cluster the information when the rest of the group takes a short break.

5. When the Prouds and Sorries are clustered and have headings, ask representatives from each group to read aloud all the information in the categories they created.

6. Debrief Prouds and Sorries. You might ask the group, for example, "As you listened to the other groups, what common threads did you hear? What in particular stood out for you? What can we learn from this information?"

OPTION: Ask your group to create a priority list of the proudest Prouds and the sorriest Sorries. This list can be used to summarize the feelings of the group and is especially helpful with large groups or groups with long lists of Prouds and Sorries.

7. Use this information to establish norms, goals, and objectives for the future.

OPTION: This technique is frequently followed by Keep/Throw, technique 47, as a tool to move toward goal setting.

Summary

The Prouds and Sorries technique can help a group articulate both its positive and negative feelings about events that happened in the past.

Before the Meeting

1. Assemble sticky notes, marking pens, and chart paper.

2. Create the charts you will use.

During the Meeting

1. Explain the purpose of the exercise and introduce the Prouds and Sorries technique.

2. Ask group members to write their responses to "What are you proud of?" and "What are you sorry about?" on the topic under consideration. Set ground rules for the exercise.

3. Ask the group to bring the ideas forward and place them on the appropriate charts labeled Prouds and Sorries.

4. Split the participants in two, and ask them to cluster their ideas with similar ideas, one group for Prouds and one group for Sorries.

5. After clustering and giving each cluster a heading, ask participants to read the responses in the categories they created.

6. Debrief the information with the goal of learning from the experience.

7. Use this information to establish norms, goals, and objectives for the future.

Source

Weisbord, Marvin. 1992. *Discovering Common Ground*. San Francisco: Berrett-Koehler.

"Our group is planning for the future. We know we need to change, but some of the things we are doing are good and shouldn't be changed. Is there a technique for helping us get rid of the bad and keep the good?"

47. Keep/Throw

What Is Keep/Throw?

Keep/Throw provides a process for a group to agree on what is working and should continue to be done and what is not working and should be discontinued or changed.

When planning for the future, a group sometimes needs to make radical changes to meet the new goals. In this situation, some people and groups will want to throw everything away and start over. This method definitely gets rid of the bad, but it doesn't acknowledge or preserve what is already good. It can also leave participants feeling that everything they have done in the past was worthless.

Keep/Throw allows for a healthier, more productive approach to change that supports past successes by honoring what is good.

When to Use Keep/Throw

- When your group is planning for the future
- When your group wants to identify methods to work together more effectively
- When your group is finished with one project and beginning another

NOTE: This technique is often used as a final step in Prouds and Sorries, technique 46.

How to Use Keep/Throw

Before the Meeting

1. Assemble the necessary materials: sticky notes, marking pens, and chart paper.

2. Create the charts you will use.

During the Meeting

1. Introduce the technique. You might say, for example, "Some of what we have done in the past definitely needs to be changed. But some of what we have done has been very effective, and we should keep these things. Let's use a technique called Keep/Throw

to help us differentiate between the two as a first step toward planning how to work together in the future."

2. Ask the group to individually brainstorm answers to the following two questions on sticky notes, one answer per sticky note. "What things are we currently doing that you would like to *Keep* and carry into the future?" "What things are we currently doing that you would like to *Throw* away and leave behind?" Post a chart or overhead similar to figure 6-17 for support.

KEEP/THROW

1. What things are we currently doing that you would like to Keep and carry into the future?
2. Which things are we currently doing that you would like to Throw and leave behind?
3. Write one idea per sticky note.

10 minutes

Figure 6-17. Instructions chart for Keep/Throw.

OPTION: An alternative to Keep/Throw is Stop/Start/Continue. In this version, you ask the group three questions: What should we stop doing? What should we start doing? And what should we continue doing?

3. Ask the group to bring their ideas forward and attach them to the charts you have labeled Keep and Throw.

4. Ask the group to cluster the ideas with other similar ideas. Split the group in two, one to cluster Keeps and one to cluster Throws. Allow about ten to fifteen minutes for clustering. Ask the two groups to give each cluster a heading.

5. After each group is finished, ask them to review the work of the other group. When participants have read all the clusters in both the Keep and Throw categories, ask them to sit back down.

6. Debrief the exercise with these or similar questions: "What stands out in your mind as you read this Keep/Throw information?" "What conclusions can we draw?" "What should we do with this information?"

7. Incorporate the information as the group suggests based on their response to the final question, "What shall we do with this information?" For example, you might want to keep the lists as a reference when the group creates goals and plans actions in the future.

Summary

Keep/Throw is a technique that provides a process for getting participants to consciously think about what they do that works and what doesn't work. It leads them to make choices about their behavior and work processes as they plan for the future.

Before the Meeting

1. Assemble sticky notes, marking pens, and chart paper.

2. Create the charts you will use.

During the Meeting

1. Introduce the exercise.

2. Ask the group to brainstorm answers to the questions "What things are we currently doing that you would like to *Keep* and carry into the future?" "What things are we currently doing that you would like to *Throw* away and leave behind?"

3. Ask the group to bring the ideas forward and place them on the appropriate charts labeled Keep or Throw.

4. Split the participants into two groups, and ask them to cluster their ideas with similar ideas, one group for Keep and one group for Throw.

5. Ask them to read the work of the other group.

6. Debrief the exercise.

7. Incorporate the information as the group suggests.

Source

Weisbord, Marvin. 1992. *Discovering Common Ground.* San Francisco: Berrett-Koehler.

"Sometimes my participants use meeting time to discuss private, one-on-one issues that don't include the rest of the group. How can I prevent this from happening?"

48. Working Break

What Is Working Break?

Working Break is a technique that provides your meeting group with a designated period of time for addressing private, one-on-one issues during the meeting without wasting the time of the other participants. This is a short, informal time specifically set aside in the meeting to take care of private and/or small-group business. It also allows for stretching and refreshing beverages.

The reality is that when colleagues get together, they tend to use the opportunity to catch up on personal pieces of business not related to the agenda at hand. Unfortunately, it is oftentimes more convenient and faster for them to take care of this business during your meeting rather than somewhere else. Moreover, this behavior occurs even if it uses other people's time unwisely.

When people know that there is time set aside for their private business, they tend to stay more focused on the tasks at hand. The Working Break technique provides that time.

When to Use Working Break

- When meeting participants come from long distances and are not able to see each other on a regular basis
- When several group members have small pieces of one-on-one business with each other
- When your meetings are getting sidetracked by people sharing information that is not pertinent to the entire group

How to Use Working Break

1. When appropriate, create a specific time during your meetings (perhaps ten to fifteen minutes) that allows individual participants or small groups to take care of their private business not related to the agenda of your meeting. This time can be used as a regular break for those not needing to use it for working purposes.

2. Post ground rules, as illustrated in figure 6-18.

WORKING BREAK GROUND RULES

- Avoid discussing issues relevant to entire group.
- Stick to brief issues, such as making an appointment or checking a deadline.
- Please stand up and move around the room.
- Socialize if you have no relevant business. Stay available for others who might have business with you.
- If a person is engaged, stand nearby to indicate that you are waiting.
- Please return to your seats when the time has expired.

Figure 6-18. Ground rules for Working Break.

NOTE: Until your group is very familiar with Working Break, bring a preprepared Working Break ground rules chart with you to all your meetings.

Summary

Working Break is a technique that provides a designated time period during your meetings for participants to take care of their private business with each other without wasting the time of other group members.

1. When appropriate, provide a short period of time specifically designed to allow your participants to deal with private, individual, or small-group business.

2. Post Working Break ground rules.

"Participants in our meetings sometimes ask themselves, 'Is anybody listening?' This tends to happen especially during heated debates. How can I be sure that people are truly listening and that everyone feels that they have been listened to?"

49. New Shoes

What Are New Shoes?

The New Shoes technique helps ensure that people in your meeting groups are listening, are understanding, and can explain the other perspectives being presented in the room. This is accomplished by asking participants to summarize what they heard to the satisfaction of the people who originally presented an idea or point of view.

This process doesn't necessarily mean the participants agree with everything that has been summarized but is designed to ensure that people are listening and understanding.

When to Use New Shoes
- When there are contentious situations in your meetings
- When people are doing a better job of stating their side of the story than of listening to the other sides
- When you want to reinforce to all participants that they have been listened to

How to Use New Shoes
1. Introduce New Shoes during a part of your meeting when it is particularly important that the opinions of all parties are understood.

2. As a group, listen to all points of view.

3. Ask people to state what they heard from the other participants' points of view. Have them include facts and feelings. Note that they can summarize accurately without agreeing with what the person has said. Post ground rules for this exercise similar to those shown in figure 6-19.

NEW SHOES

- Summarize what you heard the person say.
- Include not only facts, but also how you perceive that the person feels about what he or she said.

GROUND RULES

- Honor the self esteem and personal perspectives of the other participants.
- Use supportive vocal intonations. Sarcasm is not acceptable.
- Look at the person when you are summarizing their perspective.

Figure 6-19. Instructions and ground rules chart for New Shoes.

4. After the summary, ask the person whose viewpoint was being summarized to approve of the summary. That person or the facilitator can ask questions for clarification if appropriate. They may also make corrections if the summary is inaccurate.

   NOTE: Give all participants the opportunity to have their viewpoints summarized by the others in the room.

5. Move forward with problem solving or whatever goal you were working toward on the agenda.

   OPTION: When participants offer solutions, ask them to offer solutions that they believe would be acceptable to those with other opinions as well as from their own perspectives.

Summary

New Shoes helps participants believe that their viewpoint and position has been heard by other participants.

1. Introduce New Shoes during a part of your meeting when it is particularly important that the opinions of all parties are understood.

2. Listen to all participants' points of view.

3. Ask people to summarize what they heard from participants presenting another point of view.

4. Ask the people whose viewpoints were summarized to approve of the accuracy of the summary.

5. Move forward with problem solving or whatever goal you were working toward.

"Sometimes I feel as though we haven't done a very good job of getting to the bottom of a problem. Is there a quick technique to identify the core cause of a relatively simple problem?"

50. Five Whys

What Are Five Whys?

The Five Whys technique is designed to get to the core source of problems in minimum time. Research shows that to get to the core of a problem one will need to ask why an average of five times. Five Whys involves asking this basic question until your meeting group is satisfied that the root cause of a problem is stated and understood.

When to Use Five Whys

- When you are unsure of what specifically caused a situation to be as it is
- When you want a systematic way to lead a group to understand the real reason why a problem is occurring or has occurred

How to Use Five Whys

1. Simply ask the question "Why?" or "What caused that to happen?" about the specific problem under analysis.

2. Continue to ask why until your meeting group feels it has come to the core reason for the problem or is getting responses that seem trivial or banal. Chart the responses as appropriate.

   NOTE: This may involve talking to several people at several layers of the organization before the problem is fully understood.

3. Use the resulting information to address the issue.

Summary

The Five Whys technique gets to the source of uncomplicated problems in minimum time.

1. Identify a problem, and ask the question "Why?" or "What caused that to occur?"

2. Continue to ask why until your group feels it has come to the root of the problem.

3. Use the information to address the issue.

"We want to set goals, but we can't agree on how or where to focus our efforts. We all have our favorite areas, but there must be a better way. We need a method for gathering information so that we can get the most mileage from our efforts. What do you suggest?"

51. SWOTs

What Are SWOTs?

SWOTs help you gather information for strategic planning and other goal-setting meetings. SWOT information (**S**trengths, **W**eaknesses, **O**pportunities, and **T**hreats) provides data to accurately determine your group's current performance. A group can mean any organization and/or team, unit, department, or division within that organization. SWOT information also provides a foundation for effectively and intelligently setting goals and priorities and making other key decisions for the group's future.

Strengths and **W**eaknesses examine the internal environment of the group. Examples of the internal environment include: how effectively employee skills and other resources are being used, the effectiveness of technology and data management systems, levels of creativity and risk taking, approaches to competition, and the organization's functionality as a unit.

Opportunities and **T**hreats focus on the external environment affecting the group. The external environment can include industry, competitor, economic, social, or political information. Additionally, it could include potential changes in technology, products, markets, financing, raw materials, and labor; threats from new competition; bargaining power of suppliers and buyers; and customer expectations.

When to Use SWOTs

- When an organization, or group within an organization, wants feedback on its performance
- When your group wants to gather information before setting long and/or short term goals

How to Use SWOTs

Before the Meeting

1. Prepare for the SWOT analysis.

   a. Define what information should be collected.

Some groups are very detailed in their analysis and develop a long series of specific questions to explore. Others perform better with fewer specific questions. You, along with those participants selected to help plan your SWOT analysis, determine the best approach for your group.

Most groups simply ask four questions. What are our internal strengths? What are our internal weaknesses? What are our external opportunities? What are our external threats?

NOTE: Be sure to ask only Open-Ended Questions. (See technique 34 for details.)

NOTE: There is a danger in asking very specific questions. Specifics can influence what is considered and can narrow the potential range of responses. On the other hand, an incomplete SWOT assessment can result in a false sense of security. Do as much in-depth investigation as is feasible for your group. SWOTs should be an annual event, and the next round can be more in-depth and sophisticated if necessary.

b. Determine who should be asked for SWOT information. Ask the group: "Which stakeholder groups should be included?" "What other sources of data should be included?" "Financial?" "What else?"

SWOT information is gathered by asking your stakeholders a series of questions. Stakeholders include all people who have a stake in the success of the group. These people include internal and external customers, employees from as many layers as feasible within the organization, managers at all levels, suppliers, stockholders, and lenders.

NOTE: It is critical that information be gathered from *all* stakeholders, not just from the group that will be analyzing the information in the meeting.

NOTE: Mind Mapping, technique 29, works well to brainstorm stakeholder categories.

NOTE: Information on external opportunities and threats can also be obtained from journals, magazines, newsletters, trade shows, conventions, federal reports, and private research groups.

c. Decide how the SWOT analysis will be conducted.

SWOT questions are usually asked in face-to-face interviews or by questionnaire.

d. Determine roles, responsibilities, and time frames for collecting SWOT data.

Agree on who will be responsible for contacting stakeholders and preparing questionnaires, cover letters, memos, and so on. If you are using financial or other written data, determine how and when it will be collected.

2. Gather SWOT information.

NOTE: If you use written questionnaires, ask people to write in complete sentences and explain themselves so the data can be clearly understood. If you are using face-to-face interviews, ask interviewers to be precise in recording responses. (See Individual Interviews, technique 35, and Questionnaires, technique 37, for more information.)

NOTE: If there is a lack of trust and openness in the organization, take extra care to keep responses confidential. If people are afraid of having their handwriting recognized or e-mail messages traced, consider having participants send their SWOT comments directly to an outside facilitator.

3. Compile the accumulated SWOT data for your meeting.

Accumulate SWOT responses by category—one section each for strengths, weaknesses, opportunities, and threats. Each person's response should be recorded verbatim, even if there are duplicate responses. Information, if extensive, may be subdivided within each SWOT category.

OPTION: Some groups find it helpful to code the responses by stakeholder category—that is, E=employee, M=manager, UM=upper management, C=customer, and so on.

NOTE: Categorize and label responses before the meeting, and validate them with participants during the meeting.

OPTION: Send out the SWOT information for the group to read before the meeting.

During the Meeting

1. Review the purpose, process, and expected payoff for the SWOT exercise. (See Three P Statements, technique 8.)

   For example: "The purpose of today's meeting is to analyze our SWOT data and use it as a basis for setting our group's goals for the next two years. After our analysis, we will identify ways to maximize our strengths and opportunities and minimize our weaknesses and threats. This process will focus our efforts for improving our competitiveness."

2. Break participants into four groups, one group to analyze strengths, another for weaknesses, another group for opportunities, and the fourth group for threats.

   OPTION: Consider preassigned groups to ensure a mixture of opinions and levels of the organization. (See Small Groups, technique 20, for details.)

3. Give the groups specific exercise instructions. Post a chart with instructions, such as those in figure 6-20, as a visual aid.

SWOT SMALL GROUP INSTRUCTIONS

1. Introduce yourselves. Pick a recorder, reporter, and a timekeeper.   2 minutes

2. Individually read the information on your SWOT area.   14 minutes

3. Categorize the information.   14 minutes

Use short phrases to describe categories. Be specific.

Total time: 30 minutes

Figure 6-20. Small group instructions for SWOT.

   a. Ask each group to pick a reporter, recorder, and timekeeper. (See Self-Management, technique 10, for details.)

b. Ask each group to read the information on their area—strengths, weaknesses, opportunities, or threats.

NOTE: Participants are to read only their section for now. If you haven't sent the SWOT out for participants to preread, you can provide the raw data for all SWOT categories for anyone who is interested after the meeting.

NOTE: To determine how much time is appropriate for this exercise, read a section closely and time yourself.

c. After all individuals in each group have finished reading the information in their SWOT section, ask each group to categorize their information into headings with short phrases. For example, the strengths group might identify "skilled employees" instead of "employees." The weaknesses group might identify "overworked employees." This avoids later confusion. When in doubt, participants should create two categories instead of one. For instance, "skilled and dedicated employees" should be two categories. The recorder should write each category on a flip chart, leaving substantial space between categories for the next exercise.

NOTE: This exercise should take approximately twenty minutes for every ten pages of data. If the groups need more or less time, adjust accordingly.

OPTION: Categorize the information yourself before the meeting and have each group review your work and make changes as necessary.

4. Ask the small-group reporters to succinctly summarize their group's results for the rest of the participants. Leave time for questions or additions from other groups but keep the report session snappy to maintain the group's energy. Figure 6-21 illustrates the instructions.

REPORT BACK

Please give us a succinct report of the categories your group identified.

10 minutes per group

We will leave a few minutes for questions at the end.

5 minutes per group

Figure 6-21. Instructions chart for SWOT reports.

5. As a group, review the results of your SWOT analysis. Lead a group discussion. For example, you could ask, "What are your reactions to the results of our SWOT analysis?" "What in particular stands out for you?" "What did you find surprising/ not surprising?"

6. Summarize the group's discussion, and prepare for your goal-setting session.

Summary

SWOTs (Strengths, Weaknesses, Opportunities, and Threats) determine the present status of a group's performance. This provides a foundation for collectively and intelligently setting goals.

Before the Meeting

1. Prepare for the SWOT analysis.

    a. Define what information should be collected.

    b. Determine who should be asked for SWOT information.

    c. Decide how the SWOT analysis will be conducted.

    d. Determine roles, responsibilities, and time frames for collecting SWOT data.

2. Gather SWOT information.

3. Compile the accumulated SWOT data for your meeting.

During the Meeting

1. Review the purpose, process, and expected payoff for the SWOT exercise.

2. Break participants into four groups, one each for strengths, weaknesses, opportunities, and threats.

3. Give the groups specific exercise instructions.

4. Ask the small-group reporters to succinctly summarize their group's results.

5. As a group, review your SWOT results.

6. Summarize the group's discussion, and prepare for your goal-setting session.

"We need to make significant changes in our organization in order to successfully compete in the future. Our leaders have a fair idea of the challenges we face, but we'd like to gather input from the employees in some way that will help us gain a full picture of our issues and opportunities and also start to mobilize the organization for the changes ahead. What is the most effective way to accomplish this?"

52. Road Shows

What Are Road Shows?

While most meetings involve a smaller number of participants, Road Shows can involve whole departments, divisions, or geographical locations of an organization. The purpose of Road Shows is to gather ideas for improvement and hear reactions to work in progress. Road Shows are usually travelling exhibits that are held in multiple locations. This allows for gathering a full range of views and perspectives and is part of the process for mobilizing relevant parts of the organization for change. Road Shows are almost always part of a larger project design and its communication plan.

Road Shows are held in a large common area, either on or off site, with displays or booths along the perimeters and also in the middle of the room if space is adequate. Each part of the Road Show is usually staffed by a project team member or member of the executive steering team (see Project Teams, technique 71, and Executive Steering Teams, technique 73, for more information). The preparation for Road Shows is significant, but the payoff is huge.

Facilitating the design, planning, and implementation of a Road Show is not for beginners. If you are not a seasoned professional, strongly consider using an outside consultant or someone from within your organization who has such experience.

When to Use Road Shows

- When your organization faces a significant challenge that will require changes on all or most levels of your business
- When you need input from many perspectives to determine the best solutions for future success
- When you want high visibility and involvement in your project
- When a smaller group of people, for instance, a project team, has done some level of preparation and wants reactions and further input

How to Use Road Shows

Before the Meeting

1. Determine the scope and objectives of your Road Show.

2. Agree on the scope and objectives with your Project Sponsor and Executive Steering Group (if one exists) and engage their active support.

3. Determine who will support you in the preparation for your Road Shows. These people will likely be Project Team members. If your Road Show isn't part of a larger project, then recruit representatives from each of your stakeholder groups. These people will help build the presentations and materials for the Road Show and/or will present their section during the Road Show itself.

   NOTE: Presentation sections and their materials should be self-explanatory, but you should also have a person or two staffing each booth or display. You may choose for these people to provide brief, formal presentations during the Road Show or just to draw people into their part of the event and to answer questions. They should always be credible representatives of their topic, be enthusiastic about sharing information on their topic, and encourage feedback from participants.

4. Hold meetings to design your Road Show. You will likely need to hold a series of planning meetings, starting with the big picture and then working down to the details.

   a. Confirm the purpose and scope of your Road Show with your planning team.

   b. Determine the key communication topics and the logical flow of the room.

      See figure 6-22 (next page) as an example of a room setup for a Road Show.

   c. Plan how people will participate in each part of your Road Show. This could involve asking for feedback on sticky notes, placing dots on priority areas, and so on.

   d. Confirm that the overall design of the Road Show and the details of each presentation/display/booth are appropriately consistent in their level of detail and that together they tell a compelling and intriguing story to their various audiences.

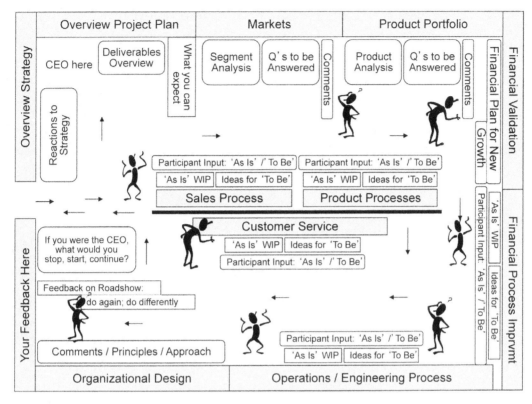

Figure 6-22. Example of a Road Show room setup.

e. Agree on roles and responsibilities for each person on the planning team.

f. Check the progress and draft materials during their development to ensure consistency and quality.

g. Allow plenty of time for printing materials and preparing displays.

   NOTE: Displays can be prepared on large pieces of paper. This makes them easy to roll up and transport from location to location.

5. Invite the participants to your Road Show. Invitations should come from the Project Sponsor or another person of influence and authority. Send invitations well in advance. Consider various modes of communication—i.e., e-mail, wall posters, and so on.

6. Set up the room well in advance of your Road Show. Staging the room takes time. Ensure there is plenty of room to move around and that all topic areas are clearly marked.

7. Do a walk-through/dry run of the Road Show with those presenting. Have them share their key points and presentations with other presenters. Do this is for two reasons: (1) Other presenters will then know the content and key points from all parts of the Road Show, which will help them communicate to participants as required during the day, and (2) it allows a time for presenter feedback and a review for consistency of messaging.

During the Meeting

1. Greet people when they come in and explain the purpose and flow of the Road Show room.

2. Ensure that all is going according to plan—that is, presenters are doing a good job of staffing their booths, adequate materials such as sticky notes are available, and refreshments are replenished. Make last-minute course corrections if required.

3. Thank people for attending as they leave.

After the Meeting

1. Hold a debriefing session with all involved in preparing for and presenting at your Road Show. Ask the group what went well and where they see opportunities for improvement. See technique 78 for details.

2. Determine how to make improvements to future Road Shows.

3. Gather and document the information received during your Road Show. Individual presenters should be accountable for collecting and documenting feedback from their own part of the Road Show, or you can appoint one or more people to collect data from all booths. Also appoint an overall coordinator to confirm that nothing is lost. Have a method in place to be able to distinguish feedback from different sessions. Feedback may vary by geography or company division.

4. Analyze the feedback you received in the Road Shows and determine how to use it.

5. Communicate back to participants, thanking them for their participation and providing highlights of your findings and next steps.

Summary

The purpose of Road Shows is to gather ideas for improvement and hear reactions to work in progress. Road Shows can involve whole departments, divisions, or geographical locations of an organization.

Before the Meeting

1. Determine the scope and objectives of your Road Show.

2. Agree on the scope and objectives with your Project Sponsor and executive steering group (if one exists) and engage their active support.

3. Determine who will support you in the preparation for your Road Shows.

4. Hold meetings to design your Road Show.

   a. Confirm the purpose and scope of your Road Show with your planning team.

   b. Determine the key communication topics and the logical flow of the room.

   c. Plan how each part of your Road Show will be participative.

   d. Confirm the overall design of the Road Show and the details of each presentation.

   e. Agree on roles and responsibilities for each person on the planning team.

   f. Check the progress and draft materials during their development.

   g. Allow plenty of time for printing materials and preparing displays.

5. Invite the participants to your Road Show.

6. Set up the room well in advance of your Road Show.

7. Do a walk-through/dry run of the Road Show with those presenting.

During the Meeting

1. Greet people when they come in and explain the purpose and flow of the Road Show room.

2. Ensure that all is going as planned.

3. Thank people for attending as they leave.

After the Meeting

1. Hold a debrief session with all involved in preparing for and presenting at your Road Show.

2. Determine how to make improvements to future Road Shows.

3. Gather and document the information received during your Road Show.

4. Analyze the feedback you received in the Road Shows and determine how to use it.

5. Communicate back to participants, thanking them for their participation and providing highlights of your findings and next steps.

7

Ten Techniques to Make Decisions

Roberta's board of directors takes forever to make decisions. "They hem and haw, analyze and reanalyze. They debate and debate, and then they debate some more. Even the simplest decisions can take hours. I know I'm not using their time wisely, but what can I do to help?"

Making decisions is a key activity in participative meetings. Once a problem has been defined and analyzed, and the potential solutions brainstormed, decisions must be made. How can a meeting group or organization improve its quality of decision making and do so with a minimum amount of stress? This chapter provides ten techniques to ensure that organizations make the best decisions, that they understand and agree upon the decisions, and that when organizations make multiple decisions, they prioritize those decisions for the most effective implementation.

Techniques include:

53. Vroom Yetton Decision-Making Model
54. Multivoting
55. Negative Voting
56. Dots
57. One Hundred Votes
58. Nominal Prioritization
59. Three For/Three Against
60. Criteria Matrix
61. Impact and Changeability Analysis
62. Business Case

"I'm all for participation, but sometimes it doesn't seem logical that every decision should be made as a group. It's overkill, and sometimes the payoff is marginal. Is there a technique that will help our organization to effectively determine the most appropriate person or group to make each decision we are confronted with?"

53. Vroom Yetton Decision-Making Model

What Is the Vroom Yetton Decision-Making Model?

The Vroom Yetton Decision-Making Model is a technique for determining how much participation is needed or desired to make a specific decision. Even in this age of participation, not every decision should be made participatively. The most appropriate level of decision making depends on the specific issue and situation.

The Vroom Yetton Decision-Making Model offers a spectrum of decision-making choices that range from authoritarian to consultative to group participative. In most cases, the group leader consciously or subconsciously uses the Vroom Yetton Decision-Making Model to decide individually how to make a given decision. It is wise for the facilitator to agree to the decision-making authority of the group with the meeting owner/group leader in advance of the meeting. This clarity helps the facilitator design the workshop appropriately and avoid any confusion or uncomfortable situations during the meeting itself.

Alternatively, the following instructions illustrate how a meeting group, for example, a project team, can use this model to determine the most appropriate level of participation for any decision facing them.

When to Use the Vroom Yetton Decision-Making Model
- When the appropriate level of participation in making a specific decision is not clear
- When you are not sure if a specific issue is worthy of meeting time

How to Use the Vroom Yetton Decision-Making Model
1. Articulate the decision or decisions to be made.

2. Outline the Vroom Yetton Decision-Making Model to your meeting group. Vroom and Yetton, the creators of this model, identified five distinct procedures for making decisions. Figure 7-1 illustrates the categories of these methods. In this figure, A stands for Authoritarian, C for Consultative, and G for Group:

VROOM YETTON DECISION-MAKING MODEL

A1   Leader makes decision alone without input.

A2   Leader informally requests information from employees, then makes decision alone

C1   Leader formally requests information or opinions from employees in one-on-one meetings, then makes decision alone.

C2   Leader holds a group meeting to discuss the issue, then makes decision alone.

G2   Leader holds a group meeting to discuss the issue and group makes the decision.

Figure 7-1. The Vroom Yetton Decision-Making Model.

3. Lead a group discussion on how to address the decision(s) under consideration based on the choices displayed in figure 7-1.

4. After the discussion, ask the participants to vote for what they each consider to be the best choice within the model for the specific decision(s) to be made. Have them make tick marks on a prepared chart similar to figure 7-2.

HOW SHOULD THIS DECISION BE MADE?

A1 ----- A2 ----- C1 ----- C2 ----- G2

Please come forward and place a tick mark next to the method that you think is most appropriate for making this decision.

Figure 7-2. Vroom Yetton voting chart.

OPTION: Provide each participant with a preprepared voting ballot so that each participant can vote privately.

OPTION: Vote by e-mail.

5. Proceed accordingly. If the entire meeting group is not involved in making the decision(s), agree on a communication plan to keep participants informed.

Summary

The Vroom Yetton Decision-Making Model is a technique for deciding what level of participation is most appropriate when making a given decision.

1. Articulate the decision or decisions to be made.

2. Introduce the Vroom Yetton Decision-Making Model.

3. Lead a group discussion on how the decision should be made.

4. Ask the participants to vote for what they each consider to be the best choice within the model for the given decision to be made.

5. Proceed accordingly.

Source

Vroom, Victor, and Philip Yetton. 1973. *Leadership and Decision Making.* Pittsburgh: University of Pittsburgh Press.

"After we brainstorm, it almost always takes too long to narrow down our options to a few of the most realistic ideas for discussion. What can we do to save time in this situation?"

54. Multivoting

What Is Multivoting?

Multivoting is a technique for narrowing a wide range of ideas or choices down to the few most appropriate, feasible, and important. This technique saves time while still considering every idea that has been generated.

While Multivoting is not a technique for making a single, specific decision, it is a fabulous technique for prioritizing large amounts of information without losing energy or wasting time.

When to Use Multivoting

- When your group has to narrow down a range of alternatives for closer analysis
- When a selection or prioritization step is necessary after brainstorming

How to Use Multivoting

1. Brainstorm your subject or issue, recording all ideas.

   NOTE: See the Old-Fashioned Way, technique 28, for details.

2. Briefly review all brainstormed ideas to make sure that everyone understands them. Combine any duplicate ideas. Clarify each idea as required with a brief explanation.

   NOTE: Do not allow any analysis or criticism of the ideas at this point.

3. When all the ideas are clear, ask your participants to come forward and place checks by all ideas on the brainstorming chart that they feel are worthy of further discussion. Create a designated area on your chart for this exercise.

   NOTE: When you start charting your list of brainstormed ideas, leave plenty of room on the chart both to the left and right of the idea and plenty of room between ideas to make room for voting.

   NOTE: At this point there is no cap on the number of ideas each person can vote for.

4. Tabulate the votes. Any issue that receives at least half of all possible votes remains in contention for the next round of voting. For example, if twenty people in total are voting, any one idea must receive at least ten votes to remain in contention. Circle or otherwise distinguish each of the ideas that passes this test, and count the total number of ideas still remaining on the list.

    NOTE: If your charts are too messy to be comprehensible, have the group take a break while you rewrite the charts with the remaining ideas.

    NOTE: Although the other ideas are shelved at this time, let the group know that you will keep the complete list available for review and consideration again at a later date. This avoids any potential rework if the group needs to analyze more ideas in the future.

5. Ask your participants to vote again but this time for only the top half of the remaining ideas. In other words, if there are twenty-four remaining ideas, each person gets twelve votes.

    NOTE: Vote using the same method as before, with participants coming forward and placing a check beside their favorite ideas.

6. After the second round of voting is completed, continue voting as outlined in steps 4 and 5 until the group members arrive at what they consider to be an appropriate number of ideas for further analysis.

    NOTE: An appropriate amount is typically between three to five remaining ideas. It is possible that the group could arrive at this number after step 3 or after one round of steps 4 and 5.

    NOTE: Multivoting is not a technique for choosing one option. To do so would create a false sense of consensus. Don't narrow your choices down below three before beginning more in-depth analysis.

7. Discuss and analyze the remaining ideas at length.

    OPTION: Analyze each idea together as a group, either in small or large group discussions.

OPTION: Allow participants to place their remaining votes all on one option, between a few of their favorite options, or each on completely different options.

OPTION: Create task force groups to research each idea. Then establish a time and date for the whole group to discuss the ideas again.

8. Proceed with appropriate next steps.

Summary

Multivoting is a technique for narrowing down many brainstormed ideas to a smaller number for further analysis and discussion.

1. Brainstorm your issue, recording all ideas.

2. Briefly review each brainstormed idea.

3. Ask your participants to vote for all the issues they believe are worthy of further discussion.

4. After the vote, identify each of the ideas that has received at least half of the total number of possible votes.

5. Have your participants vote again but this time for only half of the ideas remaining.

6. Continue voting as in steps 4 and 5 until the group arrives at an appropriate number of ideas for further discussion.

7. Discuss and analyze the remaining ideas at length.

8. Proceed with appropriate next steps.

"A majority of our group generally agrees which solutions are best without too many problems. But sometimes I'm not so sure we are in complete harmony. Is there a simple technique that will help ensure that we have full consensus?"

55. Negative Voting

What Is Negative Voting?

Negative Voting is a technique that identifies which people do *not* support a proposed decision, instead of those who do.

By identifying those who don't support a given decision, the meeting group can talk to those people, discover their specific concerns, and identify methods to alleviate these concerns. By doing so, it is possible to gain consensus among the group before moving forward. This is an excellent way to proactively solve problems before they occur.

When to Use Negative Voting

- When you want to make a decision by consensus
- When you need to decide between a few difficult choices
- When you want to enhance the acceptability of your decisions
- When group members might be pressured to agree with the majority

How to Use Negative Voting

1. After adequate discussion and analysis concerning a specific decision or option under consideration, ask your meeting group, "Who *cannot* live with this option?" Count and chart the number of people who raise their hands. Ask the same question for all options being considered by the group.

2. After this process, identify which options have accumulated the least number of negative votes. Obtain permission from the group to eliminate the options with the highest number of negative votes.

3. Taking one option at a time, ask each dissenting voter what concerns he or she has about the remaining options. Chart their concerns. Leave ample chart space between each listed concern because it will be utilized in the next step.

4. When finished, ask the entire group to brainstorm ideas that will alleviate the listed concerns. For example: "Who can think of a way to alleviate this problem for Har-

old?" or "What ideas do you have to alleviate this list of concerns about option one?" Document all ideas in the spaces you provide between each listed concern on your chart.

NOTE: Use a different color pen to distinguish between the concerns and the brainstormed ideas.

NOTE: If you haven't left sufficient room to write on your existing chart, create a new chart for the ideas brainstormed. Be sure to clearly label which ideas go with which concerns.

NOTE: If necessary, remind the group of the rules for brainstorming. See the Old-Fashioned Way, technique 28, figure 5-1, for details.

5. After you are finished brainstorming, ask each dissenter if the group's suggested changes now allow him or her to support the option. For example: "What do you think, Harold? How do these ideas work for you? . . . Do they provide enough information or changes so that you can support this option?"

NOTE: If you are voting on more than one option, ask these questions for all of the options.

6. Do a second negative vote. "Who cannot support option one when it includes these changes?"

NOTE: If appropriate, paraphrase the changes that were suggested.

NOTE: It is unlikely that all options will still receive negative votes, but if this does happen, discuss with the group how to handle the situation. You may want to repeat steps 3, 4, and 5, or you may decide to brainstorm new, more creative ideas.

7. If your group is aiming for a single decision and arrives at more than one option that everyone now supports, follow up with a positive vote. You might introduce this by asking, for example, "Which of these two choices do you think is best?"

Summary

Negative Voting is a technique for discovering who does not support a decision instead of who does. This allows the group to proactively address and resolve any concerns so it can reach true consensus.

1. Ask if there is anyone in the group who *cannot* support the options as stated.

2. Identify the options that have the fewest number of negative votes. Determine if some of these options should be eliminated at this point.

3. Taking one option at a time, ask each dissenter what his or her concerns are regarding the remaining options.

4. Ask your group to brainstorm ideas that will alleviate the concerns.

5. Ask the dissenters if the group's suggested changes allow them to now support the option.

6. Do a second negative vote including the changes for each specific option under consideration.

7. If more than one option remains that everyone supports, follow up with a positive vote to ascertain which one of the choices is the best.

"There are times when we need a quick read on our initial reactions to potential decisions. Is there a technique I can use to accomplish this?"

56. Dots

What Are Dots?

The Dots technique helps you visually ascertain a meeting group's immediate reactions to proposed solutions or goals.

Dots can be especially effective when you want to accurately capture the personal sentiments of everyone within your meeting group. Like Negative Voting, technique 55, it allows for dissenting voices to be heard, while also allowing the group to understand who is feeling neutral on any option and who needs further information to form a decision.

Dots can be used as a normal voting tool as well. However, in this technique Dots are not used as a final decision-making tool, but rather as a tool for understanding the initial reactions of the group before final decisions are made.

When to Use Dots

- When you want to ensure that everyone has his or her opinion considered
- When you want to gain feedback on the group's opinions in a short amount of time
- When you have completed a goal-setting or action-planning discussion

How to Use Dots

Before the Meeting

1. You will need to purchase enough colored Dots for the exercise. These can typically be purchased at minimal cost at most office supply stores.

   NOTE: Be sure to buy Dots that are large enough to be seen from across a large room.

   OPTION: If Dots aren't available, purchase stars instead. If the colors you want are not available it is perfectly acceptable to use other colors.

2. Prepare the charts you plan to use.

During the Meeting

1. After brainstormed ideas have been discussed and clarified, ask the group to come forward and Dot vote for every idea under consideration. You might say in explanation, for example, "Using these color-coded dots will give us an indication of which ideas are agreed upon, which have no support, and which need further discussion." Use a chart or overhead, as illustrated in figure 7-3, to support your instructions.

DOT VOTE

- Vote for all ideas.
- One dot per idea.
- Vote with the dot that best communicates your opinion.

Green Dot = Yes, I support this.

Red Dot   = No, I do not support this.

Yellow Dot = I am neutral on this.

Black Dot   = I need more information before I can form an opinion.

10 minutes

Figure 7-3. Instruction chart for Dots.

OPTION: Depending on the situation, you might only want to use red and green dots.

2. After the dot vote, ask the group for feedback using Open-Ended Questions, technique 34. You might say, for example, "What are your reactions to what you see?" "What stands out for you?" "What conclusions can we draw from our dot vote?" "What are the logical next steps?"

3. Summarize all the information from the Dots exercise and move on accordingly.

Summary

Dots help you quickly learn the level of group support for a series of ideas or issues that are being considered for decision.

Before the Meeting

Purchase enough colored Dots for your meeting group. Prepare the charts you plan to use.

During the Meeting

1. After all brainstormed issues have been discussed and clarified, ask your meeting group to come forward and Dot vote.

2. After the vote, ask the group for feedback on the results.

3. Summarize the information and move forward.

"The groups I facilitate often need to prioritize their ideas. It would be helpful to understand where the group's true energy and priorities are so that our decisions are more likely to be implemented. Is there a technique I can use to accomplish this?"

57. One Hundred Votes

What Are One Hundred Votes?

There are times when all meeting groups need to establish priorities. The One Hundred Votes technique helps determine a group's preferences among a number of different ideas or potential choices.

One Hundred Votes involves each participant distributing a total of One Hundred Votes among the available choices presented. The resulting information can then be used to make decisions about what projects to take on, which ideas to pursue, what direction to go, or which actions to take. This is a very effective decision-making technique, as it reveals what a group will most likely implement.

When to Use One Hundred Votes

- When you want to create a short list of priorities
- When you need to know where the group's energy is regarding a number of ideas

How to Use One Hundred Votes

1. After a number of potential options, goals, or actions have been identified, charted, and clarified, give all participants one hundred votes each that they can allocate to this list according to their priorities. To explain the technique, you might say, for example, "Now we're going to prioritize the ideas we have generated using a technique called One Hundred Votes. You each have One Hundred Votes to allocate among what you believe to be the best ideas. In this case, the best ideas are the ones that you would give priority. You will want to designate the majority of your votes to those. There will also be some ideas that you think don't deserve any effort or consideration. Don't give any votes to those. And there may be some ideas that you think have less merit but deserve some attention. Place the rest of your votes with those. But remember that you only have One Hundred Votes. The point of the exercise is to use your votes in a way that accurately weights your individual priorities regarding the ideas we are considering."

NOTE: All the potential choices need to be posted on chart paper around the room so that everyone will be able to easily cast his or her votes. The participants should write their number of votes directly on the charts in a predesignated area.

2. Tally the votes, and display a summary for each choice with the number of people voting and number of votes cast for each issue. For example, "5/58" means five members cast a total of fifty-eight votes. Ask for a few volunteers to help with the addition to maintain a fast pace.

3. Ask your participants to take a few minutes to visually review the data they have just generated.

4. Ask the group for reactions. You might ask, for example, "What are your reactions to what you see?" "What surprises you?" "What questions or concerns do you have?"

5. Decide as a group which issues to focus on and which to put aside.

6. Create an action plan as appropriate.

Summary

The One Hundred Votes technique identifies and focuses on a group's preferences and priorities.

1. Give each participant one hundred votes that he or she can allocate to this list according to his or her priorities.

2. Tally the votes and display a summary indicating the total number of people voting for each issue along with the total number of votes for each issue.

3. Ask your participants to visually review the data.

4. Ask the group for reactions.

5. Decide as a group which issues to focus on and which issues to put aside.

6. Create an action plan as appropriate.

"Our group is usually able to generate a list of goals and actions very easily. But after our meetings, we find that we have too much extra work. As a result, nothing gets done. Is there a technique that will help us prioritize our ideas so that we spend our time on only the most important issues?"

58. Nominal Prioritization

What Is Nominal Prioritization?

Nominal Prioritization is a technique for measuring and thereby identifying the priority of issues, decisions, or action plans.

The demands placed on organizations are such that not all issues can be dealt with equally. Some issues are simply more important to a group or organization than others and need to be given top priority.

Nominal Prioritization quickly and accurately reveals the priorities of a meeting group.

When to Use Nominal Prioritization
- When the group cannot accomplish everything and must set priorities
- After a list of goals or objectives has been created and priorities must be established

How to Use Nominal Prioritization
1. After brainstorming a complete list of issues, ideas, goals, or actions, ask your meeting group for help in prioritizing these choices.

   NOTE: All choices must be visually displayed to the group on chart paper. Be sure to create enough voting space for each choice.

   Ask each person to rank each item under consideration using the following ratings:
   1 = most importance and greatest impact
   2 = medium importance and impact
   3 = least importance and impact

   All choices can theoretically be given the same rating. Participants should not consider this a forced ranking decision. Use figure 7-4 as a visual aid for your instructions.

PRIORITIZE OUR CHOICES

- Vote for each item under consideration.
- All items could theoretically receive the same score. (This is not a forced-choice decision.)

  1 = most importance/impact

  2 = medium importance/impact

  3 = least importance/impact

- Mark your rating in the box near each listed choice.

10 minutes

Figure 7-4. Nominal Prioritization rating instructions.

NOTE: You could also ask participants to give their rankings by private ballot or by electronic voting.

NOTE: Remember that you should also vote unless you are an outside, neutral facilitator.

2. After everyone is finished with his or her ratings, determine the average of each choice by adding up the scores for that choice and dividing by the number of persons voting. Ask the group to help you with this by delegating some of the options to a few participants. Ask them to round to the nearest tenth. For example, 1.67 becomes 1.7, and 2.23 becomes 2.2.

NOTE: Be sure that each group writes the average or mean for each choice large enough to be seen by everyone in the group.

NOTE: If members of your group don't have phones with calculators on them, bring a few handheld calculators to distribute for use.

3. Ask the group for their reactions to the prioritized rankings.

4. Ask the group to agree on how to prioritize the issues based on the results of the rating process. You might ask, for example, "What decisions seem logical based on the results of this exercise?" "What level of priority should we seek to achieve? Only

issues with group priority ratings of 1.0, 1.5, and so on?" "Which options should we choose?"

NOTE: Most groups will drop the items with the lowest ratings or put them aside for discussion at a later date. Allow time for lobbying if necessary, and decide as a group how to handle any issues of disagreement.

5. Create action plans for all issues selected by the group as priorities.

Summary

Nominal Prioritization is a technique for prioritizing the choices that are facing a meeting group.

1. After brainstorming a complete list of choices, ask the group to prioritize the choices based on the ratings illustrated in figure 7-4.

2. After the voting, determine the average score for each choice.

3. Ask the group for reactions to the results of the exercise.

4. Prioritize the issues based on the ratings.

5. Create action plans for all items chosen as priorities.

"Because all sides of an issue don't get equal discussion time, the most vocal and opinionated people in my group always seem to get their way. Is there a technique that can help me alleviate this problem?"

59. Three For/Three Against

What Is Three For/Three Against?

Three For/Three Against is a technique for assuring that all sides of an issue are heard.

By design, Three For/Three Against asks for both the pros and the cons for every option or issue being discussed. This ensures that any decisions to be made are based on all of the information available, not just the opinions of the most vocal contingents.

When to Use Three For/Three Against

- When you want to be sure that all sides of an issue get equal discussion time
- When you are planning to present an idea for approval

How to Use Three For/Three Against

1. Introduce the Three For/Three Against technique, and describe how it will be used in your meeting. You might say, for example, "It is important that we hear all sides of all available options before we decide the right option for us. In the past, we have not done a very good job of this. Today let's try a new technique that will ensure that both sides of the issue are discussed. It's called Three For/Three Against. When we discuss an issue, please note that for every three comments we hear in support of an option, we will also generate three against that option. These Three For and Three Against can be offered by one person or by any of you within the group. Three is an arbitrary number. The point is to systematically hear both sides of the issue."

   NOTE: Your group may feel that always sticking to the number three is limiting and inappropriate. Be flexible. Remember that in the final analysis, the primary goal of this process is to elicit comments on both sides of an issue.

2. When an issue is being discussed, ask your group to provide three reasons why the issue should be supported and then three reasons why it should not be supported. Chart the responses. If you are discussing many options, use the technique for each option.

3. After the discussion, ask your participants to decide upon the best option for the group.

Summary

Three For/Three Against is a technique for hearing all sides of an argument before making a decision.

1. Introduce the Three For/Three Against technique, and describe how it will be used in your meeting.

2. Introduce the issue to be considered, and ask your group to provide three reasons why a specific issue should be supported and three reasons why it shouldn't be supported. Chart the responses.

3. After the discussion, ask your participants to decide upon the best option for the group.

"I want to make sure that the groups I facilitate are making sound decisions based on agreed-upon criteria, not just on the whims and fancies of the moment. What do you suggest?"

60. Criteria Matrix

What Is Criteria Matrix?

Criteria Matrix is a technique designed to prioritize a group of potential alternatives under consideration. This is accomplished by identifying and weighing agreed-upon criteria against each of those alternatives. Establishing criteria forces a group to articulate and examine their values, rationales, and assumptions before making a decision.

Criteria are standards from which one makes judgments or decisions, and their identification becomes the basis for evaluation. For example, if your work group wants to buy a specific piece of equipment, and you have a maximum of $20,000 to spend, this amount becomes a criterion. Any equipment over that amount does not meet your price criterion, and therefore you would not likely choose it. Once you identify and agree upon all the criteria for the equipment you want to purchase (costs, specifications, quality, warranties, maintenance schedules, etc.), your group can investigate the alternatives more objectively.

It is much easier to reach consensus when making a decision if the criteria are identified and agreed upon beforehand. People are much more willing to give up their favorite choices when they see that these favorites don't meet the necessary criteria. If there is no agreement on the criteria up front, it is less likely that there will be agreement on the best alternative when it comes time to make the decision.

It is important to recognize that not all criteria are of equal importance, and they should therefore have different weightings during the decision-making process.

When to Use Criteria Matrix
- When a decision has many components or criteria which must be factored
- When a potential decision is going around in circles without being resolved
- When several opinions and perspectives must be considered
- When it is difficult to choose between many choices or alternatives to make a decision

How to Use a Criteria Matrix

Before the Meeting

Prepare a chart or overhead for the Criteria Matrix you plan to use in your meeting. Refer to figures 7-5, 7-6, and 7-7 for templates.

During the Meeting

1. Brainstorm and agree on all criteria that must be satisfied to make the best decision for the problem or situation under consideration. Include criteria from all stakeholders in addition to any emotionally based and political criteria.

   NOTE: Stakeholders are defined as anybody who has a stake in the end result or anyone who will be impacted by the decision to be made.

   NOTE: If necessary, help the group understand the criteria by asking them some open-ended questions. You might ask, for example, "What are the qualities or attributes of a good solution?" "What distinguishes between a good and a bad alternative in your mind?" "What standards does an alternative have to meet in order to be acceptable?"

2. Brainstorm all options to a specific problem or situation. Create a short list of serious contenders.

   NOTE: You could use Multivoting, technique 54, to arrive at a short list of options.

   NOTE: It is preferable to determine the criteria before creating the short list of options. This will diminish the chance of forcing criteria to fit a favored option.

3. Introduce the Criteria Matrix you have selected to use for this meeting. Variation 1 functions best when all criteria have basically the same weight, and the decision is not terribly complex. Use Variation 2 when clear veto criteria exist. Variation 3 is your best choice when no veto criteria exist, the decision is quite complex, and criteria differ widely in importance.

   NOTE: You might want input from some participants in advance of the meeting on which Criteria Matrix to use.

4. Rate your short list of choices against your criteria using one of the three following variations:

Variation 1

Criteria	Choice One	Choice Two	Choice Three
TOTAL NO. OF Ys			

Figure 7-5. Criteria Matrix for Variation 1.

a. List your criteria down the left side of the chart.

b. List your potential choices along the top.

c. Analyze each choice against each criterion. If the criterion is met, mark a Y for yes in the box. If the criterion is not met, mark the box with an N for no.

d. Count the number of Ys for each choice. Write that number in the space provided at the bottom of the chart.

Variation 2

List of Criteria	Criteria Weight	Option One		Option Two		Option Three	
"Must Have" Criteria							
	VETO						
	VETO						
	VETO						
"Important to Have" Criteria		Rate 1–10	Multiply x 2	Rate 1–10	Multiply x 2	Rate 1–10	Multiply x 2
	x 2	/		/		/	
	x 2	/		/		/	
	x 2	/		/		/	
	x 2	/		/		/	
"Would Like to Have" Criteria		Rate 1–10	Multiply x 1	Rate 1–10	Multiply x 1	Rate 1–10	Multiply x 1
	x 1	/		/		/	
	x 1	/		/		/	
	x 1	/		/		/	
TOTALS	—						

Figure 7-6. Criteria Matrix for Variation 2.

Variation 2: Continued

a. Create three categories for your criteria, as illustrated in figure 7-6, and list your criteria based on these categories down the left side of the chart.

   (1) The must-have section: if these criteria are not met, the choice is immediately dropped, as noted by the *veto* in the weight section along the top of the chart.

   (2) The important-to-have section: failure to meet these criteria is important but not important enough to assure a veto of the choice. You will note that each of these criteria is weighted times two, double the weight of the next category.

   (3) The want-to-have section: these criteria are important enough for mention but not as important as the other two categories, as noted by the times-one weighting.

b. List your brainstormed choices along the top of the chart.

c. Compare each potential choice against all the selected criteria.

   (1) If a choice doesn't meet a veto criteria, it is dropped from further consideration.

   (2) In the times-two weighting section, apply a numerical rating from one to ten to show how well the group believes that the option meets the specific criteria. One would indicate that the option poorly meets that criterion. Five would indicate that it satisfactorily meets the criterion. Ten would mean that the criteria were exceeded. Write those numbers on the left side of the column.

   (3) In the times-one weighting section, apply the same numerical rating from one to ten to show how well the group believes that the option meets the criteria. Write those numbers on the left side of the column.

d. Multiply all choices that weren't vetoed by their weighting factor. Place the resulting number on the right side of the appropriate box.

e. Add all the resulting factored numbers from each choice at the bottom of each column to arrive at a final rating.

Variation 3

Criteria List All Criteria Below	Weigh the Importance of Each Criterion 1–10 1=low 10=high	Option One		Option Two		Option Three	
		Rate 1–10	Multiply x weight	Rate 1–10	Multiply x weight	Rate 1–10	Multiply x weight
		/		/		/	
		/		/		/	
		/		/		/	
		/		/		/	
		/		/		/	
		/		/		/	
		/		/		/	
TOTALS	—						

Figure 7-7. Criteria Matrix for Variation 3.

a. List your criteria down the left side of the chart as illustrated in figure 7-7.

b. Have the group rate the importance of each of these criteria on a scale of one (low—not important) to ten (high—very important).

NOTE: More than one criterion could receive the same rating.

c. List your brainstormed choices along the top of the chart.

d. Weigh each choice against each criterion on a scale of one (low in meeting this criterion) to ten (high in meeting this criterion). Write this number in the left side of the column for each choice.

NOTE: When there is controversy about a rating, take time to understand the points of all participants. Sometimes your group will need to further clarify the meaning of a specific criterion or the components of a specific choice. Once all opinions are understood, look for a number that all your participants can support. This is usually the mean number.

e. Multiply the weight of each criterion by the weight given to each choice, and write the resulting number in the right side of the appropriate column.

f. Add the resulting numbers together, and write the total at the appropriate location at the bottom of the chart.

NOTE: For all choices, please modify the Criteria Matrix grids based on the number of criteria and choices your group will analyze.

5. Using the completed Criteria Matrix, analyze the results as a group. Use this as data for helping the group make the final decision.

NOTE: The Criteria Matrix provides information to help guide your group to make the best decision. It is possible, although not probable, that groups will make a decision that is not the option supported by the Criteria Matrix.

NOTE: If none of your options ranked well against the criteria, your group may need to consider starting over again.

Summary

Criteria Matrix is a technique designed to prioritize a group of potential alternatives under consideration.

Before the Meeting

Prepare a chart or overhead for the Criteria Matrix you plan to use in your meeting.

During the Meeting

1. Brainstorm and agree upon all criteria to be considered.

2. Brainstorm all options to a specific problem or situation, creating a short list of serious contenders.

3. Introduce the Criteria Matrix you have selected.

4. Rate your short list of choices against your criteria using one of the following three options.

Variation 1

a. List your criteria down the left side. Refer to figure 7-5.

b. List your brainstormed choices along the top.

c. Analyze each criterion against each choice. If the criterion is met, mark a Y for yes in the box. If the criterion is not met, mark the box with an N for no.

d. Count the number of Ys for each choice. Write that number in the space provided at the bottom of the chart.

Variation 2

a. Create three categories for your criteria, as illustrated in figure 7-6, and list your criteria based on these categories down the left side of the chart.

(1) Must-have/veto criteria

(2) Important-to-have criteria

(3) Want-to-have criteria

b. List your brainstormed choices along the top of the chart.

c. Compare your choices against all the selected criteria.

(1) If a choice does not meet any of the veto criteria, drop it from further consideration.

(2) In the important-to-have section, apply a numerical rating from one to ten to show how the group feels each option meets the specific criteria.

(3) In the want-to-have section, apply the same numerical rating from one to ten to each option.

d. Multiply all choices that were not vetoed by their weighting factor.

e. Add together the resulting multiples from each choice at the bottom of each column to arrive at a final rating.

Variation 3

a. List your criteria down the left side of the chart as illustrated in figure 7-7.

b. Have your group rate these criteria by their importance on a scale of one to ten.

c. List your brainstormed choices along the top of the chart.

d. Weigh each choice against each criterion from one to ten, writing this number in the left side of the column.

e. Multiply the weight of each criterion by the rating given to each choice, writing the number in the right side of the appropriate column.

f. Add the resulting numbers together, and write the total at the bottom of the chart.

5. Using the completed Criteria Matrix, analyze the results as a group. Use this data for helping the group make the final decision.

Variation 2 Source

Daniels, William. 1986. *Group Power.* San Diego: Pfeiffer.

"Sometimes our group makes decisions to pursue things that we later find don't make a lot of difference, or could make a difference but are out of our control. How can we avoid these problems?"

61. Impact and Changeability Analysis

What Is Impact and Changeability Analysis?

Impact and Changeability Analysis is a decision-making technique that helps a meeting group isolate and focus on the options that will have the most impact on its organizational goals. In addition, this technique identifies the options that are within the group's authority to change. This technique results in increased efficiency of effort and improved implementation.

When to Use Impact and Changeability Analysis

- When your group must choose between options
- When not all options under consideration will have a high impact on organizational goals
- When not all options under consideration are within the control of the group

How to Use Impact and Changeability Analysis

1. After your group has brainstormed a list of options, goals, or solutions to a problem, introduce Impact and Changeability Analysis, and describe its purpose. You might say, for example, "In order to make sure that any actions we take will have a significant impact and also that they are within our control to change, let's use a technique called Impact and Changeability Analysis to help us focus our efforts."

2. Ask the group to numerically rate each of the proposed options on a scale of one to ten, and on the two following variables:

   a. High or low impact on the business. You might ask, for example, "If this option is successfully implemented, will the impact on the business be high or low? Which number between one and ten seems most appropriate?"

   b. High or low level of changeability. "Does our group have a high or low level of authority in fixing this problem? If it is well within our control, we would rate it high; if it is not, we would rate it low. If the effort to implement is difficult, rate it low. If it would be easy to implement, rate it high. What number between one and ten seems most appropriate here?"

Assign each option a specific letter (A, B, C, etc.) for identification so that it can be easily recognized when plotted on a preprepared chart or overhead similar to the one illustrated in figure 7-8.

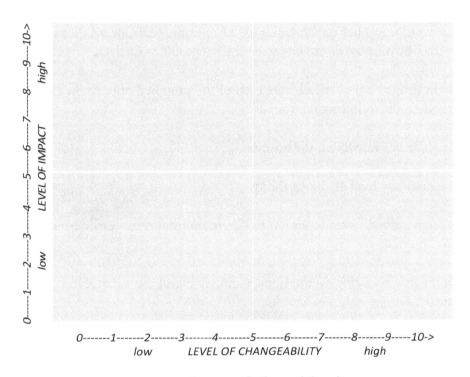

Figure 7-8. Impact and Changeability chart.

3. Once the group has identified the numerical rating for each of the two variables, plot the group's rating on the Impact and Changeability chart. Do this for each option.

4. After all the options have been plotted on your chart, analyze the results as a group. You might ask, for example, "What conclusions can we draw from what you see? What seem like the logical options on which to focus our energy?"

5. Decide as a group where to focus your energy and efforts. Create action plans to support implementation.

NOTE: See the techniques described in chapter 8, "Fifteen Techniques for Implementing Decisions," for support.

Summary

Impact and Changeability Analysis is a decision-making technique that helps a meeting group isolate and focus on the options that will have the most impact on its organizational goals. In addition, this technique identifies the options that are within its authority to change.

1. After your group has established a list of options, goals, or solutions to a problem, describe the purpose of the Impact and Changeability Analysis.

2. Ask the group to numerically rate each of the proposed options on a scale of one to ten and on the following two variables:

   a. High or low impact on the business.

   b. High or low level of changeability.

      Assign each option a letter (A, B, C, etc.) so that it can easily be identified when it is plotted.

3. Plot the group's rating on the Impact and Changeability chart. Do this for each option.

4. After all the options have been plotted on your chart, analyze the results as a group.

5. Decide as a group where to focus your energy and efforts. Create action plans to support implementation.

"I've been having trouble getting approval for important changes to the way we do business. I can't seem to get the leadership team on the same page. What can I do?"

62. Business Case

What Is Business Case?

A Business Case describes the goals, costs, and benefits of making a change with the purpose of influencing decision makers to approve the change. Although Business Cases are usually expressed in financial terms and written with the chief financial officer (CFO) in mind, a strong business case is one that addresses not only the financial rationale for a change, but also the nonfinancial and unquantifiable components of the change. The ability to tell a compelling story about the rationale for the change can be used both to gain approval for the change and also to motivate people to implement the change.

A strong Business Case will include the goal/purpose, the benefits, costs, time frame for payback, measures and targets, and risks and plans to mitigate them.

A business reason for any change is always required. But the level of proof required to make a decision will differ depending on the amount of money and time and the degree of risk involved. Regardless of the size or scope of the change, the Sponsor or owner of the proposed change should always be able to articulate the rationale to all key stakeholders in a manner that establishes enough dissonance between the "as is" state and the "to be" state to motivate support and action.

When to Use Business Case

- When the desired decision is considered large, expensive, or difficult to implement
- When a level of persuasion is required to gain leadership approval
- When the benefits of a decision are not clear to all involved in making the decision

How to Use Business Case

Preparing the Business Case

1. Determine the Owner/Sponsor of the proposed decision and its business case. If you are not that person, work closely with the Owner/Sponsor on every step. Determine who else to include in the development of the Business Case, and hold a meeting to design it together.

2. Determine the key stakeholders—that is, who will be involved in making the decision and implementing it. Think in advance about how to address their concerns and motivations. The CFO will have different issues than the human resource (HR) director, sales director, or head of customer service. Gain insight into the drivers of executive decisions, and align your business case accordingly.

3. Be clear on the vision or goal of the decision. Be able to describe the future state once the change is made in a compelling way to all stakeholders. Also be able to describe the do-nothing, status quo scenario and the risks of doing nothing.

4. Define the financial and nonfinancial benefits, both quantifiable and unquantifiable. Use figure 7-9 as an example.

THE BUSINESS CASE: ILLUSTRATIVE EXAMPLE

	Financial	Nonfinancial
Quantified	**Financial impact is clearly identified and measurable:** • Increased sales • Increased availability • Reduced handling costs	**Nonfinancial but measurable impact:** • Customer satisfaction • Service quality • More stable field force • Employee morale
Unquantified	**Financial impact that cannot be estimated accurately:** • Customer retention • Store alignment with strategy • Effective work processes	**Nonfinancial benefits difficult to measure:** • Improved communication • Increased teamwork • Enhanced reputation with suppliers and customers

Figure 7-9. Business Case example.

5. Outline the costs to get the benefits.

6. Describe the time frame for payback and overall financial impact. Provide measures of success, along with targets and time frames for achieving them.

7. Describe risk areas, possible impacts, and how to manage these risks.

8. Consider overlapping initiatives and how to handle them.

Gaining Agreement on Your Business Case

1. Be sure to validate your Business Case before presenting it. Test your case by arguing the other side.

2. Pre-present your Business Case to key stakeholders, and gain feedback and alignment. Tell a compelling story. Gain personal credibility with key decision makers. Make it real.

3. Never assume support. Get sign-off in writing from key decision makers.

Implementing Your Business Case

1. Refer back to your Business Case before, during, and after implementation to ensure that it is met as per your original promise.

2. If there are positive or negative changes, communicate them proactively to key stakeholders and decision makers.

3. Course correct as necessary.

Summary

Business Case describes the goals, costs, and benefits of making a change with the purpose of influencing decision makers to approve the change.

Preparing the Business Case

1. Determine the owner/Sponsor of the proposed decision and its Business Case. Determine who else to include in the development of the Business Case, and hold a meeting to design it together.

2. Determine the key stakeholders—that is, who will be involved in making the decision and implementing it.

3. Be clear on the vision or goal of the decision.

4. Define the financial and nonfinancial benefits, both quantifiable and unquantifiable.

5. Outline the costs to get the benefits.

6. Describe the time frame for payback and overall financial impact.

7. Describe risk areas, possible impacts, and how to manage these risks.

8. Consider overlapping initiatives and how to handle them.

Gaining Agreement for Your Business Case

1. Be sure to validate your Business Case before presenting it.

2. Present your Business Case to key stakeholders in advance, and gain feedback and alignment.

3. Gain sign off in writing from key decision makers.

Implementing Your Business Case

1. Refer back to your Business Case before, during, and after implementation.

2. If there are positive or negative changes, communicate them proactively.

3. Course correct as necessary.

8

Fifteen Techniques for Implementing Decisions

Malcolm manages the marketing department of a freight shipping company. "Ideas and decisions come easy for us. But nothing ever seems to happen after we make our decisions. Our intentions are good, but it seems like all our time goes to dealing with the crisis of the hour. Our customers are getting frustrated, and some major accounts are talking about leaving. We need to move fast."

Meetings are more powerful and effective with an implementation, next steps, or action component. But while many groups agree on where they want to go and what they need to do, few plan how to get there. This often results in conflict, confusion, and diminished effectiveness. Gaining agreement on how these group decisions will be carried out strongly increases the likelihood of success.

The fifteen techniques described in this chapter demonstrate how to efficiently move a meeting group toward action. These techniques ensure agreement on actions, clarify roles and responsibilities, and formulate plans for review and follow-up.

Techniques include:

63. Chart Actions
64. SMART Goals
65. Test for Support
66. Individual Action Planning
67. Force Field Analysis
68. Goal Plan Go
69. Transformation Maps
70. Project Charters
71. Project Teams
72. Project Plans
73. Executive Steering Group (ESG)
74. Progress Reviews
75. Roles and Responsibility Charting: RACI
76. Stakeholder Identification and Planning
77. Sustainability Analysis

"We often agree to do things in our meetings but forget exactly what the agreements were by the time the next meeting begins. We get in arguments about when things are supposed to be finished and who is supposed to do them. Is there a technique that can help us avoid these problems?"

63. Chart Actions

What Are Chart Actions?

The Chart Actions technique enables you to document agreed-upon actions as they are discussed in a meeting. This technique articulates "who will do what by when" and is an excellent way to move from vague action statements to specific action plans.

The Chart Actions technique clarifies exactly what actions are agreed upon and when these actions will be accomplished. The process also publicly identifies the person(s) who are accountable for each action, thus providing incentive that the actions will be fulfilled. These elements, when coupled with effective follow-through and monitoring, will contribute to the success of any action plan.

When to Use Chart Actions

- Whenever your group is discussing issues that require action

How to Use Chart Actions

1. When your meeting group will be discussing issues that require action, create a chart labeled Actions or Next Steps at the beginning of your meeting. Include three columns, headed by What, Who, and By When, as shown in figure 8-1 (next page). Place the chart at a convenient spot near the front of the room.

2. As ideas for action come up during the meeting, write them down in the What category. At that time, add both the Who and By When if they are clear. If the Who and By When are not clear, wait until the end of the meeting for clarification to avoid disrupting the flow of the meeting.

3. As one of the last agenda items at the end of the meeting, go back to your chart. Lead a discussion to affirm "who will do what by when" for each action item displayed.

   NOTE: Sometimes draft actions will be ideas that the group will not want to follow through on, and sometimes actions will be tabled until a later meeting. It will be appropriate, however, to document a next step for most actions.

ACTIONS		
WHAT	WHO	WHEN

Figure 8-1. Chart Actions chart.

NOTE: Don't get bogged down. If an action is controversial, and you don't have time to discuss it during your meeting, make an agenda item to discuss this action at a later date, such as at the next scheduled meeting.

4. Follow up as appropriate and necessary for each action item. Ensure actions are distributed to participants after the meeting. This can be as a subset of the minutes of the meeting or as a stand-alone document.

NOTE: It is beneficial to return to this action list at the beginning of each subsequent meeting until all actions are complete. Public follow-up greatly motivates people to accomplish what they promised to do.

Summary

The Chart Actions technique enables you to document actions or next steps as they are discussed and approved in your meeting. More specifically, the process identifies "who will do what by when."

1. Create a chart labeled Actions or Next Steps at the beginning of your meeting. Include three columns, headed by What, Who, and By When.

2. As ideas for action come up during the meeting, write them down in the What category. Add the Who and By When if they are clear at this time.

3. As one of the last agenda items at the end of the meeting, go back to your Chart Actions chart to affirm who will do what by when.

4. Follow up as necessary with each action item.

"I think the goals we set are clear and agreed upon during our meetings, but even hours later there seems to be little consensus about exactly what we agreed to. How can we avoid this problem?"

64. SMART Goals

What Are SMART Goals?

The SMART Goals technique helps you obtain clear agreement from your meeting group about exactly what any particular goal means. This technique is also excellent for improving the likelihood that a specific goal will be implemented to the satisfaction of everyone who is involved.

The SMART in SMART Goals is an acronym for **S**pecific, **M**easurable, **A**greed Upon, **R**ealistic, and **T**ime-bound. The SMART Goals technique requires the inclusion of these five elements in the communication of every goal so that there will be understanding, agreement, and action at every level of the organization.

Oftentimes, broad organizational goals are set on a corporate level and then need to be translated into more detailed, operational goals as they cascade throughout the organization. These goals communicate what the priorities of an organization, group, or individual should be. SMART Goals make this process more manageable and trackable. The following simple example shows how SMART Goals work and might cascade through an organization. The original corporate goal could be simple: "Increase profits." The SMART Goal for the organization as a whole might then be written as: "Increase our current profit margin of 5 percent to 15 percent by December 31, 2016." As a result of this corporate goal, a SMART Goal for a support service department of the organization might then be defined as: "Decrease departmental operating costs by 10 percent by December 31, 2016." Perhaps after the support service department has done some investigation on how to reach their goal, a specific area within that department might have a subsequent SMART Goal: "Decrease the cost of producing and distributing marketing materials by 25 percent by October 1, 2016." And an individual within the department that produces and distributes marketing materials may have an individual SMART Goal: "Create and lead a work team to identify methods to decrease the costs of producing and distributing marketing materials by 25 percent by October 1, 2016."

But to get the most from your SMART Goals, you must proactively monitor the progress and results of each specific action plan designed to meet your originally defined goal.

There are serious consequences if this monitoring step doesn't occur. First, without effective follow-up, the specific actions may simply be forgotten. Second, a lack of sincere follow-up indicates a lack of seriousness about goal achievement. This speaks volumes to the people who work in the organization. It is unlikely that employees will follow through when actions are not tracked or rewarded.

When to Use SMART Goals
- When you want to be sure that your goals are clear and easily tracked
- When goals must cascade down throughout an organization
- When you need to measure and evaluate the performance of a group or individual

How to Use SMART Goals
1. After your group has brainstormed and agreed upon goals, introduce the SMART Goals technique. In addition to explaining what makes a goal SMART, lead a brief discussion on the value of smartening goals. You might say, for example, "In order to make sure that we all agree on exactly what each of these goals means, what our measurable targets are, and in what time frames, let's take the time to make these goals SMART goals. SMART is an acronym that stands for **S**pecific, **M**easurable, **A**greed upon, **R**ealistic, and **T**ime-bound." Write the acronym and its meanings on a chart like the one in figure 8-2.

"SMART" GOALS

Specific
Measurable
Agreed Upon
Realistic
Time-bound

Figure 8-2. The SMART Goals acronym.

Then you might say, "What do you see as the advantages of having SMART goals?"

2. Lead a discussion in which your meeting group creates a SMART Goal for each of the goals originally agreed upon.

OPTION: When you have several goals and a large group, break the group into smaller groups, assign one or two goals to each small group, and ask each one to report back their drafted SMART Goals to the larger group for approval. This saves time and increases the participation of everyone in the group. Use a chart similar to figure 8-3 for support.

CREATE "SMART" GOALS

1. Pick a recorder and a timekeeper for your group.   1 minute

2. "Smarten" each goal by creating a short sentence or
   phrase which is:

   Specific
   Measurable
   Agreed Upon
   Realistic   10 minutes
   Time-bound   per goal

3. Pick a spokesperson who will report back to the other
   participants.

                                                                        1 minute

---

Figure 8-3. Instruction chart for SMART Goals.

3. Plan specific actions to reach your goals. Depending on the breadth of the goal, either develop action plans within your group or determine how to cascade the goal(s) throughout the organization. Plan how to communicate your goals. Determine how best to monitor progress for each SMART Goal.

NOTE: As implementation begins, actions may need to be fine-tuned and prioritized to ensure goals are achieved. See Project Plans, technique 72, for more information.

NOTE: Instead of waiting to check results after the goal deadline, it's better to have logical checkpoints, especially for large and long-term SMART Goals. See Progress Reviews, technique 74, for more details.

Summary

SMART Goals help you obtain clear agreement from your meeting group about exactly what any particular goal means. SMART Goals are designed to be **S**pecific, **M**easurable, **A**greed Upon, **R**ealistic, and **T**ime-bound and act as a vehicle to establish organizational, group, and individual priorities.

1. After your group has brainstormed and agreed upon goals, introduce the SMART Goals technique.

2. Ask your group to create a SMART Goal sentence or phrase for each of the goals originally agreed upon.

3. Plan specific actions to reach your goals.

"Even though our group approves a decision for implementation, sometimes I get the feeling that there isn't total support for that decision. Is there a technique that would better ascertain true levels of support before we begin implementation?"

65. Test for Support

What Is Test for Support?

Test for Support is a technique that provides a process for discovering how much true support exists for a decision, goal, or action plan that has already been approved.

One cannot assume enthusiastic support from all group members simply because the group has approved a decision. This misguided assumption has been the downfall of many an implementation plan.

The Test for Support technique involves people voting for their specific levels of support for a decision, goal, or action plan. By doing so, a group can effectively measure this support and respond appropriately to secure the consensus required for successful implementation.

When to Use Test for Support

- When you want to clarify the true sentiments of meeting participants
- When a decision or group of decisions has been made
- When you feel you must have full support before moving forward

How to Use Test for Support

1. Introduce the Test for Support technique and its purpose. You might begin by saying, for example, "Let's take a few minutes to discover the true level of support and enthusiasm we have for the decisions we have just made. Sometimes the approval of specific decisions is not enough. If we go forward with a false sense of enthusiasm about these decisions, their implementation will very likely fail."

2. Explain how the technique works. You might say, "I am going to give each of you a piece of paper. Please write your true sentiments about this decision." Hand out a piece of paper to each participant. Then you might say, for example, "Based on the categories written on this chart, write down the number that best describes your position." Display on an overhead or chart one of the two following options. Option 1 is illustrated in figure 8-4, and option 2 is shown in figure 8-5.

NOTE: Voting can also be done electronically.

TEST FOR SUPPORT

Write down the response that best describes your true feelings.

1- I support these actions.

2- I feel neutral about these actions.

3- I do not support these actions.

?- I don't know.

Figure 8-4. Instructions for Test for Support, Option 1.

TEST FOR SUPPORT

Write down the response that best describes your feelings.

4- I will do everything I possibly can to support these actions.

3- I agree with these actions and plan to put time toward its success.

2- I agree but I'm not willing to do much.

1- I don't really care if it works or not.

0- I will smile and quietly sabotage these efforts.

Figure 8-5. Instructions for Test for Support, Option 2.

3. When finished, participants should fold their papers and pass them to the front.

4. Ask a participant near the front to read the scores while you record the vote numbers on a prepared chart. Voting charts for both options 1 and 2 are shown in figures 8-6 and 8-7, respectively.

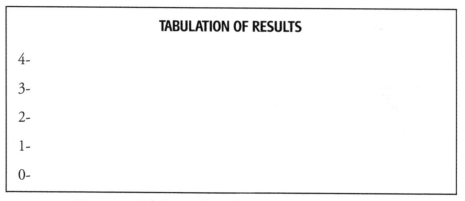

TABULATION OF RESULTS

3-

2-

1-

?-

Figure 8-6. Tabulation chart for Test for Support, Option 1.

TABULATION OF RESULTS

4-

3-

2-

1-

0-

Figure 8-7. Tabulation Chart for Test for Support, Option 2.

5. Debrief the results of the exercise. You might ask the group, for example, "What are your reactions?" "Given this information, what changes are necessary to ensure success?" Ask for information from the group as needed. You may need to ask, for example, "What causes so many of you to be ambivalent?" "What makes you unwilling to spend the time necessary to make these decisions work?"

   NOTE: Not everyone will be honest in their responses, but having the discussion will increase your level of implementation success.

6. Alter or further examine your decisions if appropriate. Only move forward in your implementation planning when you see a high level of support and enthusiasm.

Summary

Test for Support is a technique for discovering the true level of support and enthusiasm within your meeting group for a decision or plan that is to be implemented.

1. Introduce the Test for Support technique and its purpose.

2. Explain how the technique works, and ask your participants to write down their true feelings based on the choices outlined.

3. When finished, group members should fold their papers and pass them to the front.

4. Ask a person near the front to read the scores while you record the vote numbers.

5. Debrief the results.

6. Alter or further examine your decisions if needed.

"Sometimes I wish people would take responsibility for their own part in implementation. We have people from different areas of the organization in the room, and I wish they would say what they will do to help us achieve our goals. Do you have any suggestions?"

66. Individual Action Planning

What Is Individual Action Planning?

Individual Action Planning is a simple technique for identifying individual commitments and contributions to the implementation of a goal.

In this process, each individual in the meeting group publicly states what he or she intends to do to support the newly agreed-upon goal. This Individual Action Plan communicates the specific commitments that each participant will undertake as his or her contribution to overall success.

When to Use Individual Action Planning

- When the individual contributions to a goal can be completed independently of each other
- When public commitment to a goal or action is key to increasing the effectiveness of implementation

How to Use Individual Action Planning

1. After the group has identified a goal or goals, introduce Individual Action Planning.

2. Ask the participants in your meeting group to think about specifically what they will do to support that goal. Give everyone approximately ten minutes to write down his or her personal Smart Goals relative to the goal under consideration.

   NOTE: Have participants write their goals on a piece of paper large enough to be seen from across the room. (See Smart Goals, technique 64, for details.)

   Post an instruction chart similar to the one illustrated in figure 8-8 for reference during steps one and two.

DEFINE YOUR PERSONAL ACTIONS TO ACHIEVE THIS GOAL

- Think about what you specifically can and will do to support this goal.
- Write down your personal contributions as a "SMART" goal or action.

  SMART stands for Specific, Measurable, Agreed upon, Realistic, and Time-bound.

- Write this "SMART" goal on paper. Include your name.
- You can have more than one commitment, but be realistic.
- Be ready to communicate your commitments to the rest of the group.

10 minutes

Figure 8-8. Instruction chart for Individual Action Planning.

3. Ask each individual to stand up, one by one, state his or her written commitments, and place them on a wall. Public commitment to a goal will enhance the likelihood that it is accomplished.

NOTE: Unless you are a neutral facilitator, remember to participate in the exercise along with everybody else.

OPTION: If your group is large or time is short, ask individuals to turn to the person next to them to share their goals, or ask individuals at a table to share their goals with the others at their table.

4. Debrief the individual statements of commitment. You might ask, for example, "What are your reactions to what you have heard from your colleagues?" "How satisfied are you with the level of commitment from yourself and the others?" "How comfortable are you about the progress we will make if everyone honors his or her commitments?" "What might get in the way of your group achieving what you have committed to?" "What should be done to eliminate those roadblocks?"

5. Plan when and how to monitor progress. Visible follow-up on progress and results will increase the likelihood that individuals will follow through on their commitments.

6. Type up the commitments, and send them out to the team after the meeting.

Summary

Individual Action Planning is a simple technique for identifying individual commitments and contributions to the successful implementation of a goal.

1. After a group has agreed on a goal or goals, introduce the Individual Action Planning technique.

2. Ask your participants to think about specifically what they will do to support that goal, and give everyone approximately ten minutes to write down his or her personal SMART goals or actions on pieces of paper.

3. Have each participant stand up, one by one, state his or her commitments, and put them on the wall in a predesignated area.

4. Debrief the individual statements of commitment.

5. Plan when and how to monitor progress.

6. Type up the commitments, and send them out.

"There are a number of competing groups within my organization. Sometimes a good idea can be squelched because the people who thought of and developed the idea did not consider its potential opposition. Is there a systematic process to deal with this type of potential problem?"

67. Force Field Analysis

What Is Force Field Analysis?

Force Field Analysis is a technique that involves identifying both the forces that support and the forces that resist a decision or change and then determining how to strengthen the positive forces and weaken the negative forces so that the change can be implemented.

The forces you identify will likely include individuals or groups within your organization or industry, your customers, your suppliers, or any other stakeholder group. Forces will include tangible items such as budgets, physical restrictions, and personnel, as well as intangible items such as politics, feelings, and attitudes.

As any arm wrestler knows, when two competing forces work against each other, the force that is strongest and endures the longest is the force that wins. In the case of organizations, competing forces can be strong enough to kill even the best ideas.

When to Use Force Field Analysis

- When an idea is likely to face opposition
- When your group wants to test the pros and cons of a decision before presenting it to upper management or other decision makers
- When you want to increase the likelihood that goals will be implemented

How to Use Force Field Analysis

1. Explain the purpose of Force Field Analysis. You might say, for example, "We want to make sure that we are ready for both positive and negative responses to our decision [or suggestion for change]. In order to best prepare ourselves, let's take a few minutes to analyze the forces that will likely support our idea as well as the forces that likely will not. We can then look for actions to build on the forces that support us and actions to diminish the arguments against the change."

2. Draw a chart or display a prepared chart similar to the one in figure 8-9, and ask your group to brainstorm the forces for and forces against your proposed idea or change. Write the forces on the appropriate area of the chart.

FORCES FOR (+)	FORCES AGAINST (-)

Figure 8-9. Force Field Analysis template.

NOTE: If it is unclear whether a force is for or against the proposal, put it aside on another sheet for later analysis.

NOTE: Leave enough space between the forces to brainstorm strategies in the next step, and use different colored pens to differentiate the two.

3. After your lists are complete, brainstorm actions to strengthen the forces for your proposed change and actions to weaken the opposition to that change.

   NOTE: It may be helpful to ask yourselves some questions about each force to help you with your brainstorming. You might ask, for example, "Who specifically is involved?" "What is the history of this?" "How do we know this actually exists?"

   NOTE: Spend the most time focusing on the strongest forces on each side.

4. After you have finished brainstorming the actions, have your meeting group select the most effective actions to strengthen the forces for and diminish the forces against. Refer to figure 8-10 (next page) for a completed, hypothetical example of a Force Field Analysis chart on the purchase of new equipment.

5. Create action plans as necessary. Plan how to incorporate these plans into your presentation to management or next steps toward implementation. See Chart Actions, technique 63, for details.

FORCES FOR (+)	FORCES AGAINST (-)
Safety problems	No budget
Document problems and costs	*Show the cost benefits and time needed to recoup the money.*
Downtime	Skills training necessary—will disrupt work flow
Document problems and costs	
Improve productivity	*Vendor chosen provides off hours training, will not interrupt work flow. Employees are willing to train off-hours.*
Calculate productivity increases over time. When will equipment pay for itself?	

Figure 8-10. Finished example of Force Field Analysis chart.

Summary

Force Field Analysis is a technique that involves identifying both the forces that support and the forces that resist a decision or change and then determining how to strengthen the positive forces and weaken the negative forces so that the change can be implemented.

1. Introduce and explain the purpose of Force Field Analysis.

2. Ask the group to brainstorm forces for and forces against the proposal under consideration.

3. After your lists are complete, brainstorm actions to strengthen the forces for your proposed change and actions to weaken the opposition to that change.

4. After you have finished brainstorming the actions, have your group select the most effective ones to strengthen the forces for and diminish the forces against.

5. Create action plans as necessary.

Source

Lewin, Kurt. 1951. *Field Theory in Social Science.* Chicago: University of Chicago Press.

"I have read that there is a higher likelihood that goals will be obtained if the work to achieve those goals is started immediately. I have a goal-setting meeting coming up with a large group of people. After we set goals, I would like to start some of the implementation planning as soon as possible. Is there a technique that will help me do this?"

68. Goal Plan Go

What Is Goal Plan Go?

Goal Plan Go is a technique that invites your meeting participants to take responsibility for transforming the group's goals into action. The process allows individuals to choose which planning team they would like to join and to have the first meeting of that planning team immediately.

Because enthusiasm and momentum are at their peak at the time when goals are defined and approved, the likelihood for effective implementation increases dramatically when the action planning can begin immediately. Goal Plan Go allows this process to take place.

When to Use Goal Plan Go

- When no specific skills or experience are required to achieve the selected goal(s) and leaders do not need to handpick team participants. (In those cases, see Project Charters, technique 70.)
- When it is difficult for the participants to regularly meet together
- When your group has a history of good intentions but poor follow-through

How to Use Goal Plan Go

1. Be sure that your meeting group has agreed upon a list of goals. Write a list of these goals on a few pieces of chart paper with plenty of space between each of the goals. Display them around the room.

   NOTE: If possible, use existing charts from previous exercises.

2. Ask your participants to help create planning teams for each goal. You might say, for example, "We are going to take some time in today's meeting to plan how to turn our goals into action. To do so, we will create planning teams, one for each of our goals. Each planning team will be made up of a group of volunteers. Take a few minutes to think about which specific goal you would like to work on. Then write your name in the space under that goal. If you want or need to participate on the planning team

for more than one goal, you can do so, but you will need to choose which one you will focus on today. Write your name under each goal you are interested in, but place an asterisk behind your name under all but the goal of primary interest. This will indicate that you are interested in being a part of that planning team but will not be attending today's planning meeting." Exhibit a chart similar to figure 8-11 to illustrate your instructions.

CREATE ACTION PLANNING TEAMS

- Think about which goals you want/need most to support into action.
- Write your name under those charted goals.
- If you write your name under more than one goal, put an asterisk behind your name under all goals *except* the goal of primary interest. This signifies that you are interested but will *not* be a part of today's planning discussion for that group.

5 minutes

Figure 8-11. Instructions for creating action planning teams.

3. Designate a part of the room for each planning team to meet.

4. Give the groups guidelines for their discussions, and ask them to begin their planning processes. Refer to figure 8-12 for an example of these guidelines.

PLANNING TEAM GUIDELINES

- Pick a leader for your team.
- Choose a recorder and timekeeper for today's meeting.
- Begin to create a detailed action plan to accomplish your goal. Include "who does what by when." Concentrate on planning the work instead of doing the work.
- Establish your next meeting time/place during this planning session.
- Be ready to report back your progress and actions by xx o'clock.

Figure 8-12. Planning team guidelines.

5. After an appropriate period of time (depending on the amount of time available in your meeting), ask each group to report the results of their progress. Have them include any agreed-upon next steps or actions as well.

6. Determine as a group how and when to monitor the progress of the implementation efforts.

Summary

Goal Plan Go is a technique that invites your meeting participants to take responsibility for transforming the group's goals into action. The process allows individuals to choose which planning teams they would like to join and to have the first meeting of that planning team immediately.

1. Be sure that your meeting group has agreed upon a list of goals. Write a list of these goals on chart paper with plenty of space between each of the goals.

2. Ask your participants to think about which specific goals they would like or need to work on as part of the planning team that will transform these goals into action.

3. Designate a part of the room for each planning group to meet.

4. Give the groups guidelines for their discussions and have them begin their meetings.

5. Ask each group to report back on the progress of its planning efforts.

6. Determine how and when to monitor the progress of implementation.

"My leadership team and I have a pretty clear idea of where we want to be in the next five years, but we don't know exactly how to get there. There are so many issues and improvements to address that it's hard to get our heads around them. What suggestions do you have?"

69. Transformation Maps

What Are Transformation Maps?

A Transformation Map is a one-page visual depiction of the plan for implementing a strategy or goal. It describes the major results, actions, and milestones required to achieve your strategic goal along with the expected timing for each of them. It is a tool to build alignment with your leadership team. Because it describes the components of the change, it demystifies the path forward. This is a great discussion and decision-making tool for use in a workshop or strategy meeting. Its results are used to guide future actions and priorities.

Transformation Maps are best created with a group in a workshop-type setting. The process of developing the Transformation Map with the appropriate stakeholders is as important as the map itself. Simply presenting a finished map without significant stakeholder input and involvement will not have nearly the same level of ownership, understanding, or consensus and therefore will not achieve the same level of results.

An example of a Transformation Map appears on the next page.

When to Use Transformation Maps
- When you want to agree and communicate the multiple components of your strategic plan with your key stakeholders
- As part of your company's strategic planning process, and before your budgeting process begins, as a tool for prioritizing

How to Use Transformation Maps

Before the Meeting
1. Determine who needs to attend the meeting. Be sure that all stakeholder groups are represented, even if they are not all at the same level of the organization.

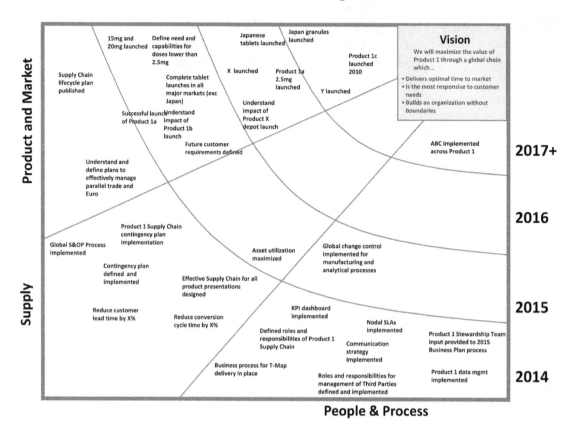

Figure 8-13. Transformation Map example.

2. Determine who will facilitate the meeting. If you are the group's leader, you will want to participate in the discussion, but be aware that it is very difficult to focus on the content of the discussion and facilitate at the same time. Nonetheless, if the meeting will have only a few people, it is possible that you might want to facilitate the meeting yourself.

3. Forecast how much time you will need for the meeting. At least a few hours will be required.

4. Create a wall-sized Transformation Map template to be used in the meeting. A sample template is below. You will need to customize both the time frames and the categories to suit your specific purpose.

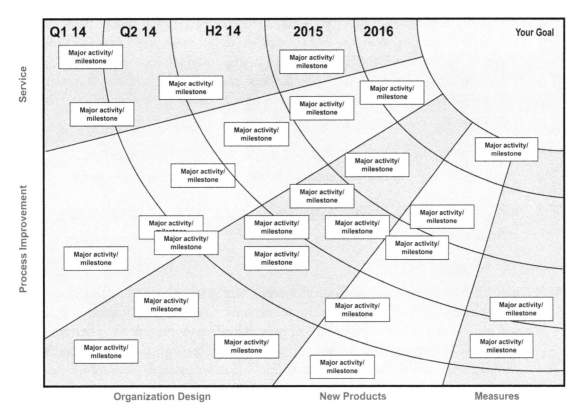

Figure 8-14. Sample Transformation Map template.

a. Draft the goal or vision statement that will go in the top right corner.

b. Determine the length of time for achieving this goal or vision—that is, three years, five years, and so on.

c. Determine the time frames for the Transformation Map. For example, if the time for achieving your goal is three years, your time frames could be broken down as Q1-2014, Q2-2014, H2-2014, H1-2015, H2-2015, 2016. You will usually have a higher volume of activities and milestones as you begin, so you will have shorter time frames at the beginning of your journey.

NOTE: Q1 refers to quarter 1 of the year, H1 refers to the first half of the year.

d. Determine the categories for your map. These categories will change based on the nature of your goal or vision. For example, a supply chain project may include categories such as vendors, technology, customers, and organizational design. Choosing the right categories for your situation can be difficult. Don't worry if you change them a few times. It is helpful to have draft categories in mind in advance as a starting point for the group's discussion.

NOTE: You may want to use sticky notes to document your time frames and categories so they can easily be changed based on feedback from your group.

5. Bring the materials required to the meeting—that is, the template, sticky notes, pens, and masking tape.

During the Meeting

1. Describe the purpose of the Transformation Map with your group. You might say, for example: "In order to define and agree on how we will reach our strategic goal, we will use a tool called a Transformation Map. The Transformation Map describes the major results, actions, and milestones required to achieve your strategic goal, along with the expected timing of each of them." Share an example of a Transformation Map if you think it will be helpful.

2. Agree on the ultimate goal or vision with your stakeholder group. Document this goal or vision in the upper right hand corner of the page. Examples include: "double sales in three years" or "increase market share by 50 percent."

3. Confirm the time frames and categories you will use.

NOTE: At this point the time frames and categories are academic since you haven't started to use the framework yet, so don't get too bogged down. If you need to, you can modify the time frames and categories as you get into defining actions and milestones.

4. Discuss as a group which actions and milestones should occur and when, working backward from the goal. Use sticky notes for the actions and milestones. This allows people to move them freely during the discussion.

5. Watch for interdependencies between them—for instance, technology that will need to be in place before a product launch can occur. Be conscious of the magnitude of

each change—that is, which resources will be required and for which period of time. Be sure to include projects that are already in process or planned to start in the future. You want a complete and realistic picture. Avoid unrealistic plans, but also balance the need for quickness.

6. Agree with the group on who will be accountable for each element of your transformation plan. This might involve creating Project Charters, technique 70; Project Teams, technique 71; and an Executive Steering Group, technique 73. At the minimum, use Chart Actions, technique 63. Also agree on your communication and follow-up plan.

After the Meeting

1. Communicate the plan outlined on your Transformation Map to the appropriate persons within your organization.

   NOTE: After your key stakeholders agree on the decisions, use the Transformation Map as a visual aid when describing plans to wider audiences. However, because of its detailed nature, it is not a document that should be used as part of a presentation projected on the wall unless people have copies of it in front of them as well.

2. Follow up on a regular basis to ensure that actions and milestones are achieved.

Summary

Transformation Maps are a great way to gain alignment with key stakeholders about the integrated plan to achieve a long-term goal.

Before the Meeting

1. Determine who needs to attend the meeting.

2. Determine who will facilitate the meeting.

3. Forecast how much time is required.

4. Create a wall-sized Transformation Map template.

5. Bring the materials required to the meeting.

During the Meeting

1. Describe the purpose of the Transformation Map with your group.

2. Agree on the ultimate goal or vision.

3. Confirm the time frames and categories you will use.

4. Discuss as a group which actions and milestones should occur and when, working backward from the goal. Use sticky notes for the actions and milestones.

5. Watch for interdependencies. Avoid unrealistic plans, but also balance the need for quickness.

6. Agree with the group about who will be accountable for each element of your transformation plan.

After the Meeting

1. Communicate the plan.

2. Follow up on a regular basis to ensure that actions and milestones are achieved.

"I've been asked to lead a change project within my company, but I'm not really sure what is expected. What should I do?"

70. Project Charters

What Are Project Charters?

A Project Charter is a one-page document that describes the new project's:
- Objectives
- Measures and targets—both financial and nonfinancial
- Deliverables
- Assumptions regarding support requirements, risks, interdependencies, and so on
- Project Sponsor (the leader ultimately accountable for the project's success), Project Manager (the person who leads the project on a day-to-day basis), team members (people assigned to the project either full or part time), and the time required for their participation
- Scope

The Project Charter serves as the written agreement among key stakeholders, the Project Sponsor, the lead, and the team. Having this agreement up front avoids conflicts and confusion later on and will increase the likelihood of success from the very start.

When to Use Project Charters
- When you want to make sure that your project is clearly defined and agreed upon with key stakeholders from the start
- When you want to assemble a special project team to accomplish a specific goal (See Project Teams, technique 71, for details.)

How to Use Project Charters
1. The Project Sponsor and Project Manager agree on the categories in the charter template, draft the Project Charter, and gain input and alignment with key stakeholders.

2. If there is an Executive Steering Group, the ESG should sign off on the charter. See Executive Steering Group, technique 73, for more details.

3. Use the Project Charter to create a more detailed project plan with support from and alignment with the project team.

4. Refer back to the charter from time to time to ensure that the direction of the project remains consistent with original expectations.

Objectives	Measures and Targets	Deliverables	Assumptions
• Establish strong Industrial Operations capabilities in China • Build a complete factory capable of handling the complete line • Lead thinking in process design for complete line operations • Drive low cost sourcing for the group	FINANCIAL • Reduce landed costs by 20 to 30% by 2015 • Increase addressable market share from 47 to 56% by 2015 • Note: 2014 financial target to be defined • Performance against Business Case NON-FINANCIAL • Completion of assembly of 8 blowers and 3 fillers in 2015 • Reduce lead time by four weeks for delivery to Chinese market by Dec. 2015 (linked to location plan) • 194 local and ex-pat people hired in Industrial operations by end of 2015 • Future KPI: customer satisfaction	Phase 1 • Designed and constructed plant (including new model for plant organization) • New organization design and deployment to accommodate complete line • Process and information flow design and installation (to support SAP deployment) • Local sourcing of components Phase 2 • Project mode to end of 2015 to drive sustainability and to deliver on targets on equipment delivery and key learning • Build a 'one company' culture in China, including consistent processes with the Group • Build End of Line and Tooling capabilities in 2014, and Labeling in 2015	• We will continue to create strong synergies with Market Operations and Strategic Sourcing • Project will deliver according to the original business case • IS and processes at global level are implemented • Intellectual Property issues must be proactively and carefully addressed to avoid company risk

Team Members & % Time		Out of Scope	In Scope
Role	% Time	• Market Operations sales in China	• Industrial operations in China
Sponsor: Sam Sneed	5%	• Strategic Sourcing activities in China (but links and consequences secured)	• Local sourcing operations
Lead: Margaret Thatcher	100%		• Contribution/synergies with Sales activities
Team Members			• Contribution/synergies with Strategic Sourcing activities
Tom Hanks	60%		
Gregory Hines	40%		

Figure 8-15. Project Charter example.

Objectives	Measures and Targets	Deliverables	Assumptions
·X	·X	·X	·X

Team Members & % Time		Out of Scope	In Scope
Role:	% Time	·X	·X
Sponsor:			
·X			
Initiative Manager:			
·X			
Team Members:			
·X			
·X			

Figure 8-16. Project Charter template.

Summary

A Project Charter is a great way to gain agreement on the objectives and parameters of a new project.

1. The Project Sponsor and Project Manager agree on the categories in the charter template, draft the Project Charter, and gain input and alignment with key stakeholders.

2. If there is an Executive Steering Group, the ESG should sign off on the charter.

3. Use the Project Charter to create a more detailed project plan.

4. Refer back to the charter from time to time.

"I've just been asked to lead a change project within our company. I know I don't have all the skills and information to achieve the expected results on my own. It's going to be especially tricky because a lot of groups are going to be impacted by the change, and I'm sure they are going to resist. What can I do to lower my risk and improve my chances of success?"

71. Project Teams

What Are Project Teams?

Most significant decisions require changes to people, processes, or technology when they are implemented. Therefore, they require significant effort to design, prepare for, transition to, and implement. Forming a Project Team specifically to support these efforts is a great way of lowering risk and improving your chances of success. Project Teams are made up of a diverse group of people called together to analyze the current situation, design the elements of the change, identify the steps to achieve it, and support implementation. Individuals are asked to be members of a team either instead of or in addition to their current responsibilities.

When to Use Project Teams

- When a change is considered high risk or difficult to implement.
- When your project impacts several different stakeholder groups—that is, divisions or geographies—and will involve significant changes to your existing ways of working
- When your organization has a history of poor delivery on previous initiatives

How to Use Project Teams

1. Confirm the purpose and scope of the Project Team. See Project Charters, technique 70, for more details.

2. Determine the skills and expertise required on the team. Be sure to consider all stakeholder groups and their required involvement.

3. Look around the organization for those individuals with the required skills and expertise. Look beyond your favorites. Participation on a project is a great way to grow your next generation of leaders. Team members must not only have the required skills and expertise but must also be considered credible representatives of their part of the organization.

4. Determine if you need the team to work on your project full-time or part-time.

5. Work with proposed team members' direct managers to gain support for their involvement in the project. Ensure that the workload of team members is distributed to someone else or stopped.

6. Launch the team. Involve team members in designing the details of your Project Plan. See technique 72 for more information.

7. Hold regular meetings throughout the project. Use the techniques outlined in this book to support your success. Take time to have fun along the way.

8. Celebrate the end of the project, and ensure that team members are successfully reintegrated into old or new jobs.

Summary

Most changes require significant effort to design, prepare for, transition to, and implement. Forming a Project Team specifically to support these efforts greatly lowers risk and improves your chances of success.

1. Confirm the purpose and scope of the Project Team.

2. Determine the skills and expertise required on the team.

3. Identify individuals with the required skills and expertise.

4. Determine if you need the team to work on your project full-time or part-time.

5. Work with proposed team members' direct managers to gain support.

6. Launch the team.

7. Hold regular meetings throughout the project.

8. Celebrate the end of the project, and ensure that team members are successfully reintegrated into old or new jobs.

"We seem to have a difficult time moving from large, complex goals into detailed action plans. Is there a technique that can help us better organize our efforts in this type of situation?"

72. Project Plans

What Are Project Plans?

The Project Plans technique helps you effectively prepare a complex action plan. After an organization or group has agreed upon and approved a goal, it needs to create an action plan for achieving that goal. If the goal is large and complicated, the resulting action plan will have several levels and categories of activity.

A Project Plan is an extremely efficient technique for establishing the levels and categories of a complex action plan in a systematic and easy-to-understand form. Sometimes the details of a plan of this type will be completed on different levels and by different departments within an organization. A Project Plan serves this purpose well and also provides an easy-to-follow process for visually tracking what actions will be done by whom and by when.

When to Use Project Plans
- When planning the details of how to reach a complex goal
- When the actions required to achieve a goal are multifaceted and multilayered
- When you want agreement between those involved in a plan's implementation and also other key stakeholders

How to Use Project Plans

Before the Meeting

Prepare an Excel spreadsheet using the template on the following page as a starting point. Customize it for your purposes.

NOTE: You may also use Microsoft Project if you prefer, and if all team members have access to Microsoft Project software.

Be sure to include the individuals who will deliver your project at the meeting. If this is not possible, plan subsequent meetings to include all appropriate people.

(Your Team Name Here) Project Plan				Q1 2014					
Task	Start Date	Finish Date	Who Leads Task	6-Jan	13-Jan	20-Jan	27-Jan	3-Feb	ETC.
MAJOR ACTIVITY									
subactivity									
subactivity									
subactivity									
MAJOR ACTIVITY									
subactivity									
subactivity									
ETC.									

Figure 8-17. Project Plan template.

During the Meeting

1. Review the SMART Goal or Project Charter for which you are creating your action plan. See SMART Goals, technique 64, or Project Charters, technique 70, for details.

2. Display your project plan template on a large screen. Explain the process of building the project plan; you will start with the list of primary activities and then fill in the details. This keeps the meeting from getting bogged down in detail too quickly and allows participants to see the big picture first.

3. Have your meeting group list the primary activities or categories of activities that will need to be accomplished in order to reach the goal. Type the replies into your Project Plan as you go. Use verbs to start each phrase to ensure clarity of the action. Don't worry about typing perfection at this point. You can clean up your document after the meeting is over.

   NOTE: You may also ask another participant with good typing skills to manage this task for you.

4. Once the primary activities are documented, ask the group to identify the next level of activities that will need to be accomplished. Type their responses as you go.

295

5. Continue the process as described in steps 3 and 4 to whatever level of detail is required and appropriate for the situation.

   NOTE: The appropriate level of detail is usually at the point where individuals are clear about the actions or next steps required from them and where the interdependencies of tasks are clear.

6. Add Who and By When information for every branch of your Project Plan.

   NOTE: When estimating time frames, it is often helpful to work backward from the goal. In other words, begin from the last required action in the process toward the first actions. By doing so, you are more likely to create time frames that meet the original time commitment.

7. Review and complete your Project Plan.

8. Agree with the group on how to launch the project plan and monitor progress.

After the Meeting

1. Clean up your document, and send it to participants. Ask for feedback to ensure that the Project Plan articulates agreements and is a feasible plan.

2. Follow your Project Plan as agreed.

Summary

Project Plans provide a means for effectively detailing a complex action plan, usually involving more than one person.

Before the Meeting

Create a template for the meeting. Invite your project team or other appropriate persons to the meeting.

During the Meeting

1. Review the SMART Goal for which you are creating your action plan.

2. Explain the process you will use.

3. List the primary activities or categories of activities that will need to be accomplished.

4. Identify the next level of activities that will need to be accomplished.

5. Continue the process as described in steps 3 and 4 to the level of detail that is appropriate for the situation.

6. Add Who and By When information for every branch of your Project Plan.

7. Review and complete your Project Plan together as a team.

8. Agree on how to launch the project and monitor progress.

After the Meeting

1. Clean up your document, send it to participants, and ask for feedback on its accuracy and feasibility.

2. Follow your Project Plan as agreed.

"I got approval for an important change in the way we do business, but now we're stalled. The people on our project team don't have the clout to break through the logjams and resolve cross-functional issues. What should I do?"

73. Executive Steering Group (ESG)

What Is Executive Steering Group?

Executive Steering Groups (ESGs) are groups that are called together to oversee a specific project or program. Your ESG should represent your major stakeholders and have the decision-making authority to direct your project. ESGs usually consist of individuals in leadership positions who are credible and influential enough to make change happen. The ESG meets on a regular basis—that is, monthly or quarterly—for the duration of the project. They are accountable for achieving the Business Case and implementing the project as planned. (See Business Case, technique 62, for details.)

The Sponsor (the ultimate owner of the project) is normally the chairperson of ESG meetings. The Sponsor may want to have a facilitator run the ESG meetings so he or she can participate fully. If you are not the Sponsor of the project or initiative, work closely with the Sponsor on every step to ensure alignment on the content and process of each meeting.

When to Use an Executive Steering Group

- When a change is considered high risk or difficult to implement
- When your project has several different stakeholder groups involved—that is, divisions and geographies—and will involve significant changes to your existing ways of working
- When your organization has a history of poor delivery on previous projects and change initiatives
- When people on your project team will need help to break through logjams and make cross-functional decisions

How to Use an Executive Steering Group

1. Identify the key stakeholders/stakeholder groups impacted by the proposed project's results.

2. Determine who would be appropriate Executive Steering Group members. These members could all be part of an existing leadership group, a subset of a leadership group, or a group that has never met before nor will again.

3. Draft a purpose statement for the group's existence. Include time commitments, roles, and expected outcomes.

4. Invite each person individually to be part of your ESG. Discuss the Project Charter (technique 70) with him or her, and describe why you want each person to be on the ESG. If you are not the Project Sponsor, have that person invite individual ESG members.

5. Launch the Executive Steering Group. Invite members well in advance. Start the meeting by reviewing the charter and explaining why each person is at the table. If members do not know each other, be sure to take the time to introduce each person and describe the contribution each will make to the team.

6. Ensure that the ESG signs off on the Business Case (if one exists), Project Charter, and Project Plan and agrees who is on the Project Team. See Business Case, technique 62; Project Charters, technique 70; and Project Teams, technique 71, and Project Plans, technique 72, for more details.

7. Ensure that each meeting is a valuable use of time for each member and is a forum for decisions and direction setting. Meetings that only update members without giving them something to do are a waste of time. Plan your ESG meetings to coincide with project milestones. Be sure that you can justify each agenda item. In other words, why is the item on the agenda? What relevance does it have to the steering group members? This question will eliminate boring updates on activities that have no interest to the steering group members.

   NOTE: The Sponsor should be in alignment with the Project Manager and the facilitator in advance of each meeting. The Sponsor should never go into an ESG meeting without knowing the agenda, being prepared, and, when required, having prepositioned the ESG members in advance so the meeting can be a productive use of time. You want to avoid any conflicts or nasty surprises in public.

8. When the project has been fully and successfully implemented, be sure to have a closing meeting, dinner, or celebration to thank the ESG members for their contributions. You want a strong ending as well as a strong beginning.

9. If the project starts to crumble after implementation, resurrect the ESG to help get the changes back on track. If there are issues impacting sustainability—for instance,

lack of resources or training, conflicting goals and measures, etc.—it is the ESG's responsibility to make the required changes to ensure the Project Charter's objectives are met.

Summary

Executive Steering Groups (ESGs) are groups that are called together for purposes of overseeing a specific project or program. These groups should represent your major stakeholders and have the decision-making authority to drive the direction of your project.

1. Identify the key stakeholders/stakeholder groups impacted by the proposed project's results.

2. Determine who would be appropriate Executive Steering Group members.

3. Draft a purpose statement for the group's existence.

4. Invite each person individually to be part of your ESG.

5. Launch the Executive Steering Group.

6. Ensure that the ESG signs off on the Project Charter and Project Plan.

7. Ensure that each meeting is a valuable use of time.

8. When the project has been implemented, have a closing meeting, dinner, or celebration to thank the ESG members for their contributions.

9. If the project starts to crumble after implementation, resurrect the ESG to help get the implementation back on track.

"A few months ago my company made me responsible for running a project. I'm doing my best, but the project is already running out of steam and so am I. My boss hasn't asked me about the project even once, so maybe it's no longer a priority. I'm not really sure. Maybe I should just put the project on the back burner and see what happens. What do you think I should do?"

74. Progress Reviews

What Are Progress Reviews?

Progress Reviews are the mechanism for tracking a project's progress and results. When done on a timely and regular basis, Progress Reviews can help maintain momentum and ensure that results are achieved. The Project Manager uses his or her Project Plan as a guide and, depending on the project structure, updates the Sponsor, Executive Steering Group, and/or key stakeholders, including his or her boss on a regular basis. Typical Progress Review meeting topics include:

- Progress according to plan
- Measures and accomplishments versus targets
- Risks and issues, specifically those needing Sponsor or ESG support
- Decisions to be made
- Next steps/expected accomplishments before the next meeting

When to Use Progress Reviews

- When your project lasts more than a few weeks in length

How to Use Progress Reviews

Project reviews are conducted and prepared by the Project Manager for meetings held with the Project Sponsor and/or the Executive Steering Group (ESG). If there is no formal Project Sponsor or ESG, proactively schedule and hold these meetings with your boss. The schedule for the Project Reviews should be part of the initial project plan and coincide with project deliverables, milestones, and decision-making points.

The Project Manager should be well prepared for each progress review meeting. It is appropriate to bring bad news forward proactively in a problem-solving manner.

It is often helpful to also send written progress updates between meetings. A useful method for written progress reviews is the ABCD report. ABCD stands for:

A = Accomplishments	These are accomplishments for the week.
B = Benefits	This section outlines what went especially well.
C = Concerns/Issues	This section is used to call attention to critical matters that are impeding or might impede progress.
D = Do Next	These are action items for the coming week or two; each entry should appear as an accomplishment within two weeks.

Figure 8-18. ABCD definition.

Using a green, yellow, red format is also helpful for reporting on overall status. Use the actual color in a box to emphasize the point.

Overall Status	
Green	We are on-track to achieve our goals and deliverables.
Yellow	There is the potential of missing project deadlines without close attention.
Red	We are behind schedule, and there is a need for immediate action/intervention to get back on track.

Figure 8-19. Overall Status definition.

Summary

Progress Reviews help track a project's progress and results. When done on a timely and regular basis, Progress Reviews can help maintain momentum and ensure that results are achieved. Progress Review options include meetings; ABCD reports; and green, yellow, red status summaries.

"We will need to change some of our existing processes and ways of working with other departments when we implement new technology next month. I'm expecting complete chaos. How can I avoid confusion and bad feelings?"

75. Roles and Responsibility Charting: RACI

What Is Roles and Responsibility Charting: RACI?

Roles and Responsibility Charting: RACI is a method for coordinating and documenting roles and responsibilities.

RACI stands for:

R = Responsible	Persons involved in doing the work, or making the decision.
A = Accountable	The buck stops here. The person who is ultimately accountable. Only one A is allowed.
C = Consulted	Persons who are consulted before a decision is made or action is taken.
I = Informed	Persons informed after the decision is made or action is taken.

Figure 8-20. RACI definition.

Where most other methods document only the person who is accountable for a decision or activity, RACI also documents who will be involved in doing the work, who will be consulted before a decision is made, and who will be informed after the decision is made or action taken.

When to Use RACI
- When working across departments, groups, or organizations where roles and responsibilities are not clear and therefore duplication occurs or nothing gets done
- When changing a process or way of working
- When you want to communicate the difference between how something was done in the past and how it will be done in the future
- When introducing a new way of working
- When decision-making authority is unclear
- When tasks are performed or decisions made at the wrong level of the organization
- When managing the interfaces is difficult
- Where finger-pointing occurs when things go wrong
- Where ambiguities exist

Key
R=Responsible
A=Accountable
C=Consulted
I=Informed

	ACTIVITY	President	Regional Director	District Sales Manager	Dealer Dvlpmt Manager	Region Specialist Manager	Region Specialist	MD Director	SC Specialist Manager	SC Specialist	MD Solution Mgr	Sales Support Comm
				Sales					**Market Development**			
Sales Strategy	Develop national sales strategy	A	R	I	I	I	I	R	C	I		
	Implement national sales strategy and conduct quarterly updates	A	R	R	R	R	R	R	R	C	R	
	Establish annual sales targets	A	C	C	C	I	I	R	C	I	R	
Key Accounts	Determine and maintain Key Account List	I	A	I	I	C	R	I	R	I		
	Establish definition of key accounts	A	R	R	I	I	I	C	C	I		
	Define 80/20 Strategy	A	R	I	R	I	I					
	Develop strategic key account & customer sales plans	I	A	R	R	C	C	C	R			
	Communicate key account needs through to Customer Solutions	C	C	C				A	R	R		

Figure 8-21. Example of RACI.

How to Use RACI

1. Define the scope of exercise—that is, the starting and end points of a process.

2. Document the key activities in the process on an Excel spreadsheet or in a Word document.

3. Determine those people or positions involved on the other axis of your spreadsheet or document.

4. Hold a meeting with representatives of each stakeholder group to define the RACI.

   a. Review the purpose of the RACI. Explain what it stands for and how it will be used.

   b. Confirm the scope and key activities with the group.

   c. Agree who has the *A* for each activity.

   d. Fill in the *R*s, *C*s, and *I*s for each activity.

e. Review the RACI for overall accuracy.

f. Agree on the communication and implementation plan.

5. Communicate the results to all stakeholders.

6. Enforce the new roles through the use of new job descriptions, measures, targets, and so on as required.

7. Review the RACI with key stakeholders on a periodic basis to look for opportunities for improvement.

Summary

RACI is an excellent tool for articulating the roles and responsibilities of groups and individuals.

1. Define the scope of the exercise.

2. Document the key activities.

3. Determine those people or positions involved.

4. Hold a meeting with representatives of each stakeholder group to define the RACI.

5. Communicate the results to all stakeholders.

6. Implement the new roles.

7. Review the RACI with key stakeholders on a periodic basis.

"I know that our strategy is going to make significant changes to the way we work around here. I also know that there will be a lot of resistance. What can I do to ensure that our strategy actually becomes a reality?"

76. Stakeholder Identification and Planning

What Is Stakeholder Identification and Planning?

A stakeholder is anyone who has a stake in the results of your change. In a business situation, stakeholders could include employees, management, unions, customers, suppliers, the board of directors, shareholders, community interest groups, and government regulatory authorities.

Stakeholder Identification and Planning is the process of determining who your stakeholders are, learning what their needs and perspectives are, and planning how to address them in your project design and implementation.

Gaining support for any change is critical, even when you are the boss and have ultimate decision-making authority.

When to Use Stakeholder Identification and Planning

- Before your potential change starts and during each phase of the project's implementation
- When your projects have a history of failing due to unexpected or undermanaged resistance

How to Use Stakeholder Identification and Planning

1. Identify those who will be affected (stakeholders). Do this independently or with a group of people such as your Project Team.

2. Determine the stakeholders' issues through Individual Interviews, technique 35; Focus Groups, technique 36; Questionnaires, technique 37; or Road Shows, technique 52.

3. Determine how best to address those issues. Incorporate appropriate actions into your overall Project Plan. Prioritize issues as required.

4. Plan how to involve key stakeholders in the change effort in order to maximize acceptance and minimize resistance. For example, include stakeholder representatives on your project team or plan for communication at key milestones in your project.

NOTE: See Force Field Analysis, technique 67, as a tool that the stakeholder group could use.

Summary

If you do not pay attention to each stakeholder group impacted by your decision and its implementation, you will have suboptimal results at best.

1. Identify those who will be affected.

2. Determine the stakeholders' issues.

3. Determine how best to address those issues

4. Plan how to involve key stakeholders in the change.

"It seems that every time we implement a change, within a few months, people are back to their old ways of working. What can we do to make change stick?"

77. Sustainability Analysis

What Is Sustainability Analysis?

Many changes do not persist because no one has taken the time to identify and address the issues that will support or sabotage the change over the long term. Sustainability Analysis is designed to identify and address issues critical to making the change stick.

Examples of issues that can impact sustainability include:

- Ensuring that the right people are in the right jobs, including:
  o Effective leadership
  o People with skills and expertise to do the job
  o Performance management, proactively addressing poor performance
- Adequate training and communication about the change
- Alignment of rewards and recognition
- Projects prioritized, ensuring the most important actions are taken first
- Organizational structure aligned
- Processes aligned
- Cultural issues addressed
- Technology issues addressed

When to Use Sustainability Analysis

For every change, some level of analysis will be necessary. The bigger the change, the more time will be required to ensure sustainability.

How to Use Sustainability Analysis

1. Analyze the issues by asking yourself and the stakeholders, "What will get in the way of this change being a success over the long term?" This analysis should be part of the original project plan.

2. Document and prioritize the issues and discuss ways to overcome them. Discuss your plan with decision makers, for example the Executive Steering Group and Project Sponsor, and gain their support in addressing sustainability issues.

You can customize the sample checklist on the following page.

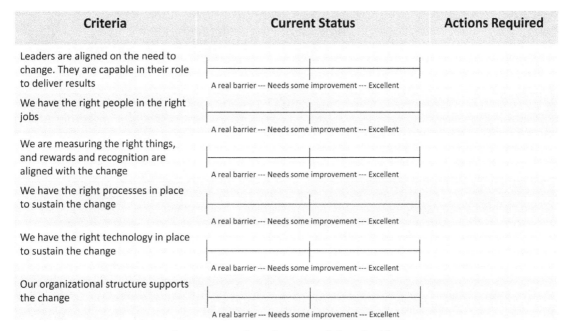

Criteria	Current Status	Actions Required
Leaders are aligned on the need to change. They are capable in their role to deliver results	A real barrier --- Needs some improvement --- Excellent	
We have the right people in the right jobs	A real barrier --- Needs some improvement --- Excellent	
We are measuring the right things, and rewards and recognition are aligned with the change	A real barrier --- Needs some improvement --- Excellent	
We have the right processes in place to sustain the change	A real barrier --- Needs some improvement --- Excellent	
We have the right technology in place to sustain the change	A real barrier --- Needs some improvement --- Excellent	
Our organizational structure supports the change	A real barrier --- Needs some improvement --- Excellent	

Figure 8-22. Sample sustainability checklist.

3. Assign accountabilities for recommended changes, and follow up to ensure the changes are made. In some cases, some elements of your sustainability plans may need to become independent projects—for instance, improving performance management or improving leadership effectiveness.

4. Review on a regular basis.

Summary

Sustainability Analysis is designed to identify and address issues critical to making the change stick.

1. Analyze the issues that will get in the way of your project's success.

2. Document and prioritize the issues, and discuss ways to overcome them.

3. Assign accountabilities for recommended changes, and follow up to ensure the changes are made.

4. Review on a regular basis.

9

Four Techniques to Evaluate Meeting Effectiveness

Ralph's engineering meetings are good, but with a little help they could be even better. "We evaluate the effectiveness of almost everything we do, but we never evaluate our meetings. I think some feedback would help us, and I want to show that I'm willing to walk the talk."

As with other products and services, meetings need feedback from their customers (in this case the participants) in order to continually increase their effectiveness. This chapter provides four techniques that give meeting facilitators specific processes to obtain accurate information about the effectiveness of their meetings. These technique alternatives ask for different types of information in different ways, but all provide the meeting facilitator with the data necessary to accurately measure and consistently improve the quality of his or her meetings.

These four techniques include:

78. What Went Well/Opportunities for Improvement
79. Once Around the Table
80. Team Effectiveness Chart
81. Written Questions

"I've been leading our team meetings now for almost a year, but I've never asked for feedback on how I'm doing. Is there an accurate, fast, and easy way to get input from my group about how well our meetings are going?"

78. What Went Well/Opportunities for Improvement

What Is What Went Well/Opportunities for Improvement?

What Went Well/Opportunities for Improvement is a technique for gathering feedback on how well your meetings work. This type of technique, sometimes called a process check, is usually scheduled at the end of a meeting, but it can be used at any time you feel it is necessary.

The What Went Well/Opportunities for Improvement technique primarily analyzes the effectiveness of the processes and techniques that the specific meeting under consideration has utilized. This technique also gathers feedback on other aspects of the meeting, such as the quality of the content and results, participant behavior, and participation in general.

This type of feedback gives important information to the meeting facilitator. The information helps provide a basis for technique selection in subsequent meetings with the same meeting group and also challenges the facilitator to work consistently to improve the product he or she delivers.

When to Use What Went Well/Opportunities for Improvement
- When you want to receive honest feedback about the quality of your meetings
- When you want to improve the caliber of your meetings
- When you want meeting feedback to be open and shared by all

How to Use What Went Well/Opportunities for Improvement

Before the Meeting
1. Put What Went Well/Opportunities for Improvement on the meeting agenda.

2. Determine which option you want to use in your meeting. Variation 1 is designed to obtain verbal feedback from the whole meeting group; variation 2 obtains this verbal information from small groups; and variation 3 provides individual, written feedback. You may choose to use all of these variations with the same meeting group over time to keep participants from tiring of the same technique.

NOTE: You will need to allot between five and twenty minutes for this exercise, depending on the size of your meeting group and the specific technique option you choose to use. Variation 1 should require ten to fifteen minutes, variation 2 twenty minutes, and variation 3 about five minutes.

3. Prepare two charts, one that looks similar to the one illustrated in figure 9-1. Also include an instruction chart for the technique option you will use. See figures 9-2 through 9-4.

+ What Went Well	++ Opportunities for Improvement

Figure 9-1. What Went Well/Opportunities for Improvement chart.

NOTE: When creating their What Went Well/Opportunities for Improvement charts, some facilitators write a plus sign at the top of one column for What Went Well and a minus sign or two plus signs in the Opportunities for Improvement column.

During the Meeting

1. Introduce the What Went Well/Opportunities for Improvement technique. If this is the first time your group has used this technique, take a minute to describe the purpose, process, and payoff of the exercise. (See Three P Statements, technique 8, for more information.) You might say, for example, "The purpose of What Went Well/Opportunities for Improvement is to hear from each of you how you feel our meeting went today. I'd like to hear about both what you thought went well, or was

effective, and what you thought didn't go so well, or where there are opportunities for improvement. Here's how we will do it." Display and explain your prepared instructions from variations 1, 2, or 3 outlined below. Then you might say, for example, "I hope the payoff of this exercise will be a better meeting the next time we meet. I plan to incorporate your ideas, building on what went well, and look for ways to capitalize on our opportunities for improvement."

2. Lead the exercise, using one of the three following options.

Variation 1: Obtain Verbal Feedback as a Group

This works well when your group is under twenty participants and you have about ten to fifteen minutes at the end of your meeting.

a. Explain the exercise to the group, using a chart similar to the one shown in figure 9-2 as a visual aid. You might say, "In one or two brief sentences, tell us what you think went well and what you feel are our opportunities for improvement for this meeting."

WHAT WENT WELL/OPPORTUNITIES FOR IMPROVEMENT

Briefly, give us your feedback on today's meeting.

- What went well?
- What are our opportunities for improvement?

Let's hear from everyone, no passing, please.

Figure 9-2. Instruction chart for Variation 1.

b. Ask for a volunteer in the group to begin. Suggest the round-robin method (hearing from everyone in sequence) or popcorn method (anyone speaks up whenever he or she wants, and no specific sequence is required or expected) for listening to everyone's comments.

NOTE: You could also ask for anyone who has feedback to bring it up when he or she is ready instead of asking everyone to participate. This is an especially good option when time is short or the group is large.

c. Document all comments on your prepared chart.

d. Debrief the information, and obtain agreement on what can be done differently for the next meeting.

NOTE: Consider going through each item on the "opportunities for improvement" side of the chart to help the group identify specific actions for the next meeting.

NOTE: Make sure that the tone of your voice supports your openness to questions and concerns. If your voice doesn't support your words (due to sarcasm and defensiveness, for example) you will lose credibility.

Variation 2: Obtain Verbal Feedback from Small Groups

If your group includes over twenty participants, break your group into a few small work groups. Be sure that each group has an easel, chart paper, and markers.

a. Explain the exercise to the groups, using a chart similar to figure 9-3 as a visual aid.

WHAT WENT WELL/OPPORTUNITIES FOR IMPROVEMENT

- Pick a recorder and reporter.
- Round robin—no passing please.
- Briefly give your feedback on what went well and opportunities for improvement in today's meeting.

5 minutes

Figure 9-3. Instruction chart for Variation 2.

b. Give the groups five minutes to share and chart their feedback.

c. Ask each group for a two-minute report back.

d. Debrief the information shared by each small group. To help the groups, you might ask, "What are the commonalities?" "Which seem to be our strengths?" "Which areas should we concentrate on in order to make the greatest improvements?"

Variation 3: Obtain Individual, Written Feedback

This option works well with small or large groups. Use it when you do not have or do not want to take time in the meeting for verbal feedback. The feedback can be reviewed at the next meeting or as part of the minutes of the meeting. This is an excellent feedback technique to use right before lunch in an all-day meeting so that corrections and modifications can then be made in the afternoon.

a. Explain the exercise, using a visual aid like the one shown in figure 8-4. Be sure that there are enough sticky notes within reach of all participants.

WHAT WENT WELL/OPPORTUNITIES FOR IMPROVEMENT

Please give us your feedback on today's meeting.

- What went well?
- What are our opportunities for improvement?

Please write all ideas on sticky notes. One idea per sticky note.

Stick them on the chart as you leave.

Figure 9-4. Instruction chart for Variation 3.

b. Begin the exercise. Place the prepared chart paper and easel by the door so that it is easy for participants to quickly stick their feedback on the chart as they leave the meeting.

c. After the participants have left, read and cluster the feedback. Decide what actions are appropriate given the feedback from the group. Decide how to incorporate their ideas and how to communicate your intentions, either as part of the minutes of the meeting or at the beginning of the next meeting.

NOTE: If you use this option, give participants the results of the feedback when the meeting reconvenes, at the next meeting, or in the meeting minutes. It's best to cluster similar comments together, so you can say, for example, "Seven people made comments about the effectiveness of our brainstorming session," before you read the comments verbatim. See Card Clusters, technique 31, for details. Be sure not to sugarcoat the results or you will lose credibility. Consider stating your action plan for improvement based on these comments.

Summary

What Went Well/Opportunities for Improvement is a technique for gathering feedback from meeting participants on the strengths and weaknesses of the meeting you just facilitated.

Before the Meeting

1. Put What Went Well/Opportunities for Improvement on the agenda.

2. Determine ahead of time which of the variations you will use in your meeting. Variation 1 obtains verbal feedback from the full group, variation 2 obtains verbal feedback from small groups, and variation 3 obtains individual, written feedback.

3. Prepare the charts you will need to support you.

During the Meeting

1. Introduce the What Went Well/Opportunities for Improvement technique.

2. Lead the exercise using one of the three following options.

   Variation 1: Obtain Verbal Feedback as a Full Group

   a. Explain the technique to the group.

   b. Ask for a volunteer in the group to begin the exercise.

   c. Document all comments on your prepared chart.

   d. Debrief the information shared from each group, and obtain agreement on what can be done differently to improve the next meeting.

Variation 2: Verbal Feedback in Small Groups

a. Explain the exercise to the small groups.

b. Give the small groups five minutes to share and chart their feedback.

c. Ask each group for a two-minute report back.

d. Debrief the information shared from each group.

Variation 3: Individual, Written Feedback

a. Explain the exercise.

b. Individuals provide feedback on sticky notes and place them on the prepared chart by the door.

c. Read and cluster the feedback. Decide how to incorporate the ideas into your next meeting and how to communicate your intentions.

"I wish I knew what participants were thinking as we close the meeting. I'd like to hear not just about the meeting itself and the decisions we've made but also their general thoughts. What can you suggest?"

79. Once Around the Table

What Is Once Around the Table?

Once Around the Table is a simple and powerful technique that provides participants with the opportunity to first reflect and then communicate their thoughts as the meeting comes to a close. This technique usually creates a good sense of closure and completeness to the session. But don't use it if you think the group will be hostile for some reason or you are running behind schedule. One of the other techniques would be better in those situations.

When to Use Once Around the Table

- When you want to hear opinions from everyone in the room
- When you want the meeting leader to hear the thoughts of others to help him or her prepare his or her own closing remarks

How to Use Once Around the Table

1. Once you have finished all agenda items, briefly summarize what the group accomplished during the meeting.

2. Set up the Once Around the Table exercise. Use figure 9-5 as a template for your instructions to the group.

ONCE AROUND THE TABLE

Take a moment to silently reflect on today's session. Think about your final thoughts as the meeting closes.

Be prepared to share one or two short sentences on your thoughts.

When we start, we will listen to everyone's thoughts without comment or question, and we will end with session with X (leader's name).

Figure 9-5. Once Around the Table instructions.

3. Give participants one to two minutes to reflect individually and silently on the meeting and their impressions of it.

4. When the majority of the participants appear ready, start the exercise. You may ask for a volunteer to start or choose someone to start. Since the exercise ends with the leader, you may want to start with one of the participants sitting next to the leader. If you are not a neutral facilitator or the leader, you may also start if you like. Remind the group members that they are to share one or two short sentences and that no comments, rebuttals, or discussion are allowed. Participants should only listen to the comments of others.

5. After all participants have shared their reflections, the leader should close the session.

   NOTE: If you are not the leader yourself, please ensure that you have properly positioned the leader so he or she knows that he or she will close the session and how the exercise will work.

   NOTE: Neutral facilitators do not usually offer their reflections unless the leader has agreed in advance.

Summary

Once Around the Table is a great technique that allows you to hear from everyone as the meeting closes.

1. Briefly summarize what the group accomplished during the meeting.

2. Set up the Once Around the Table exercise.

3. Give participants one to two minutes to reflect individually.

4. Start the exercise.

5. Have the leader end the session.

"My team is very exacting and likes to use quantitative ratings. Is there a meeting evaluation technique I can use that satisfies this criterion?"

80: Team Effectiveness Chart

What Is a Team Effectiveness Chart?

A Team Effectiveness Chart visually and quantifiably measures specific aspects of your meeting, such as level of open communication, satisfaction with results accomplished, the degree to which the group honors the ideas of others, or other components of the meeting. A chart with different grids with numerical rankings displays the resulting measurements.

A Team Effectiveness Chart incorporates Movement, technique 16, and creates a chart that serves as a visual aid to display quantified group ratings. This chart can also be used as a benchmark for later evaluations.

When to Use a Team Effectiveness Chart

- When you want to get feedback on specific criteria
- When you want feedback that is measurable
- When you want to include everyone in nonverbal feedback
- When you want to get feedback quickly about the quality of your meetings

How to Use a Team Effectiveness Chart

Before the Meeting

1. Add Team Effectiveness Chart to the end of the meeting's agenda. Allow fifteen minutes for rankings and a debriefing discussion.

2. Decide which components of your meeting are appropriate for the group to measure for effectiveness. You may want to consult with other meeting participants to determine these categories. Your group's ground rules (see Ground Rules, technique 3, for more information) will offer a springboard for ideas. Possible examples of these components include:
   - How well we listened to each other
   - How well we stayed on track
   - How satisfied we are with the results of our meeting
   - How well we followed our ground rules
   - How well we brainstormed creative ideas

- How open and honest our communication was
- How well we encouraged and accomplished full participation
- How comfortable participants felt about speaking their mind

3. Create charts similar to the two illustrated in figures 9-5 and 9-6.

    NOTE: If your meeting group is large, consider duplicating the information on two or three charts instead. This will avoid crowding while participants place their marks.

    NOTE: This process could also be done electronically.

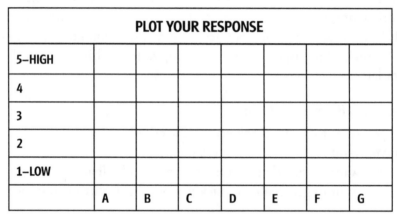

PLOT YOUR RESPONSE							
5–HIGH							
4							
3							
2							
1–LOW							
	A	B	C	D	E	F	G

Figure 9-6. Team Effectiveness Chart.

KEY	
A	How well did we listen to each other?
B	How well did we stay on track?
C	How satisfied are you with our meeting results?
D	How well did we follow our ground rules?
E	How well did we brainstorm creative ideas?
F	How open and honest was our communication?
G	How well did we encourage and accomplish full participation?

Figure 9-7. Team Effectiveness Chart questions key.

During the Meeting

1. Introduce the Team Effectiveness Chart technique. If this is the first time your group is using this technique, explain what it is used for and how to use it. You might say, for example, "The Team Effectiveness Chart is a technique for visually measuring your feedback about our meeting. These measurements will allow us to look at our strengths and weaknesses as a meeting group. We can then look for methods to improve our effectiveness in our upcoming meetings. We can also use these measurements as a benchmark. After we work to improve, we can measure ourselves again and see what progress we have made." Share the measurements you will be employing, using your charts to support you. Explain how and why the components being measured were determined.

2. Ask every participant to come forward and mark how well he or she thinks the team did in each category under consideration. They should indicate their ratings by putting a large dot on the chart in the appropriate place. You may provide sticky dots or markers for this exercise.

3. After everyone is finished and seated, debrief the information as a group. Here are some sample questions that may be appropriate. "As you look at our chart, what stands out for you?" "What conclusions can we draw from this information?" "What are we particularly good at?" "What would you say are our major opportunities for improvement?" "What should we target as actions for improving our meetings?" "How should we accomplish these actions?" Chart the group's responses, and create a list of action items based on the major opportunities for improvement.

4. After the meeting, keep the charts your team has developed. Be sure to write the date on each of them.

5. Benchmark your group's progress in the next meeting or in whichever future meeting you and your group feel is appropriate. Compare your progress against the first measurement.

    a. Repeat steps 1 and 2 on a new chart.

    b. To debrief, bring out the old chart, and place it next to its counterpart from today's meeting.

c. As a group, numerically measure the difference between your previous rankings and this meeting's rankings.

d. Use or modify the debrief questions in step 3. Create a new action plan as necessary. You might also consider bringing out your old action plan to see if you have accomplished those actions yet.

e. Keep the charts or a summary of the charts (or photos of them) for benchmarking in the future.

Summary

A Team Effectiveness Chart is a technique with which your meeting participants measure the effectiveness of specific meeting components.

Before the Meeting

1. Add Team Effectiveness Chart to the end of the meeting's agenda.

2. Decide which components of your meeting are appropriate for the group to measure.

3. Create charts similar to those in figures 9-6 and 9-7.

During the Meeting

1. Introduce the Team Effectiveness Chart technique, using your charts to support you.

2. Ask every participant to come forward and mark how well he or she thinks the team did in each category under analysis.

3. Debrief the information as a group, and create an action list based on the major opportunities for improvement.

4. After the meeting, date and keep the charts for step 5.

5. In a later meeting, benchmark your group's progress.

a. Repeat steps 1 and 2 on a new chart.

b. To debrief, bring out the old chart, and place it next to its counterpart from that day's meeting.

c. As a group, calculate the difference between your previous rankings and this meeting's rankings.

d. Use or modify the debrief questions in step 3, creating a new action plan as necessary.

e. Keep the charts or a summary of the charts for benchmarking in the future.

"In addition to meeting together, sometimes our group meets by phone or across locations and even via e-mail. Is there a meeting evaluation technique that I can use both inside and outside a face-to-face meeting?"

81. Written Questions

What Are Written Questions?

The Written Questions technique gathers written feedback on your meeting's effectiveness from each individual in the meeting. The technique requires each participant to complete a meeting evaluation questionnaire that has been prepared in advance.

Written Questions, like the other meeting evaluation techniques described in this book, do more than simply analyze and measure the effectiveness of your meetings. Like a good antivirus program for your computer, these techniques expose problem areas in your meetings as well as provide the insights to correct those problems and weaknesses. Their importance to meeting success and their recommended consistent use, therefore, cannot be overemphasized.

When to Use Written Questions

- When you don't have time to evaluate the meeting as a group
- When you have participants in different locations
- When you want to use an alternative to verbal feedback in your meeting

How to Use Written Questions

Before the Meeting

1. Reserve a few minutes near the end of your meeting agenda for the Written Questions evaluation technique.

2. Prepare the Written Questions that you would like to use in your meeting. Figures 9-8 and 9-9 illustrate two example questionnaires.

MEETING QUESTIONNAIRE

As you reflect back on our meeting, what are your thoughts?

How effective was this meeting for you?   Please circle one:

1 - very effective

2 - somewhat effective

3 - somewhat ineffective

4 - very ineffective

Why?

What do you think we did well?

What would you suggest we do differently next time?

What additional comments do you have?

Figure 9-8. Meeting questionnaire, Variation 1.

MEETING QUESTIONNAIRE

On a scale of 1-10 (1=very poor 10=excellent), how would you rate your satisfaction with our meeting's results?

1-------2-------3-------4-------5-------6-------7-------8-------9---------10

On a scale of 1-10 how would you rate our use of your time?

1-------2-------3-------4-------5-------6-------7-------8-------9---------10

Comments:

Figure 9-9. Meeting questionnaire, Variation 2.

Create a questionnaire that meets the specific needs of your meeting group.

NOTE: When creating your questionnaire, be sure to ask Open-Ended Questions (see technique 34 for details).

During the Meeting

1. Near the conclusion of your meeting, introduce the Written Questions technique, and review the instructions and contents of your questionnaire.

   NOTE: It is best to schedule the meeting evaluation as the second-to-last agenda item. End the meeting with another short agenda item, such as planning the next meeting. If you ask people to complete a meeting evaluation questionnaire as you are about to dismiss the meeting, only a few people will stay to do so or take the time required to make it a meaningful exercise. A short agenda item afterward will ensure that everyone will take the time to complete the questionnaire.

2. Ask your participants to complete the questionnaire and return it to you as they leave the meeting.

Variation 1: Use the format shown in figure 9-8 as a chart instead of an individual questionnaire. Place this chart near the door at the end of your meeting so your participants can rate each question as they leave the meeting. Be sure to provide sticky notes so they can write and post their comments as well.

Variation 2: When your group is meeting electronically and won't be meeting face-to-face, send your questionnaire to each participant before the meeting begins. Ask them to complete and return the material electronically immediately after the meeting.

After the Meeting

Collect, compile, and communicate the data received from your Written Questions.

NOTE: In addition to providing the information generated from the questionnaire, be sure to communicate your intended actions as a result of the feedback.

Summary

Written Questions is a technique for gathering meeting evaluation information individually and silently.

Before the Meeting

1. Reserve a few minutes near the end of your meeting agenda for the Written Questions technique.

2. Prepare the Written Questions questionnaire you would like to use in your meeting.

During the Meeting

1. Introduce the Written Questions technique, and review the instructions for the exercise.

2. Ask the participants to complete the questionnaire.

After the Meeting

Collect, compile, and communicate the data generated from the questionnaire as well as an outline of any resulting actions.

In Conclusion

In this book, I have shared the 81 Techniques I find most valuable in designing and facilitating meetings. I hope you have found this book useful in your journey to becoming an expert in meeting facilitation. I too continue to work on improving my skills as a meeting facilitator. I encourage you to share additional techniques you have found useful. Please send me your favorite tips and techniques for designing and facilitating meetings. You can reach me at ava@avasbutler.com.

Index

CPSIA information can be obtained
at www.ICGtesting.com
Printed in the USA
BVHW010630080921
616246BV00034B/314